WJEC Psychology

for AS

Julia Russell and Matt Jarvis

WITHDRAWN
FROM STOCK

to be returned on or before the
below.

COLLEGE
LIBRARY

Warwickshire College

00661893

HODDER
EDUCATION
AN HACHETTE UK COMPANY

Photo credits

The author and publishers would like to thank the following for permission to reproduce material in this book:

Figure 1.5 © Roger-Viollet / TopFoto; Figure 1.7 © uwimages – Fotolia; Figure 1.8 © SCIENTIFICA, VISUALS UNLIMITED /SCIENCE PHOTO LIBRARY; Figure 2.1 © RIA NOVOSTI/SCIENCE PHOTO LIBRARY; Figure 2.2a, b and c from PSYCHOLOGICAL CARE OF INFANT AND CHILD by John B. Watson © 1928 by W. W. Norton & Company, Inc. Copyright renewed 1955 by John B. Watson. Used with permission of W. W. Norton & Company, Inc.; Figure 2.4a and b with kind permission by Prof. Albert Bandura, Stanford University; Figure 3.4 © DeVIce – Fotolia; Figure 3.7 © HaywireMedia – Fotolia; Figure 4.1 © Andrew Barker – Fotolia; Figure 4.4 © Cristian Nitu – Fotolia; Figure 5.1 © Andres Rodriguez – Fotolia; Figure 5.3 reproduced with permission. © 2011 Scientific American, Inc. All rights reserved; Figure 5.5 © Ken McKay/TalkbackThames / Rex Features; Figure 5.6 © APIC / Hulton Archive / Getty Images; Figure 5.7 from the film Obedience © 1968 by Stanley Milgram; © renewed 1993 by Alexandra Milgram; Figure 5.9 Slater, M., Antley, A., Davison, A., Swapp, D., Guger, C., Barker, C., Pistrang, N. and Sanchez-Vives, M. (2006) 'A virtual reprise of the Stanley Milgram obedience experiments.' PLOS One, December: np. / http://www.plosone.org/article/info:doi%2F10.1371%2Fjournal.pone.0000039, reproduced with permission; Figure 6.1 © Vladimirs Koskins – Fotolia; Figure 6.3 © Ken Tannenbaum – Fotolia; Figure 6.4a © Carola Schubbel – Fotolia; Figure 6.4b © Michael Eaton – Fotolia; Figure 6.5 © Steve Byland – Fotolia; Figure 6.6 © microimages – Fotolia; Figure 6.7 © Walter Luger – Fotolia; Figure © Poresh – Fotolia; Figure 7.1 © microimages – Fotolia; Figure 7.4 © Tier und Naturfotografie / SuperStock; Figure 7.5 © HO/Reuters/ Corbis; Figure 7.6 © Ovidiu Iordachi – Fotolia; Figure 8.1 © Papirazzi – Fotolia; Figure 8.2 © deanm1974 – Fotolia; Figure 8.3 © deanm1974 – Fotolia.com; Figure 8.4 © deanm1974 – Fotolia; Figure 8.5 © pressmaster – Fotolia; Figure 8.6 reproduced with permission © 2011 Scientific American, Inc. All Rights reserved; Figure 8.7 reproduced with permission © 2011 Scientific American, Inc. All Rights reserved; Figure 9.1 © TheFinalMiracle – Fotolia; Figure 9.2 © Kurhan – Fotolia; Figure 9.3 © Temych – Fotolia; Figure 9.4 © Willee Cole – Fotolia; Figure 10.1 © Dominique VERNIER – Fotolia; Figure 10.3 © Tom Davison – Fotolia; Figure 11.1 © Yuri Arcurs – Fotolia; Figure 11.3 © Sean Gladwell – Fotolia; Figure 11.4 © Anke van Wyk – Fotolia; Figure 12.1a © JoeFox / Alamy; Figure 12.1b © Antiques & Collectables / Alamy

Every effort has been made to obtain necessary permission with reference to copyright material. The publishers apologise if inadvertently any sources remain unacknowledged and will be glad to make the necessary arrangements at the earliest opportunity.

WARWICKSHIRE COLLEGE LIBRARY

NOV 11

Class No
150 RUS

Acc No
00661893

Price & Loan Type
£17.99   SL

Orders: please contact Bookpoint Ltd, 130 Milton Park, Abingdon, Oxon OX14 4SB. Telephone: (44) 01235 827720. Fax: (44) 01235 400454. Lines are open from 9.00 – 5.00, Monday to Saturday, with a 24 hour message answering service. You can also order through our website: www.hoddereducation.co.uk

If you have any comments to make about this, or any of our other titles, please send them to educationenquiries@hodder.co.uk

British Library Cataloguing in Publication Data
A catalogue record for this title is available from the British Library

ISBN: 978 1 444 13748 4

First Published 2011
Impression number   10 9 8 7 6 5 4 3 2 1
Year   2015, 2014, 2013, 2012, 2011

Copyright © 2011 Julia Russell and Matt Jarvis

All rights reserved. No part of this publication may be reproduced or transmitted in any form or by any means, electronic or mechanical, including photocopy, recording, or any information storage and retrieval system, without permission in writing from the publisher or under licence from the Copyright Licensing Agency Limited. Further details of such licences (for reprographic reproduction) may be obtained from the Copyright Licensing Agency Limited, of Saffron House, 6-10 Kirby Street, London EC1N 8TS.

Hachette Livre UK's policy is to use papers that are natural, renewable and recyclable products and made fromwood grown in sustainable forests. The logging and manufacturing processes are expected to conform to the environmental regulations of the country of origin.

Cover photo © Troyka – Fotolia.com
Illustrations by Barking Dog Art
Typeset by Fakenham Prepress Solutions, Fakenham, Norfolk NR21 8NN
Printed in Great Britain for Hodder Education, An Hachette UK Company, 338 Euston Road, London NW1 3BH

Contents

Introduction

The AS exams

At AS, there are two exams, PY 1 – Approaches in Psychology, which is 1 hour and 15 minutes long and worth 40 per cent of the AS marks, and PY 2 – Psychology: Core Studies and Applied Research Methods, which is 1 hour and 45 minutes long and is worth 60 per cent of the AS marks. These units are examined in January and in June. Make sure you know when you are sitting each module and when, exactly, the examination is.

The unit content

PY 1 – Approaches in Psychology

Four approaches are studied in PY 1. These are:

- biological
- behaviourist
- psychodynamic
- cognitive.

For each of these, you need to be able to:

- outline the main assumptions
- describe one theory
- describe one therapy and link it explicitly to an assumption or key feature of the approach
- describe and evaluate the methodology used
- evaluate the approach as a whole
- compare and contrast the approach with other approaches.

Table 0.1 The theories and therapies for each approach

APPROACH	THEORY	THERAPY
Biological	Selye's General Adaptation Syndrome	Psychosurgery or chemotherapy
Behaviourist	Social learning theory of aggression	Aversion therapy or systematic desensitisation
Psychodynamic	Freud's theory of personality development	Dream analysis or free association
Cognitive	Attribution theory	Cognitive behavioural therapy or rational emotive therapy

PY 2 – Psychology: Core Studies and Applied Research Methods

Ten core studies, two from each of five approaches, are studied in PY 2. These are listed in Table 0.2.

Table 0.2 The core studies

APPROACH	STUDY 1	STUDY 2
Social	Asch (1955)	Milgram (1963)
Physiological	Rahe *et al.* (1970)	Bennett-Levy and Marteau (1984)
Cognitive	Gardner and Gardner (1969)	Loftus and Palmer (1974)
Developmental	Gibson and Walk (1960)	Langer and Rodin (1976)
Individual differences	Buss (1989)	Rosenhan (1973)

For each core study, you need to be able to:

- describe the aims and context
- describe the procedure
- describe the findings and conclusions
- evaluate the methodology used
- evaluate the findings/conclusions in comparison with complementary/ alternative research findings.

From your understanding of research methods, you also need to be able to apply your knowledge to new situations. In brief, you should be able to:

- define and evaluate qualitative and quantitative research methods, including:
  - experiments (laboratory, field and natural)
  - correlations
  - observations
  - questionnaires
  - interviews
  - case studies
- understand and know how to ensure:
  - reliability (split-half, test-retest, inter-rater)
  - validity (experimental and ecological; content, concurrent and construct)
- understand ethical issues, including:
  - informed consent
  - deception
  - right to withdraw
  - confidentiality
  - protection from psychological and physical harm
- define and offer strengths and weaknesses of sampling methods, including:
  - opportunity
  - quota
  - random
  - self-selected (volunteer)
  - stratified
  - systematic

- define, outline the advantages and disadvantages of and draw conclusions from different ways of describing data, including:
  - coding systems
  - categorisation
  - content analysis
  - mean, median, mode
  - range
  - scattergraphs
  - bar charts
  - histograms.

Examination questions and assessment objectives

Exam questions are designed to test your skills, specifically three different types, identified as different assessment objectives, as follows.

Assessment Objective 1 (AO1): a measure of your knowledge and understanding

This tests how well you understand and can describe information, such as psychological theories, studies, concepts and research methods. Your communication should be clear and effective; you should aim for logical, well-structured answers and remember that spelling and use of psychological terms will be assessed.

Assessment Objective 2 (AO2): a measure of your ability to analyse, evaluate and apply

This tests how well you can interpret information, assess its strengths and weaknesses and apply your knowledge – including to unfamiliar situations. This can include psychological theories, studies, concepts and research methods. As for AO1, your communication should be effective.

Assessment Objective 3 (AO3): a measure of your understanding of the process of psychological investigation

This tests your knowledge of the issues involved in designing, conducting and reporting studies in psychology. It covers a range of research methods, problems of reliability, validity and ethics and how to solve them, and how to deal with data collection and draw conclusions from findings.

The weighting of these assessment objectives in the two papers is shown in Table 0.3.

Table 0.3 Weighting of assessment objectives

	NUMBER OF MARKS	% OF AS	AO1	AO2	AO3
PY 1	60	40	40%	40%	20%
PY 2	90	60	40%	40%	20%
Overall in AS	150	100	40%	40%	20%

The two papers also differ in structure.

PY 1 has five compulsory questions; the first two test AO1 and the last three test AO2 and AO3. These questions can be about:

- the approaches
- their related therapies.

The first two questions, each of which is worth 12 marks (question 1 is made up of parts a and b each worth 6 marks), will use command words such as:

- outline (give brief details without explanation or evaluation)
- describe (give a detailed account without explanation or evaluation).

The last three questions will use command terms such as:

- evaluate (assess the value or effectiveness of)
- strengths (positive evaluation points)
- weaknesses (negative evaluation points)
- limitations (negative evaluation points)
- compare (discuss similarities between)
- contrast (discuss differences between).

In these last questions you can be asked to describe and evaluate research methods (such as ethics, reliability and validity), as well as the approaches and therapies.

PY 2 has three sections (Sections A and B are about the core studies, and Section C is about research methods):

- Section A has three compulsory questions testing AO1 (each worth 12 marks).
- Section B has three compulsory questions testing AO2 (each worth 12 marks).
- Section C has a choice of two questions, each worth 18 marks. You must answer one of them.

This amounts to a lot of material, and only three hours in which to demonstrate how well you understand the course and have learned the material. Throughout the chapters that follow, there are examples of examination questions and examiner commentary and exam tips. These will help you to understand what is required and how to achieve it. More specific advice about how to study and how to revise is contained in this chapter.

Studying effectively

To perform well in exams, it is essential that you:

- understand the specification content
- learn it well enough to recall it
- can use it effectively.

The following sections will help you to achieve these aims.

Understanding the specification content

You will have been taught about each approach and core study. However, if you missed a lesson, were not concentrating, did not quite get the ideas the first time around or have simply forgotten, it will help to follow up your class work with opportunities to consolidate your learning. The following are ideas for improving your understanding. You may find that there are ones that suit you better than others, although some, like keeping your file organised, are important for everyone.

- *Use your textbook* – after a lesson, at the end of the week, or if you have missed a lesson or are unsure, look up the topic you have covered and read it though (remember to use the index rather than just flicking though and reading what looks interesting).
- *Reread your notes* – look back regularly through the notes you have taken in class to check that you still understand them. Do something active with them, like writing a list of the key terms, making them into a table of strengths and weaknesses or drawing pictures to help you to remember the main ideas. If your notes do not seem to make sense, look the topic up, ask a friend or ask your teacher for help.
- *Read a different textbook* – different people explain things in different ways so even when the books contain the same information, this can help you to understand and remember ideas better.
- *Use your psychology* – look for examples of what you have studied at home, in school or college, on TV or in books, and then talk about it! Explaining how the psychological concepts you have learned apply to everyday life will help you to become more familiar with the ideas and better at describing them.
- *Keep your file organised* – sorting your notes out helps you to understand each topic as you think about the key ideas in the approach or the study. Use a copy of the specification or Tables 0.1 and 0.2 above to decide how each unit should be structured. Make sure that you have notes on everything in the specification (your specification is WJEC GCE 2009 and you can find it on the internet at: www.wjec.co.uk/index.php?level=21&subject=97).
- *Write a word list* – using your notes, textbook and the specification, construct a list of all the terms you encounter, adding new ones as you learn new topics. Write out your own definition for each one and give an example where possible.
- *Practise answering examination-style questions* – the questions in exams follow clear patterns, so you will know what to expect. Make sure that you tackle all the different types and topics, not just the ones you find easiest.

Helping yourself to learn

You are much more likely to remember the information you have been taught and be able to use it effectively if you are an active participant in your studying – just passive reading is unlikely to be enough. Below are some ideas that you can try that will encourage you to learn actively. You will work better in a tidy space and it is useful to have some extra resources, such as highlighters, big sheets of paper, small cards (index cards are good), coloured paper and coloured pens. But beware of spending more time shopping for stationery or tidying your room than actually working.

Working on your own

There are advantages to working alone: you can go at your own pace, you can choose which topics to study and there will be no one to distract you!

Question and answer cards

You will need some small cards or you can cut sheets of A4 into four pieces. Use your notes or a book and write a question on one side of the card and the answer on the other. You could ask yourself questions such as the following:

- What are the main points for the assumptions/theory/therapy/research methods for the ... approach?
- How can the ... *approach/its methods* be evaluated?
- What are the similarities between the ... *approach* and the ... *approach*?
- What are the differences between the ... *approach* and the ... *approach*?
- What were the aims/contexts/procedures/findings/conclusions for the ... core study?
- How can the ... *core study* be evaluated in terms of *methodology/alternative evidence*?

You can then test yourself using the questions and check your progress, or help yourself if you get stuck simply by turning the card over. Both writing the cards and using them are active learning strategies.

Visual aids

Many people find that visual images and layouts help them to learn – although not everyone does, so don't worry if this doesn't work for you. Many of the topics can be represented in pictures or tables. Use a large sheet of paper to make a poster illustrating the main points of a theory or core study. You could:

- draw flowcharts to show stages (such as in the GAS)
- include diagrams of apparatus (for example, for Milgram's or Asch's studies)
- present results of studies as graphs
- illustrate key points with drawings that will trigger your memory (for example, boats with information in them for Rahe *et al.*'s study or different animals with the results of Bennett-Levy and Marteau).

Figure 0.1 Drawings of studies can help you to remember. Which group was happier in Langer and Rodin's study, and why?

Same/different

Draw up tables to compare each possible combination of approaches or research methods. How are they similar and how are they different? You could briefly describe the similarities in one colour pen and the differences in another.

Concept maps

At the end of Chapters 1–9, you will find a concept map. You could redraw these as bigger versions using different colours for each box, listing the main ideas as bullet points in each box or as smaller versions with just key words to prompt you to recall a greater level of detail.

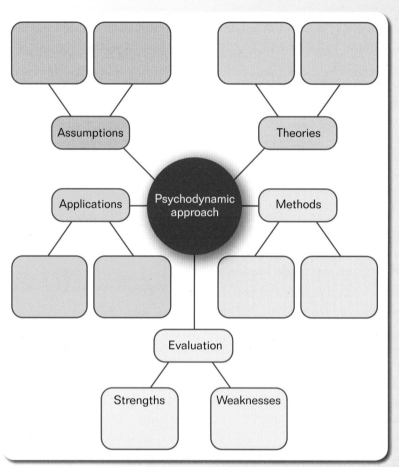

Figure 0.2 Concept map

Working with a partner

You could work either with a friend who also does psychology or with a willing person who can act as a questioner or prompt – they do not have to know any psychology at all.

Question and answer cards

If you are working with a fellow psychology student, you could write the cards as above, then test each other, only turning over if neither of you is sure of the answer. If you have a non-psychologist helping you, they can read the questions and check your answer using the back of the card.

Alphabet hat

Write the letters of the alphabet on small pieces of paper or card and put

Figure 0.3 If you are revising in a pair, use an alphabet test to check each other's progress

them in a bag or box (you can leave out X, Y and Z). Take it in turns to pull out a letter and the other person must think of a concept, term or reference (study) beginning with that letter, then describe it. It may help if the person listening to the answer has the index of the book open so that they can give prompts.

Charades

If you are working with another psychology student, take it in turns to think of a psychological concept, term or study and try to act it out without using words, just like you would when playing charades. If you think your artistic skills are better than your acting, try the same idea but using drawings (like playing Pictionary). When your partner guesses correctly, swap over. If they cannot guess, you have to name the concept *and* explain it to them.

Revising effectively

Keeping your notes organised and up-to-date during the year will make your revision much easier. If, however, like many students, you have not quite succeeded, good revision can still help.

For revision to be really effective, it needs to be well planned, so you need to give yourself enough time and use that time well. To ensure your revision time is well spent you need to:

- know what you have to know and learn it
- understand how you will be tested and practise it.

Examiners follow a mark scheme so they are looking for a demonstration of specific knowledge and skills. Your answers must be *accurate*, well *detailed* and used to answer the question *effectively* (for example, by including coherent evaluation). You may also need to demonstrate *depth* (a thorough, detailed understanding) and *range* (a variety of ideas, evidence or arguments) in your answer. This means knowing your stuff and explaining it well. Finally, your answers need to demonstrate good use of language, including grammar, punctuation and spelling, as well as be written in a well-structured, coherent and accurate way.

Managing your time

You need to make sure that you learn all the approaches and core studies – you do not want to find you run out of time.

- Start your revision early – if you are sitting the January exam, it is likely to be at the very start of the spring term; the summer exam is usually in May, before the June half-term holiday.
- Get organised – plan your revision so that you have time to learn everything you need to know. There is no point in being great at some of the approaches or core studies if you know nothing about the rest.
- Use your time well – spread your revision out but try to dedicate specific 'chunks' of time (for example, a whole morning) to working, and remember to give yourself breaks (but beware of time-wasting).

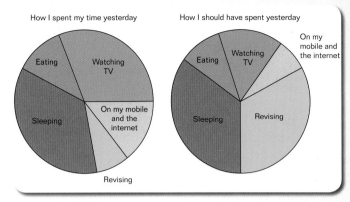

How I spent my time yesterday

How I should have spent yesterday

Figure 0.4 Time circle

Revision timetable

A revision timetable can be very simple – a list of topics with target dates. Drawing up a complex (but improbable) one is unlikely to be a good use of time. Recognise that you will have other commitments so try to be realistic – for example, about how much you can do at the weekend or when your favourite TV programme is on. Also consider how well you understand each topic – some may take more time. Using highlighters and the 'traffic light' system may help you to decide. Using tables covering the specification (such as Tables 0.1 and 0.2 above), colour each topic:

- *green* if you know and understand it well
- *orange* if you know and understand it fairly well
- *red* if your knowledge and understanding is less good.

It is vital that you stick to your plan in terms of timing in order to get everything done. If you get behind, you will need to rethink either how long you are spending doing revision (perhaps you should spend more?) or whether you may be devoting too much time to each topic – do you need to move more quickly to get everything done?

Time circles

If you are not keeping to your timetable, work out how much time you spent on each of the activities in Figure 0.4 (and anything else you spent a long time doing) the previous day. Then work out from your revision timetable how much time you intended to spend working. Draw two time circles and use them to decide whether you could be more time efficient. But watch out – drawing time circles and colouring them in is not a substitute for work!

Self-motivation

Revising is difficult because there seems to be a mountain of information. When you look at what you have to learn, either the material seems familiar so it is dull and difficult to see the need to learn it or it does not seem familiar at all, which is demotivating. Either way, you have to try to keep yourself going. Here are some useful pointers:

Do:
- set yourself achievable, intermediate, goals
- reward yourself at the end of a session – hopefully you have earned it
- have breaks – they will improve your concentration
- cheer yourself up with coloured pens and paper (and music *if* you can concentrate)
- work with a friend or get someone to read you questions, or answer them out loud
- have a 'work space' (for example, a corner of your room) so you can keep your revision separate.

Do not:

- give up too easily – reaching a short-term goal will motivate you
- work with the TV switched on to a programme you want to watch – it will distract you, so turn it off or watch it and work properly in another time slot
- spend time on 'jobs', like making an all-colour revision timetable or re-filing your notes. These are displacement activities – you should be revising!

Know when your exam is

Be sure that you know the date, time and unit that you are sitting. Plan your travel so that you arrive in good time. Take a black pen and at least two spares. Do not take your phone into the exam hall – it is not allowed. It is not enough for it to be turned off; you should not have it with you.

Time management in examinations

You must not exceed the average time for each question – 12 minutes (a mark a minute) – or you will run out of time. You have some reading time, use this for reading and planning answers.

An error made by some students in these examinations is running out of time. In PY 1 30 per cent of candidates don't finish the paper – they don't do question 5. Many others produce very short and very poor later answers. In PY 2 many candidates do not complete the critical assessment question(s) or do them very badly. All this is due to poor time management.

What is the solution? Plan your time – 12 minutes per question – and stick to it. Rehearse this timing in revision. Do not plan answers longer than the amount you can write in 12 minutes.

1 The biological approach

This chapter includes:

I should be able to:

- outline two main assumptions of the biological approach

- describe Selye's General Adaptation Syndrome as an explanation of stress

- describe how the biological approach has been put to use in psychosurgery or chemotherapy

- describe and evaluate the research methodology used in the biological approach

- evaluate the biological approach in terms of its strengths and weaknesses

- compare and contrast the biological approach with other perspectives.

What could I be asked?

There is no guarantee that future exams will keep precisely to this wording or mark allocation. However, it is likely that any questions you are asked about the approach will be much like the following:

1. (a) Outline **two** assumptions of the biological approach. [4]

   (b) **Describe** Selye's General Adaptation Syndrome as an explanation of stress. [8]

2. **Describe** how the biological approach has been applied in one therapy. [12]

3. (a) Evaluate **two** strengths of the biological approach. [6]

   (b) Evaluate **two** weaknesses of the biological approach. [6]

4. **Compare and contrast** the biological and psychodynamic approaches in terms of similarities and differences. [12]

5. **Explain and evaluate** the methodology used by the biological approach. [12]

The biological approach to psychology has its roots in the much older science of biology, so has a very long history. 'Modern' research into the structure of the nervous system began as early as the eighteenth century with the microscopic study of brain cells and investigations of the brain through autopsy. Techniques have moved on enormously with much more detailed and informative research methods, such as brain scans of people performing different actions. Nevertheless, many of the early findings about the biological structures and their functions were accurate and informative and those discoveries are still relevant today. This is not, however, the case for all aspects of the biological approach, as you will see.

Assumptions of the biological approach

The biological approach looks at psychology from a physiological perspective – that is, it considers physical changes in the body, including the influence of chemical and electrical events. The main assumptions of the approach are based on biology and include the following ideas:

- **neurons** (nerve cells) affect our thinking, emotions and behaviour
- functions in the brain are **localised**
- **hormones** affect our thinking, emotions and behaviour.

Understanding these ideas is important because it enables us to see how the mechanisms affecting thinking, emotions and behaviour are controlled. Psychologists can then use this understanding to develop therapies to help people overcome mental health problems – for example, through:

- psychosurgery – operating on the brain to control mental disorders
- chemotherapy – the use of drugs to control mental disorders.

The structure and function of neurons and the nervous system

The nervous system is made up of cells called neurons, which form connections through structures called synapses. Neurons themselves conduct minute electrical messages (called action potentials) around the brain and body. There are different types of neurons that serve to carry information in different ways:

- sensory neurons – convey information about stimuli (such as light, sound or pain) to the brain
- motor neurons – convey instructions out from the brain, for example, to make muscles contract or to stimulate the release of hormones from glands
- interneurons – are found only in the **central nervous system** (CNS) and important in thinking and decision making.

Neurons consist of a long, thin **axon**, the part that transmits the electrical message, and branched ends. The electrical message can be sent only in one direction, from the **dendrites** (the branching tree at the 'front') to the axon terminals (the branches at the 'end'). Many interconnections are formed between axon terminals and dendrites of adjacent neurons; each one of these interconnections is called a **synapse**. At this junction, the neurons do not physically touch and the electrical message from one neuron is transferred to the next by chemicals (called **neurotransmitters**) (see Figure 1.1). There are many different neurotransmitters, including serotonin, dopamine and noradrenaline.

Glossary

central nervous system – the brain and spinal cord (CNS).

hormone – a chemical released from an endocrine gland into the bloodstream which targets other body tissues and controls them, so can influence our thinking, emotions or behaviour.

localisation – some functions are controlled by specific areas in the brain.

neuron – a nerve cell.

neurotransmitter – a chemical that passes a message between one neuron and another.

receptor – location on the postsynaptic membrane of a neuron to which specific neurotransmitters (or drugs) can attach and stimulate or inhibit the action of that neuron.

synapse – the junction between two neurons.

Receptors on the post-synaptic membrane are specific to particular neurotransmitters. One consequence of this is that, in addition to neurotransmitters, similarly shaped drug molecules can also attach to specific receptor sites. This is important in understanding the action of drugs used to treat mental disorders (see page 8).

Localisation in the brain

The central nervous system (CNS) consists of the brain and spinal cord. The brain is a highly organised structure. The brain stem, which connects to the spinal cord, is surrounded by the cerebral hemispheres. These are roughly similar structures on the left and right sides, thus many (but not all) structures are found on both sides of the brain.

A surface view (without the covering of the skull) shows the brain has four 'lobes'. These lobes are areas of the outer layer called the cortex. Beneath this, there are many other structures, each with different, although complex and interacting, functions. The cortex is only the outer few millimetres of the brain and is deeply folded. The resulting 'hills' and 'valleys' give the cortex an enormous surface area. Different areas of the cortex have different functions, being devoted to vision, movement and language, for example (see Figure 1.2). The link between particular areas and functions in the brain is called **localisation**. One consequence of this is that, if damage is caused to a small area of brain tissue, specific functions may be lost.

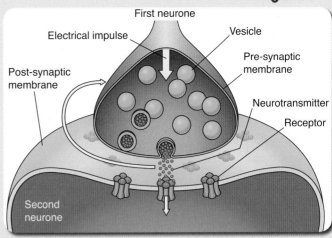

Figure 1.1 Synaptic functioning

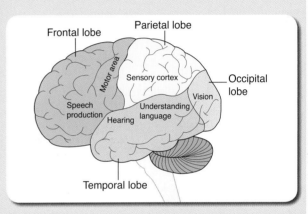

Figure 1.2 A surface view of the brain

The endocrine system

Within the body, there are two communication systems: the nervous system (a fast, electrical process) and the endocrine system (a slower, chemical one). The **endocrine system** is composed of many glands, which secrete **hormones** into the bloodstream. Hormones are chemicals that travel around the body in the blood and affect the action of target organs. As a result, hormones can influence our thinking, behaviour and emotions. For example, the hormone melatonin affects whether we feel sleepy or awake. One important role for hormones is in the coordination of our response to stress; we will look at this next.

Selye's General Adaptation Syndrome

One biological event that involves both the nervous system and the endocrine system is the body's response to stress. **Stress** is a physical and psychological response experienced when we encounter a threat that we feel we do not have

Glossary

endocrine system – a set of glands that release hormones into the bloodstream.
stress – the physical and psychological reaction to a threat that appears to be too difficult for us to be able to deal with.
stressor – a source of threat that may be internal or external that could initiate a stress response in the individual.

the resources to overcome. Such threats, called **stressors**, may be internal or external and can come from sources such as loud noise, crowds or a lot of work. These situations may be acceptable when we feel able to cope with them but become stressors when we cannot. For example, a large animal running towards us might be perfectly okay if it is a friendly horse coming in from the field, but this event is unlikely to be judged positively if it is a bull with horns (and you are not a matador). The difference is simply that, in the first situation, we assess the situation and decide we have the means to cope (a calm voice and a handful of food). In the second example, however, we are likely to decide that we might be flattened or stabbed and there would not be much we could do about it – so we experience stress.

The changes that occur in the face of a stressor are adaptive – they have evolved to help us to survive. Clearly, being able to respond to a threat in a way that will increase the chances of survival is beneficial – hence it has evolved. So, how is our response to stress beneficial?

Selye (1947) began investigating how rats responded to different unpleasant situations and stimuli that he judged to be stressful (for example, heat and fatigue). They produced the same kinds of response regardless of the stressor used (hence *general*). These responses reflected an attempt by the body to cope with the situation (i.e. resulted in *adaptation*). The responses included a range of physiological and behavioural changes rather than a single effect, so were described as a *syndrome*. The initial changes include increased pulse rate, blood pressure and breathing rate, dilated pupils and a diversion of blood away from organs such as the digestive system to the muscles. These all help to prepare the individual for an emergency, such as fleeing danger or engaging in a fight. This first response is called the alarm reaction. Selye identified a further two phases in the body's response that arise if the stressor persists (resistance and exhaustion). The sequence of the General Adaptation Syndrome is therefore:

- *alarm reaction:* the immediate activation of the body's mechanisms for dealing with a threat
- *resistance stage:* the attempt by the body to return to a steady physiological state despite the persistence of the stressor
- *exhaustion stage:* the failure of the body to return to a normal physiological state in the on-going presence of a stressor that causes depletion of bodily resources and eventual collapse.

Selye saw this syndrome as an increase in the capacity of the individual to cope with (or resist) the impact of a *specific* stressor and the failure of this coping in the final stage. He also recognised that this response was only effective against that particular threat and, in many other ways, the body became less effective at coping. He described this as the loss of *cross resistance* (see Figure 1.3).

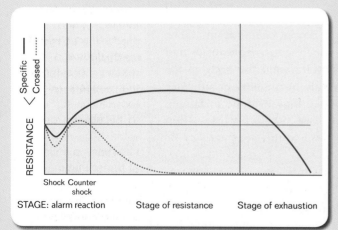

Figure 1.3 Loss of cross resistance

The alarm reaction

The immediate changes that occur in the alarm reaction are caused by the nervous system. Specifically, messages from the sensory organ that detects the threat (such as eyes seeing a ghost or ears hearing an explosion) are rapidly transmitted to the brain and the sympathetic part of the **autonomic nervous system** (ANS) is activated (see Figure 1.4). The ANS consists of two approximately antagonistic halves:

1   the sympathetic part – responsible for activating the body when arousal is high

2   the parasympathetic part – active during relaxation (for example, when we have eaten a big meal or are asleep).

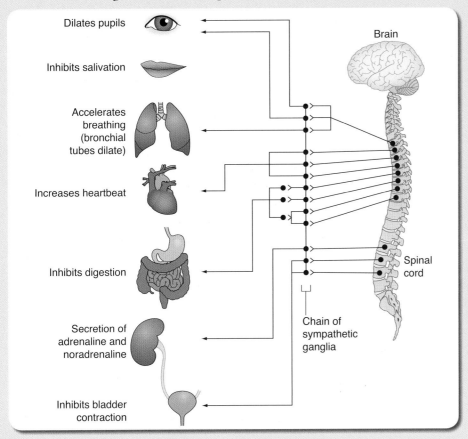

Figure 1.4 Sympathetic nervous system

The neurons of the ANS are part of the peripheral nervous system – that is, they lie outside the CNS and are distributed around the body reaching all the vital organs. The bodily changes caused by sympathetic activation help to prepare us for action. For example, a faster heart and breathing rate supplies more oxygen and the redirection of blood to the muscles assists this, so we are more likely to have the energy to fight or run away. The messages to the sympathetic system are located alongside the spinal cord. They are all together in a 'line' (called the sympathetic chain) and tend to be activated together. Activation of the different roles of the parasympathetic system tends to occur independently.

In addition to the response of the nervous system, the endocrine system is also activated. This occurs because the sympathetic nervous system (SNS) stimulates

Glossary

adrenal glands – a pair of glands, lying on top of the kidneys, that are part of the endocrine system. Each really consists of two glands: the **adrenal medulla** (which produces adrenaline) and the **adrenal cortex** (which produces cortisol).

hypothalamus – a small but complex part of the brain which interacts with both the nervous and the endocrine systems.

the **adrenal glands** (specifically the **adrenal medulla**) to release a hormone called **adrenaline**. The effects of adrenaline are similar to those of the SNS itself. The effects of the hormone, however, are slower but longer lasting than those of the SNS. This allows the defensive reactions to be maintained in the face of the danger. If the threat subsides, the parasympathetic part of the ANS can return the body to normal. The link between the sympathetic nervous system and the adrenal medulla is referred to as the **sympathetic adrenal medullary system (SAM)**. The SAM is therefore responsible for the body's reaction to acute (short-term) stressors.

The resistance stage

If the danger persists, the bodily state of alert cannot be maintained by adrenaline. Other hormones are released to sustain the body's defence reactions. Levels of these hormones may remain high for months or even years if a stressor persists. They include:

- *cortisol* (from the adrenal cortex), which makes more energy available through the breakdown of fats and release of glucose from the liver
- *aldosterone* (from the adrenal cortex), which maintains elevated blood pressure
- *thyroxine* (from the thyroid gland), which increases basal metabolic rate so maintains elevated heart and breathing rate and allows energy from food to be used quickly and efficiently.

The key hormones in this stage are the glucocorticoids, such as cortisol, released from the **adrenal cortex**. Cortisol is released in response to the presence of adrenocorticotrophic hormone (ACTH) in the blood. ACTH itself is released from the **pituitary gland** under the influence of corticotrophin releasing factor (CRF), a small protein released by the **hypothalamus**. This link between the hypothalamus, the pituitary gland and the adrenal cortex is called the **hypothalamic pituitary–adrenocortical axis** (HPA). The HPA is responsible for the body's response to chronic (long-term) stressors. However, the effects of persistently elevated hormone levels are themselves damaging and ultimately lead to illness and the exhaustion stage.

The exhaustion stage

Selye observed that, whatever the cause of stress, if the threat persisted, his animals became sick and died. The exhaustion stage reflects the body's inability to sustain attempts to cope under chronic stress. One significant impact is on the immune system, the structures and mechanisms that the body employs to fight disease. Under prolonged stress, this system becomes less effective. A high level of hormones such as cortisol appears to impair immune functioning. This is associated with an increase in allergic reactions, such as asthma and eczema, a change in the activity of lymphocytes (cells that fight diseases) and an increased risk of heart disease and cancer.

There are many internet sites offering advice about how to deal with stress. Look at a selection that explains what effects sufferers of stress are likely to experience. Use your understanding of the physiology of the response to stress to explain some of these effects.

Applying the biological approach to therapy: psychosurgery

The aims of psychosurgery

Psychosurgery is the use of surgery on the brain to treat psychological disorders. In the case of the procedures discussed below, the objective was to relieve distress and anxiety, particularly in patients that did not respond to any other treatment. Although the function of the targeted brain areas had not been identified, the effect of the surgery was deemed, at least at first, to have a specific effect.

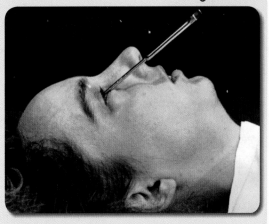

Figure 1.5 Lobotomies were sometimes performed via the eye socket

Techniques in psychosurgery

One of the first widespread uses of psychosurgery was a procedure called a **lobotomy**. Early lobotomies were called *leucotomies* (from *leuco*, referring to the white matter of the brain, and *tome*, to cut). The technique was pioneered by Egas Moniz and developed by Walter Freeman. It was based on a report that Moniz heard in 1935. A laboratory chimpanzee that became very distressed when she made errors on tests was subdued by a bilateral lesion to the prefrontal areas of her left and right frontal lobes. The safety of this treatment for highly emotionally distressed people was supported by a case in which a person's frontal lobes had been removed to destroy a tumour. This patient appeared not to suffer any intellectual impairment, despite the physical damage to the brain. These two observations, of a different species and a single human, were the basis for the development of several techniques which, in principle, aimed to destroy, or cut connections from, the frontal lobes. These included:

- *leucotomy* – an operation in which a narrow device called a leucotome was inserted (via holes made in the skull) into the frontal lobe. The 'blade' of the leucotome, a wire loop, was then extended and the device was rotated to lesion a core of tissue. This procedure could be repeated several times to destroy pieces of prefrontal cortex.
- *transorbital lobotomy* – a procedure which used a special knife, called an 'ice pick', inserted under the eye lid and into the back of the eye socket. This was used to break through the skull into the brain and moved around to destroy connections between the prefrontal area and other brain areas. This was repeated on both hemispheres.

This treatment was used on patients who were emotionally unstable and violent and did not respond to other forms of therapy. It did generally have the effect of relieving emotional distress and anxiety, thus calming the patient down. As a consequence, the surgery became common. Tooth and Newton (1961) reported that more than 10,000 such operations were performed in the UK alone. This popularity was especially true of the transorbital procedure, which did not even

Exam tip

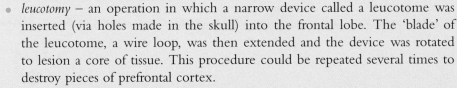

There are two therapies described here. In the exam, you will be asked to describe **either** psychosurgery **or** chemotherapy, so you only need to learn one of these therapies. Remember, to gain full marks in a question about biological therapy, you must link psychosurgery or chemotherapy back to the assumptions of the approach.

require hospitalisation. Now, however, such procedures are rare because of their severe side effects. Problems included changes in the patients' personality – for example, they became lethargic, apathetic, irresponsible or socially withdrawn. Although the patients' intellectual ability did not seem to be affected, they lacked the ability to plan their own behaviour or judge its appropriateness.

Current procedures

Despite the problems with psychosurgery, less dramatic procedures such as the **bilateral cingulotomy** are still occasionally performed. This has been used to help very depressed patients and sufferers of obsessive-compulsive disorder who do not respond to other treatments. It is also used to reduce pain in cancer patients. In this operation, the cingulate gyri, which link the **limbic system** to the frontal lobe, are destroyed. There is one cingulate gyrus on each side of the brain (hence 'bilateral'). This modern operation uses very accurate stereotactic magnetic resonance imaging to assist surgeons to identify the exact location of the area to be lesioned. The lesion can be performed with a fine electrode, which destroys the tissue directly. Alternatively, a gamma knife can be used. In this procedure, beams of radiation are focused on the location to be destroyed. So, unlike early lobotomies, a cingulotomy can be restricted to a minute area and the skull does not have to be breached.

How does psychosurgery link back to assumptions of the approach?

- As many brain functions are localised, damage to particular brain areas can have specific effects on psychological functions. This idea underlies psychosurgery because the intention is to disrupt a particular brain function. Although many areas may contribute to a particular problem behaviour, damage to a single area may be sufficient to suppress the symptoms. It might help to think of a bike: lots of parts are important to making it go – the wheels, chain, pedals, etc. – but you only have to take one pedal away and it will not work any more.
- This localisation also explains how other functions remain unimpaired – as the areas controlling those functions are separate and undamaged. In the bike analogy, even a bike with a missing pedal can be steered effectively if you free-wheel down a hill.

Applying the biological approach to therapy: chemotherapy

Neurotransmitters and the aims and techniques of chemotherapy

Drugs can affect synapses to influence emotions, cognition or behaviour to treat the symptoms of mental illness. This is *chemotherapy,* the therapeutic use of drugs. Three ways that drugs can interfere with synaptic transmission are to:

- *mimic neurotransmitters* and imitate their action at the receptor sites – for example, causing stimulation and an increase in the frequency of action potentials

Glossary

bilateral – both sides of the brain.
limbic system – an area deep within the brain that plays a role in emotional responses.

- *prolong neurotransmitter action* – for example, by preventing the recycling of neurotransmitter molecules into the pre-synaptic membrane, thus increasing the effect of the neurotransmitter
- *block receptors* – so preventing neurotransmitters from attaching to receptors, thus reducing the likelihood of action potentials occurring.

One of the earliest drugs to be understood was morphine. This works by imitating the action of neurotransmitters called **endorphins**. These 'natural opiates' are molecules that are structurally like the drug morphine and are even more powerful painkillers (think: *endo* – internal, *orphins* – morphine like). Morphine molecules attach to the receptors that naturally respond to endorphins and control our experience of pain. As morphine also causes activation at these receptors, it too has an analgesic effect. The nature of this effect was understood after the discovery of endorphin receptors in the brain by Pert and Snyder (1973). Morphine, and many related drugs (other opiates), are extensively used in medical practice for the relief of pain. One disadvantage of morphine use is that, in the long term, it causes dependence – that is, patients find it difficult to cope without the drug after prolonged use. As a result, it is only used for the control of pain in acute cases, such as after surgery, and for severe chronic pain, such as in terminal cancer patients.

The mental disorder schizophrenia is linked to a high level of the neurotransmitter dopamine. Some drug treatments for schizophrenia, such as chlorpromazine, are effective because they block dopamine receptor sites. This action reduces the access of dopamine molecules to the receptor sites so counters the effect of high dopamine levels and reduces symptoms.

In depressed individuals, levels of another neurotransmitter, serotonin, are low compared to non-depressed people. A drug group called selective serotonin reuptake inhibitors (SSRIs) blocks the return of serotonin to the pre-synaptic membrane. This means that there is relatively more of the neurotransmitter remaining in the synaptic cleft. This effectively increases the likelihood of serotonin molecules attaching to the receptors, countering the low neurotransmitter levels.

Box 1.1

Examples of mental disorders: schizophrenia and depression

Schizophrenia is characterised by the disruption of both emotions and cognition, so affects perception, thinking, language, behaviour and emotional responses. It can be identified by:

- positive symptoms – diagnosed by their presence (such as hallucinations and the belief that the individual's thoughts are being controlled or have been 'inserted')

- negative symptoms – diagnosed by the absence of responses (such as immobility or lack of speech).

Depression is a mood disorder characterised by a persistent and overwhelming sadness. This can be diagnosed by symptoms such as loss of pleasure or interest in most activities, significant loss or gain in weight, sleeping very much more or less than normal, feeling fatigued and having low self-esteem.

Glossary

meta-analysis – a review study that combines the findings of many similar previous investigations.

opiate – drug extracted from the opium poppy (morphine and codeine). Opiates work by attaching to opioid receptors.

placebo – an apparent treatment in which no active element is present (for example, a pill containing no drug or an operation that opens the skull but does not affect the brain at all).

randomised controlled trial – a design for a clinical investigation which compares the outcome for patients randomly assigned to different conditions, usually including treatment and placebo groups.

SSRI (selective serotonin reuptake inhibitor) – an anti-depressant drug which works by preventing the reabsorption of the neurotransmitter serotonin into the pre-synaptic membrane. This causes more serotonin to be available in the synapse to stimulate the post-synaptic receptor sites.

Glossary

dependent variable – the factor which is measured in an experiment.

experimental design – the allocation of participants to conditions in an experiment.

independent groups design – different participants are used for each condition of the IV.

independent variable – the factor which is deliberately manipulated in an experiment.

lab experiment – a study in which the researcher creates different conditions of the IV in an artificial, controlled environment and measures the effect on the DV. This allows the researcher to draw causal conclusions about the effect of the IV on the DV.

repeated measures design – the same participants are used in each condition of the IV.

How does chemotherapy link back to assumptions of the approach?

- As communication between neurons is chemical (using neurotransmitters), it is possible for other chemicals (i.e. drugs) to affect brain function. Some drugs act by enhancing synaptic transmission (for example, SSRIs) and others by reducing it (for example, antipsychotics).
- Different drugs have different effects because they act on different neurotransmitters – for example, SSRIs on the neurotransmitter serotonin and chlorpromazine on the neurotransmitter dopamine.

The methodology of the biological approach

Laboratory experiments on animals

Research using animals provided most of the early psychological knowledge about the structure and function of the nervous system and hormones. Moniz's ideas that led to widespread psychosurgery were based on the case of a single chimp, but the majority of animal research is not based on isolated examples but on the systematic testing of many animals under controlled conditions in which they are exposed to a range of procedures. This is the basis of a laboratory experiment. Such studies seek to demonstrate the effect of an independent variable (IV) on a dependent variable (DV). Other factors that could affect the DV are controlled. This enables the researcher to be more sure of a causal influence of the IV on the DV. The way animals (or human participants) are allocated to conditions in an experiment is called the experimental design. The same animals may be used in each condition (repeated measures design) or different ones may be used for each condition (independent groups design).

Using animals allows researchers to control potential confounding variables much more rigorously than would be the case if people were used, and a wider range of procedures can be used. We have looked at several areas of research in this chapter in which laboratory experiments using animals have played a significant part. For example:

- Studies relating to Selye's explanation of stress have explored the effect of a stressor (the IV) on animals' health (the DV). Potential confounding variables, such as diet, are controlled.
- Experiments have compared animals with deliberate lesions (areas of brain damage) to control groups to investigate the roles of specific brain areas (i.e. to demonstrate localisation of function).
- In the exploration of improved methods of psychosurgery, lesioned animals may be compared to controls who either are unharmed or have been anaesthetised and had their skulls opened without actually damaging the brain (these are called 'sham' operations).
- Drug effects may be tested on animals – for example, to compare the effect of one type of drug to another or to the absence of the drug on the animals' behaviour.

Evaluation of laboratory experiments on animals

One major strength of using animals in laboratory experiments is the extent to which potential confounding variables can be controlled. Factors such as diet, exercise, amount of sleep and social isolation may affect psychological variables, such as the consequences of stress and mental health. This means that the validity of the findings of such studies is high because the changes in the DV are less likely to be due to extraneous variables than if human participants were used. In addition, as laboratory animals are small, cheap and readily available, procedures can be replicated, thus increasing the reliability of the findings.

Similarly, the range of procedures that can be used with human participants is much smaller. For example, people's brains cannot be lesioned for experimental interest and they cannot be exposed to extreme stressors or stressed for long periods of time. Animals, therefore, provide a way to explore research questions that cannot be studied with the same degree of scientific rigour in humans.

If we are to benefit from such research, we must be confident that we can generalise from the findings of experiments using animals to humans. This seems reasonable as we have a shared evolutionary history so our hormonal and nervous systems are very similar. Having the same endocrine glands releasing similar hormones suggests our responses to stress would be alike. Mammals, including ourselves, rats, mice, cats and monkeys, have the same basic brain structure (of a hind-, mid- and forebrain). It thus seems probable that the biological processes underlying our behaviour are the same.

However, there are also important differences between the systems. For example, in the case of hormones, women differ from other female mammals in that their sexual cycle causes menstruation. There may, therefore, be differences in other hormone systems too. Our brains are also different, in both size and structure. The outer layer of the brain (the cortex) is much larger in humans relative to our size than in other animals. So generalisation from animals to humans is credible in some ways but not in others.

Another criticism of laboratory animal experiments is an ethical one, which questions whether the animal's suffering is outweighed by the benefits to humans. For some people, the answer to the question 'Do the ends justify the means?' is 'no' because they hold the view that animals should not suffer pain or distress in order to relieve such symptoms in humans. For others, the answer is 'yes', at least sometimes. Bateson (1986) suggested that when the certainty of benefit from an animal study was high, the research was of good quality and the suffering was low, research would be worth conducting (see Figure 1.6).

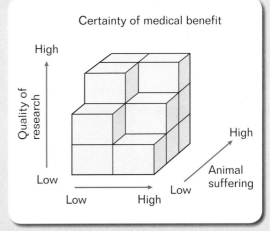

Figure 1.6 Bateson (1986) suggested determining whether any animal study should be conducted by considering a balance of factors

Glossary

extraneous variables – factors in an experiment, other than the IV, which could affect the DV so need to be controlled.
reliability – the extent to which findings are consistent (for example, the same results would be obtained if a study was repeated).
validity – the extent to which a test or task measures what it is intended to measure.

Brain scanning

Brain scanning methods fall into two types: *structural* and *functional*. Structural scans, such as computerised axial tomography (CAT) and magnetic resonance imaging (MRI), provide detailed images of living brains. They produce images showing the details of structures inside the brain without actually having to

cut through any tissue. This type of scan can be used to investigate normal and abnormal brain function by looking at the differences in structure between the brains of different individuals. For example, some studies have shown that people with schizophrenia have larger ventricles – spaces within the brain – than people without schizophrenia.

A functional scan, such as positron emission tomography (PET) or functional magnetic resonance imaging (fMRI), identifies those parts of the brain that are more or less active at a given time. This enables the researcher to link brain activity to behaviour. Such techniques can be used to investigate normal and abnormal brain function by looking at the differences between responses to different experiences or in different brain areas.

Structural scanning: MRI

MRI scans (see Figure 1.7) look like a photograph of a slice through the brain. The process of MRI uses a strong magnetic field, which causes the hydrogen atoms in water molecules to behave like compass needles and 'point' the same way when it is turned on. When radio waves are passed through the head and the hydrogen atoms return to their original positions, they emit radio waves, which are detected by the scanner. As different parts of the brain contain differing amounts of water, the emission of radio waves varies between areas, causing different 'densities' (shades of grey) on the image.

During an MRI scan, the participant lies on a narrow bed inside the tubular scanner. They must keep very still for the scan to work. They can hear and speak to the researcher through a headset but the environment inside the scanner is very noisy.

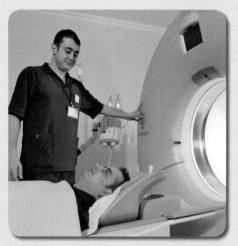

Figure 1.7 For an MRI scan, the participant lies on a bed that slides inside the scanner

Functional scanning: PET

In a PET scan, a radioactive molecule (called a tracer) is injected into the participant's bloodstream. The tracers are chemicals (like water or glucose) that are used by active brain tissues. The tracer reaches the brain in about one minute and it decays over the following 10–15 minutes. This produces radioactivity (initially as positrons, then gamma rays), which is detected by the scanner, indicating activity in that area of the brain. The doughnut-shaped scanner surrounding the participant's head detects the gamma rays and produces an image in which varying levels of brain activity appear as different colours (see Figure 1.8).

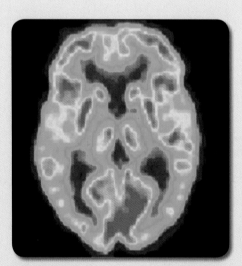

Figure 1.8 A PET scan indicates differing levels of brain activity as different colours

The participant is typically scanned several times in two conditions, such as prior to chemotherapy as a baseline, and then again after a course of treatment. The difference between the scans indicates whether there has been a change in levels of brain activity, and if so which parts of the brain are affected.

Evaluation of the use of brain scanning

One major strength of brain scanning is that it can investigate people's brains while they are still alive. This is an improvement on earlier methods, which could only investigate what the brain looked like postmortem and relate this to the way it worked. With structural scanning, we can compare images of live brains and test the 'owners' to relate differences between structures to differences in behaviours, cognition or emotion. This can help to establish whether a physical abnormality is responsible for a symptom. Functional scans are even more informative as they can measure changes in brain activity in real time. They can therefore be used for a wider variety of applications.

Modern brain scanners produce clear, detailed, accurate images and have good reliability, although structural scans have higher resolution – that is, smaller regions can be identified than on functional scans. Such techniques are also highly objective. However, the validity of evidence from brain scans depends, to an extent, on the way it is interpreted. For example, differences in brain activity levels between depressed individuals receiving chemotherapy and non-depressed individuals may be due to differences in mental health or due to the drug treatment received for depression. That is, brain scans cannot explain *why* differences exist, and this interpretation stage can threaten validity.

A significant weakness of brain scanning is the effect of the scanning process itself on the participant's behaviour or emotions. PET scanning involves being injected – a potentially emotionally arousing procedure – so findings may be confounded by anxiety. Similarly, as it is small and very noisy inside an MRI scanner, it is quite unlike day-to-day life. This not only lowers ecological validity but also limits the range of behaviours a participant can perform while inside.

Finally, there are ethical issues to consider. Scanning may be distressing for the participants (due to injections or confinement) and, in the case of PET scanning, the frequency of scans must be limited due to exposure to radiation.

Glossary

ecological validity – the extent to which findings can be applied beyond the setting in which they were obtained.
objective – being independent (for example, not affected by the researcher's personal perspective or expectations).

Evaluation of the biological approach

Strengths

1. Biological approaches are perceived to be scientific and trustworthy

The biological approach is based on the objective study of observable, measureable factors that affect behaviour. For example, hormone and neurotransmitter levels can be assessed (and manipulated) and the influence of natural (or experimental) variation can be measured. As a consequence, controlled experiments can be performed to investigate the effects of changes in environmental factors (for example, in the study of stress) or of body chemistry (for example, in the testing of drugs for mental illnesses). In the latter, further objectivity is achieved through comparisons between drug and placebo groups and the use of random controlled trials.

However, at least historically, biological approaches have not always been rigorously scientific. For example, the use of lobotomies was based on very limited

evidence and the consequences of the operation for the patient were severe. Findings from the chimpanzee would not necessarily have been relevant to humans. The species differ in both brain structure and function (for example, cognition and behaviour). The findings from the human case may not have been generalisable because the medical reason for the lobotomy was a physical not a psychological one, and a single instance is not sufficient to indicate the success of a procedure on others. Furthermore, the rapid growth of the technique was based on its effectiveness not only in reducing distress in patients but also in making difficult individuals more manageable for staff in institutions. Such manipulation is now seen as unethical. At the time, however, the treatment was perceived to be an improvement in the care of patients who were suffering severe and incurable distress or whose behaviour could not be controlled other than by confinement or restraint.

2. Explanations from the biological approach have useful applications

One application is to help to remove stigma from mental illnesses, such as the progress made with post-traumatic stress disorder (PTSD) – the 'shell shock' experienced by soldiers during the world wars – attributed at the time to a weak personality or malingering. Soldiers exposed to the horrors of the battle-field sometimes develop severe and lasting reactions, including panic, confusion and paralysis, that are now believed to be the result of physiological responses to stress.

This approach has led to research into the role of corticotrophin releasing factor (CRF), which may help war veterans. In an experiment comparing controls to Vietnam veterans, Liberzon *et al.* (1999) found that the veterans with PTSD were more sensitive to combat-related sounds than either non-veterans or veterans without PTSD. They showed greater sensitivity to stress in terms of reactions, such as heart rate and adrenaline and cortisol levels. Sautter *et al.* (2003) compared PTSD sufferers with and without psychotic symptoms. Those most severely affected (i.e. with psychotic symptoms) had higher levels of CRF. Together, the findings suggest that a drug which acts on CRF could provide a therapy for PTSD (Zorrilla and Koob, 2004).

Biological therapies are also useful in the treatment of mental illness, through psychosurgery, at least in its more recent form, and chemotherapy. While the initial claims of success by Moniz and Freeman were not substantiated, recent treatments have been more effective. In an investigation of cingulotomy for the control of pain, Cohen *et al.* (1999) found that more than 60 per cent of patients reported less pain post-operatively and most required less medication to control their pain.

There is also evidence supporting the use of chemotherapy, suggesting that the biological approach is an effective tool for investigating and treating mental illness. For example, Trivedi *et al.* (2006) found that the SSRI citalopram was effective in treating depression. Thirty-three per cent of the patients taking cital-opram experienced remission and for 47 per cent their depression score halved – often within eight weeks. However, it is possible that some of those who recovered would have gone into remission spontaneously and, as this particular study lacked a placebo group, this effect cannot be identified.

However, evidence from studies of chemotherapy is mixed. In a meta-analysis of randomised controlled trials using chlorpromazine for schizophrenia, Adams *et al.* (2005) found that chlorpromazine failed to produce global improvement in 76 per cent of patients and commonly produced adverse side effects, such as sedation, a risk of movement disorders and dizziness. Nevertheless, it is a low-cost treatment that is effective for one in seven people with schizophrenia, is still a common treatment and provides a standard against which other drugs can be evaluated.

Weaknesses

1. Is the biological approach too simplistic?

Mental illnesses such as depression and schizophrenia are often more complex than is implied by reductionist, deterministic biological explanations, so drug treatments are rarely fully effective. For example, several neurotransmitters (serotonin, noradrenaline and dopamine) are important in depression, so drugs targeting a single one, such as SSRIs, which target only serotonin, may not be sufficient. Differences in symptoms between individuals may also mean that a treatment which is effective for one patient does not work for all. Furthermore, as neurotransmitters have multiple roles in the brain, drugs often have side effects.

2. Chemotherapy only treats symptoms

Finally, chemotherapy can only treat the symptoms of a disorder, rather than identifying and eradicating the cause. This means it is likely to provide only a temporary solution. A more permanent 'cure' would need to identify and reverse or remove psychological or environmental factors that are important, for example, in maintaining a depressed mood. We will consider such issues in Chapter 4. However, if it is not possible to change the individual's past or their biology, then chemotherapy may offer a way to manage symptoms that would otherwise be distressing.

Box 1.2

Where does the biological approach stand on key issues and debates?

Reductionism

The biological approach takes a 'reductionist' stance, focusing on a narrow range of factors (for example, the level of a neurotransmitter) to explain phenomena such as mental illness. This tends to preclude other possible causal factors, such as childhood experiences or social setting. In this sense, it is a weakness of the approach, although reductionism does allow individual causal effects to be explored effectively, so it is also a strength.

Determinism

The biological approach takes a 'deterministic' view of stress, which tends to ignore factors such as individual differences. A deterministic approach says that, under a certain set of circumstances (for example, a particular stressor), a person will show signs of the GAS, progressing through adaptation and exhaustion. This is a strength as it provides a clear understanding of the process. However, this narrow view cannot explain why some people get stressed and ill but others do not, even when exposed to the same stressors. The deterministic viewpoint is therefore a weakness of the biological approach.

Nature–nurture debate

Again, the position taken by the biological approach is quite extreme, lying at the 'nature'

end of the debate, for example in the explanation of problems such as mental illnesses. As the causes of these problems are seen as biological, the solutions are also approached from a physiological angle. Thus the focus of biological psychology tends to exclude the role of nurture in the development of mental illness and, as a consequence, the importance of environmental influences (such as the part played by other people) in managing symptoms.

Psychology as a science

This is a major strength of the biological approach. Ideas from the biological approach are readily tested in scientific ways using laboratory experiments. In addition, objective and reliable measures can be used, such as scientific instruments like brain scanners.

Exam tip

To get high marks in a compare-and-contrast question, you must refer to the issues and debates.

Comparing and contrasting the biological approach

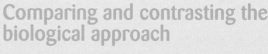

Here we are going to show an example of how to compare and contrast the biological approach with the psychodynamic approach.

Table 1.1 A plan for how to compare and contrast the biological and psychodynamic approaches

CRITERION	BIOLOGICAL	PSYCHODYNAMIC	SIMILARITY/DIFFERENCE
Assumptions	Neurons, localisation and hormones	Unconscious mind and early relationships	Difference
Applications	Psychosurgery and chemotherapy	Therapy	Difference
Methods	Lab experiments using animals and brain scanning	Clinical case studies and interviews	Difference
Nature–nurture	Mostly nature	Balance of nature and nurture	Difference
Reductionism	Reductionist	More holistic	Difference
Determinism	Deterministic	Deterministic	Similarity
Science	Very scientific	Not scientific	Difference

Summing it up

- Neurons are nerve cells that send electrical messages. They communicate across synapses using neurotransmitters that attach to receptor sites.

- The brain is part of the central nervous system. It is highly organised and different structures have different functions – this is called localisation. The nervous system is vital to our emotions, cognition and behaviour. It coordinates our responses and triggers rapid reactions.

- The endocrine system is composed of hormones released from glands into the blood. It is another important communication system in the body and is slower but longer acting than the nervous system. It is important in controlling our response to stress.

- Stress is a response to a threat that we perceive ourselves to be unable to cope with. Such threats may be internal or external.

- The GAS (General Adaptation Syndrome) was proposed by Selye and consists of three stages:

  - Alarm reaction – an initial, rapid response to a threat that mobilises bodily resources. This is effected by the sympathetic nervous system and adrenaline.

  - Resistance stage – a later and more prolonged response that allows the body to remain ready for defensive action in ways that can be sustained. It is achieved through hormones such as cortisol.

  - Exhaustion stage – the effect of prolonged attempts to deal with a stressor that diminish bodily resources and cause an elevated risk of illness.

- Psychosurgery – treats mental illnesses by operating on the brain – for example, using lobotomies and cingulotomies. The lobotomy was widely used but had a poor success rate. It was popular in part because it made it possible to control difficult patients. Cingulotomies have a higher success rate and fewer side effects but still carry considerable risks. Localisation, an assumption of the approach, is central to psychosurgery as the technique is intended to work by causing damage to a specific area in order to change a particular brain function. This explains why other functions are unimpaired as the areas controlling them are undamaged.

- Chemotherapy – treats mental illnesses using drugs. Many drugs are used to help people to cope with mental illnesses (for example, anti-depressants). They often act by mimicking or blocking the effects of a neurotransmitter. Although often very successful at reducing symptoms, they have side effects and cannot solve the cause of the condition. The assumptions of the approach relating to neuronal communication through neurotransmitters explain how drugs can alter brain function as they affect synaptic transmission either by increasing or by decreasing it and how different drugs differ in their effects – as they affect different neurotransmitters.

- Laboratory experiments on animals enable researchers to explore explanations of behaviour and test the effectiveness of drugs and psychosurgery in controlled and reliable studies. However, the findings may not generalise to humans and the animals used may suffer so the research may not be justified.

- Brain scanning can investigate structure or function of the brain. MRI uses a noisy magnet to produce a highly detailed structural scan. PET uses radioactivity to produce a less detailed functional scan. Although scans are very detailed and reliable, the scanning process is unlike normal life and the scans need to be interpreted – both of which are threats to validity.

- Overall, the main strengths of the biological approach are that it is scientific and objective, and has led to effective treatments for mental illness.

- The key weaknesses are that the approach is both reductionist and determinist, and chemotherapy treats symptoms rather than eradicating the cause of a disorder.

Consolidate your understanding

The biological approach

Use the following activities to run the information in this chapter through your mind. Each activity is designed to help you process the information in a different way, which should help you ensure you understand it and make it easier to remember.

Wordsearch

S	D	E	M	L	E	R	U	T	A	N	L	R	S	R	Y
C	E	G	R	R	S	O	S	O	L	I	O	E	O	I	O
S	T	A	Y	I	T	S	N	I	A	R	B	S	T	I	E
R	E	T	T	I	M	S	N	A	R	T	O	R	U	E	N
D	R	S	E	T	N	E	F	L	M	Y	T	E	C	O	I
C	M	E	P	S	S	R	H	E	R	M	O	P	X	L	L
O	I	C	D	A	C	T	H	P	E	O	M	A	N	B	A
R	N	N	G	U	N	S	A	M	A	T	Y	P	M	I	N
T	I	A	G	N	C	Y	O	U	C	O	M	T	R	E	E
I	S	T	C	U	L	T	S	T	T	L	R	I	Y	T	R
S	T	S	Y	S	L	E	I	M	I	U	C	M	R	E	D
O	C	I	T	E	N	O	R	O	O	G	R	S	S	Y	A
L	U	S	N	T	L	I	T	R	N	N	X	E	O	R	R
T	M	E	U	T	M	T	A	O	A	I	S	S	I	A	E
A	O	R	C	R	Y	T	U	R	M	C	S	Y	A	A	O
D	E	N	D	R	I	T	E	P	B	Y	I	T	S	T	I

synapse   lobotomy   adrenaline
brain   brain scan   SAM
GAS   PET   HPA
neurotransmitter   MRI   ACTH
stressor   reductionist   CRF
resistance stage   determinist   axon
cingulotomy   nature   dendrite
alarm reaction   cortisol

Crossword

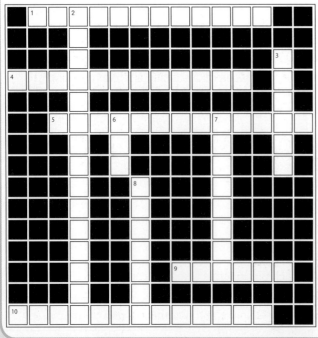

Across

1. Drugs for mental illness
4. Brain functions are limited to specific areas
5. Brain operations for mental illness
9. Reaction to an unmanageable threat
10. A research method using rigorous controls in an artificial setting (two words)

Down

2. The final phase of Selye's GAS (two words)
3. A nerve cell
6. The brain and spinal cord (abbreviation)
7. Where a neurotransmitter attaches to
8. Released from glands in the endocrine system

Wordsearch and crossword solutions begin on page 231.

Consolidate your understanding

Cloze

Neurons are nerve cells that send _____ messages. They communicate across synapses using _____ that attach to _____ sites. The _____ is part of the central nervous system. It is highly organised and different structures have different functions. This is called _____. The nervous system is vital to our emotions, cognition and behaviour. It coordinates our responses and triggers rapid reactions. The _____ system is composed of _____ released from glands into the blood. It is another important communication system in the body and is slower but longer acting than the nervous system. It is important in controlling our response to _____. Stress is a response to a threat that we perceive ourselves to be _____ to cope with. Such threats may be internal or external.

The GAS (_____ _____ _____) was proposed by Selye and consists of three stages: the _____ reaction (an initial, rapid response to a threat that mobilises bodily resources which is effected by the _____ nervous system and _____); the _____ stage (a later and more prolonged response that allows the body to remain ready for defensive action in ways that can be sustained which is achieved through hormones such as cortisol); and the _____ stage (the effect of prolonged attempts to deal with a stressor that diminish bodily resources and cause an elevated risk of _____). The biological approach takes a determinist view of stress, which tends to ignore factors such as individual differences and states that, under a certain set of circumstances (for example, a particular stressor), a person will show signs of the GAS. However, this cannot explain why some people get stressed and ill but others do not, even when exposed to the same stressors.

_____ treats mental illnesses by operating on the brain – for example, using _____ and cingulotomies. The lobotomy was widely used but had a _____ success rate. It was popular in part because it made it possible to control difficult patients. Cingulotomies have a higher success rate and _____ side effects but still carry considerable risks. Localisation, an assumption of the approach, is central to psychosurgery as the techniques are intended to work by causing damage to a specific area in order to change a particular brain function. This explains why other functions are _____ as the areas controlling them are undamaged. The biological approach takes a _____ perspective in the explanation of problems such as mental illnesses as the causes (and solutions) are approached from a biological angle. The focus of biological psychology thus tends to exclude the role of _____ in the development of mental illness and the importance of environmental influences (such as the part played by other people) in managing symptoms.

_____ treats mental illnesses using drugs. Many drugs are used to help people to cope with mental illnesses (for example, anti-depressants). They often act by mimicking or blocking the effects of a _____. Although often very successful at reducing symptoms, they have side effects and cannot solve the _____ of the condition. The assumptions of the approach relating to neuronal communication through neurotransmitters explain how drugs can alter brain function as they affect synaptic transmission either by increasing or by decreasing it and how different drugs differ in their effects – as they affect different neurotransmitters.

Laboratory experiments on _____ enable researchers to explore explanations of behaviour and test the effectiveness of drugs and psychosurgery in _____ and reliable studies. However, the findings may not _____ to humans and the animal suffering caused may not justify the research. Brain scanning can investigate structure or function of the brain. _____ uses a noisy magnet to produce a highly detailed structural scan. _____ uses radioactivity to produce a less detailed functional scan. Although scans are very detailed and _____, the scanning process is unlike normal life and the scans need to be interpreted – both of which are threats to _____.

Overall, the main strengths of the biological approach are that it is objective and has led to effective treatments for mental illness. The key weaknesses are that the approach is both reductionist and _____, and chemotherapy treats _____ rather than eradicating the cause of a disorder.

For help completing the cloze activity, see the 'Summing it up' section for this chapter.

Consolidate your understanding

Concept map

Complete the empty boxes and you will have a visual revision plan.

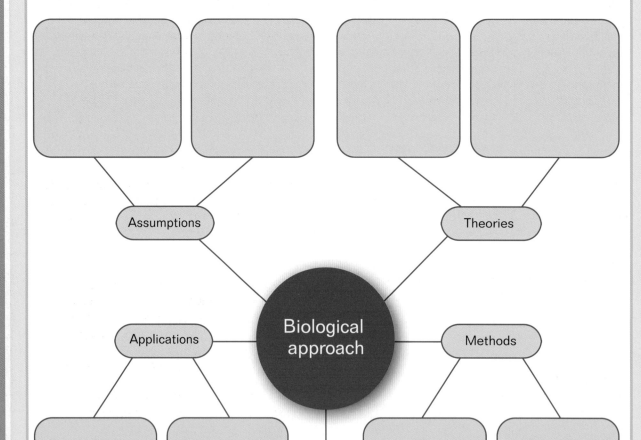

Assumptions

Theories

Applications

Biological approach

Methods

Evaluation

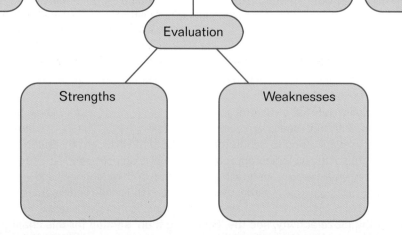

Strengths

Weaknesses

Exam focus

The biological approach

This is probably the first 'doing the exam' section you'll read. It's largely structured around the five questions you will answer in your PY 1 (Approaches in Psychology) paper and contains some handy hints and revision ideas. Don't be worried if it doesn't immediately make sense – it's probably best to come back to it once you've done a test or two.

Assumptions

As with all the approaches you will need two assumptions here. It is important to remember that the biggest assumption of the biological approach is that **evolution** has shaped everything about us: structure, biology and behaviour. Evolutionary hypotheses about behaviour are normal in this approach. There is also the linked assumption of **animal-human continuity** – that we are an animal like every other and can be studied using the ideas and methods we use for other animals.

Theory

GAS is a simple theory to describe. You need a sentence or two about Selye and what he did, then a three-stage description that includes specific information about the role of hormones and neurotransmitters, in order to get the 8 marks available. If you feel the urge to draw a diagram, go ahead. Diagrams can help produce a clear and accurate answer, but they have to be supplemented with clear, accurate text in order for the answer to go into the 'reasonably accurate and detailed category'!

Therapy

Don't forget **the link between therapy and the approach**. Here the link must be brain chemistry for an answer about drug therapies, and brain structure in an answer about psychosurgery.

Chemotherapy should have general principles of drug use (mainly to alleviate symptoms rather than cure), with a couple of good examples of such therapy in detail (for example, SSRI therapy for depression). **Don't evaluate – the 12 marks are for description only**.

Strengths and weaknesses

Remember that strengths and weaknesses will be asked about separately with part a) of the question asking about strengths and part b) about weaknesses. The two best strengths are the scientific nature of this approach and the useful therapies generated, especially chemotherapy. You could have the reductionist nature of biology as a weakness, with the neglect of individual differences and social factors.

Compare and contrast

The only difficulty here is with the cognitive approach, which in modern times is a partner in neuroscience – therefore there will be a lot of 'compare' but less 'contrast'. The biological approach is so invasive that the contrast with other approaches is easily made, and its neglect of the individual places it in direct contrast to the psychodynamic approach. It is also strongly deterministic (but say how it is and give an example).

Explain and evaluate method

A number of methods are available, and it is simply a matter of personal choice, they include: **scanning methods** (fMRI and PET are easily described and evaluated as both have strengths and weaknesses), **twin studies** and **case studies** (examples are needed, which could include Phineas Gage, or Moniz basing his techniques on the chimp and female patient with tumour).

2 The behaviourist approach

I should be able to:

- outline two main assumptions of the behaviourist approach
- describe social learning theory as an explanation of aggression
- describe how behaviourist ideas have been put to use in either aversion therapy or systematic desensitisation
- describe and evaluate the research methodology used in the behaviourist approach
- evaluate the behaviourist approach in terms of its strengths and weaknesses
- compare and contrast the behaviourist approach with other perspectives.

What could I be asked?

There is no guarantee that future exams will keep precisely to this wording or mark allocation. However, it is likely that any questions you are asked about the approach will be much like the following:

1. (a) Outline **two** assumptions of the behaviourist approach. [4]

   (b) **Describe** social learning theory as an explanation of aggression. [8]

2. **Describe** how the behaviourist approach has been applied to one therapy. [12]

3. (a) Evaluate **two** strengths of the behaviourist approach. [6]

   (b) Evaluate **two** weaknesses of the behaviourist approach. [6]

4. **Compare and contrast** the biological and behaviourist approaches in terms of similarities and differences. [12]

5. **Explain and evaluate** the methodology used by the behaviourist approach. [12]

Behaviourists focus on the observable reactions of organisms to their environments and attempt to explain psychological processes in terms of acquired responses to stimuli, so behaviourism is referred to as 'stimulus–response' psychology. It differs from introspection and from the psycho-dynamic psychology, which focuses on explaining events in terms of the unconscious. This matters as the phenomena behaviourists record, unlike thoughts or unconscious motives, are observable and measurable, so behaviourism is highly scientific. Explanations from the behaviourist approach account for the ways in which new behaviours are acquired.

Assumptions of the behaviourist approach

The main assumptions of the behaviourist approach include the following ideas:

- the role of the **environment**
- the importance of **observable events** in research
- the **common principles** in learning.

The role of the environment

The environment is a significant influence on our behaviour. It can provide stimuli that act as triggers for behaviours, such as the presence of food producing salivation. Through learning, new environmental stimuli can acquire the ability to trigger such responses. The environment is also a source of consequences that affect the likelihood that we will repeat a behaviour. Good things, such as praise, make us more likely to do something again. Receiving punishment, on the other hand, means we are less likely to do the same thing again.

The environment also provides models, allowing individuals to learn by copying. A child growing up in a home where adults have a regional accent will acquire that accent by imitation. Manipulating an individual's environment is therefore a way to alter their learning experience. Other approaches also suggest that aspects of the external environment may affect behaviour, such as the psychodynamic approach, which claims that childhood experiences are important. The behaviourist approach is different because it focuses directly on the role of the environment. Other approaches, in contrast, include internal aspects too, such as the role of the unconscious in psychodynamic psychology.

The importance of observable events in research

The behaviourist approach focuses on external rather than internal factors so its methodology is distinctive. Whereas other approaches must rely, to an extent, on assumptions about thinking, feeling, attitudes or the unconscious, the behaviourist approach relies exclusively on observable data. While behaviourists do not deny the existence of an unconscious, the emphasis of their investigations is on the visible, measurable changes that occur in behaviour in response to known manipulations of the environment.

The common principles in learning

Behaviour learned in response to one stimulus may appear in response to another, similar stimulus; this is called **generalisation**. For example, a child might learn that aggression at home makes a sibling surrender their sweets. They may then be aggressive to peers at school too.

Discrimination is the process of distinguishing between two similar but different stimuli and responding to only one of them. For example, a child may be aggressive at home to a younger sibling but not to an older one.

These ideas are central to the behaviourist approach because they apply to

> ### Glossary
>
> **introspection** – studying mental processes by looking inwardly at one's own thinking.
> **learning** – a relatively permanent change in behavioural potential that arises as a result of experience.

behaviours acquired by any mechanism – for example, classical or operant conditioning, or social learning (see below). They are also important because they have survival value for the learner. An animal that can generalise a response can apply the behaviour to new situations which might be beneficial (for example, birds that learn to open the foil tops on old milk bottles to reach the cream could generalise this to yoghurt pots, etc., and gain new sources of food). Discrimination can help the individual to avoid dangerous or unpleasant situations – for example, a bird might learn to eat only nice-tasting berries or insects on the basis of their colour.

When behaviours have been learned, they are not necessarily permanent. Following the learning period, a newly acquired behaviour may be lost from the repertoire. This is called **extinction** of the response. After a period of time during which this response is not produced, it may suddenly reappear, triggered by the original stimulus. This is called **spontaneous recovery**.

Early behaviourist theories

Classical conditioning

Classical conditioning occurs when an individual acquires the response of reproducing an action that they can already perform, but in response to a new situation. For example, a puppy will learn that going in the car leads to exciting places to walk. Soon it gets excited every time the car door is opened. The learned response becomes an automatic and unavoidable consequence of exposure to this new stimulus. In order to describe this process, you need to understand the correct terms:

- *unconditioned stimulus* (UCS) – the existing cause of a behaviour (which may be a reflex) prior to conditioning
- *neutral stimulus* (NS) – a new stimulus which, prior to conditioning, did not produce this response
- *unconditioned response* (UCR) – the pre-existing response to the unconditioned stimulus
- *conditioned response* (CR) – a response, similar to the unconditioned response, which is produced in response to the conditioned stimulus
- *conditioned stimulus* (CS) – the name given to the neutral stimulus after conditioning when it has acquired the capacity to produce the conditioned response.

The CR may differ from the UCR in terms of latency (the time it takes to start) and strength (how vigorous the response is). The CR is likely to occur more slowly and less vigorously than the UCR.

Ivan Pavlov was the first researcher to identify and explore classical conditioning (see Figure 2.1). He was a physiologist exploring digestion and knew that animals produced saliva in response to food. However, he was interested to know why his experimental dogs also salivated to the sound of footsteps, whether or not the walking person was bringing food. Pavlov (1927) investigated whether the dogs had learned that the sound was associated with food. During the experiment, salivation was measured with:

- meat powder alone
- meat powder and a ticking of a metronome (the conditioning phase)
- a ticking metronome alone.

Pavlov found that the dogs initially salivated to the meat powder (UCS) but not the metronome (NS). After the conditioning phase, during which the noise and the food were presented together repeatedly, the dogs also salivated (CR) to the metronome. The dogs acquired an association between the existing response of salivation and the new stimulus – the sound of the metronome (then a CS).

Before conditioning:
UCS (meat powder) → UCR (salivation)
During conditioning:
UCS + NS (beat of metronome) → UCR
After conditioning:
CS (beat of metronome) → CR (salivation)

Many behaviours can be classically conditioned. For example, you may find yourself looking up expectantly and considering crossing the road because you have heard the sound of the 'clear to cross' beeping – that is the product of classical conditioning. We are even conditioned to salivate. Ask someone to rattle a biscuit tin or unwrap a chocolate bar near you. Even if you cannot smell the food, you may salivate because the visual and auditory triggers act as a conditioned stimulus. Humans behaviour can also learn a fear response through classical conditioning.

John Watson, another famous behaviourist, investigated conditioned emotional responses. Watson and Rayner (1920) studied a nine-month-old boy called Albert who was initially unafraid of a range of objects, such as a white rat and wooden blocks, but was startled by a loud noise (see Figures 2.2a and b). He was classically

Figure 2.1 Ivan Pavlov with one of his dogs during an experiment

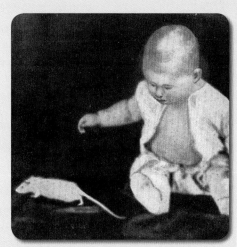

Figure 2.2a Before conditioning, Albert shows no fear of the rat

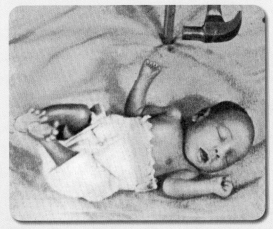

Figure 2.2b Before conditioning, Albert is afraid of the loud noise

Figure 2.2c After conditioning, Albert's fear generalises to other fluffy, white objects

conditioned by being repeatedly shown a rat and simultaneously hearing a loud noise (caused by striking a metal bar with a hammer). His response to the noise alone was observed, and to objects, such as the wooden blocks, that had not been associated with the noise. Watson and Rayner observed that the infant was afraid of the loud noise and, after the second pairing with the rat, also seemed afraid of the rat. After five days, the child cried in response to the rat and to similar white, soft objects (such as a fur coat and Father Christmas beard – see Figure 2.2c). After seven weeks, these responses were still present but at no point did he show distress to the wooden blocks. These observations suggest that Albert had acquired an association between the sight of the rat and the new stimulus – the loud noise – through classical conditioning. This response generalised to other, similar, white fluffy objects but not to different objects, such as the wooden blocks.

Operant conditioning

When an animal is placed in a new situation, it responds with a range of behaviours triggered by stimuli in the environment. Some of the responses have no effect, some produce pleasant, and others unpleasant, consequences. These consequences determine the future frequency of the behaviours that elicited them. If a behaviour results in an overall pleasant effect, this is called **reinforcement** and the behaviour will be repeated more often. When this pleasant effect is the result of something good happening, this is called **positive reinforcement**. If the pleasant effect is the result of something nasty stopping, it is called **negative reinforcement**. In either case, remember, the behaviour increases in frequency. However, if the behaviour has unpleasant effects, this consequence is called **punishment**, and the behaviour is repeated less often. Punishers can be either the end of something nice (**negative punishment**) or the start of something nasty (**positive punishment**).

These consequences may occur every time the action is performed or only sometimes (partial reinforcement). This pattern is called the schedule of reinforcement and affects both the rate of responses and extinction.

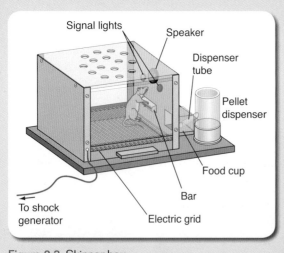

Figure 2.3 Skinner box

Much of our understanding of operant conditioning comes from the extensive work of B.F. Skinner. He devised a way to test learning in animals, minimising the need for human interference. He created a mechanised box in which an animal, such as a rat or pigeon, could perform a range of responses and (for some, but not others) gain automatic reinforcement. This apparatus, now called a Skinner box, allowed him to vary the nature and frequency of reinforcement (for example, food, which was delivered in tiny pellets). A Skinner box (see Figure 2.3) also records the frequency of the animal's responses. Skinner conducted many different experiments – for example, showing that rats receiving food for pressing the bar in a box (i.e. were reinforced) pressed the bar more often than those receiving no food. Interestingly, rats receiving food on only some bar presses (a partial reinforcement schedule) responded faster and were more resistant to extinction than those reinforced for every bar press.

The social learning theory of aggression

In addition to the processes of conditioning, humans and animals can acquire new behaviours by observation. This is explained by social learning theory. This theory says that social learning happens when one individual acquires the ability to perform a new behaviour by watching that behaviour in another (the *model*). The observed behaviour is then imitated. Behaviours acquired in this way can therefore be learned without necessarily being performed.

Box 2.1

Bandura's processes in social learning

Bandura (1977) identifies four processes in social learning. These are:

- *attention* – the model must actually be observed, rather than just present
- *retention* – the observer must remember what they have seen
- *reproduction* – the observer must be capable of doing the behaviour they have seen
- *motivation* – the observer must have a reason to perform the new action.

The first three criteria will result in the acquisition of the new response; the fourth is also required if the behaviour is to be demonstrated.

Social learning may account for the acquisition of aggressive responses. Some children may observe violent acts by their parents, and both children and adults are exposed to aggressive behaviours in the media, such as TV, computer games and films. Indeed, the more violent TV that children watch, the more aggressive they are (Eron *et al.*, 1972). This pattern becomes stronger for boys, though not girls, as they grow older and, by age 30, adults who had watched more violent TV as boys are more likely to have been convicted of violent crimes (Eron and Huesmann, 1986).

Several factors increase the likelihood that an observer will perform a behaviour that they have observed. Some factors affect whether the behaviour will be acquired – for example, learning is more likely if the model is:

- the same gender
- the same age
- of powerful or high status
- friendly or likeable.

Observers are more likely to identify with models to whom they aspire. So individuals with these characteristics, such as adults (high status), peers (same age) and characters on TV (powerful and likeable), are all potentially effective models.

In addition, the probability of the behaviour actually being performed is also influenced by external events – for example, it is more likely if:

- the observer has seen the model being rewarded for the behaviour (this is called *vicarious reinforcement*)
- the observer is rewarded directly (an effect of operant conditioning, i.e. positive reinforcement).

In films, and even cartoons, violent characters tend to have attributes such as those listed above and, furthermore, are rewarded for their actions. For example,

a cartoon 'baddy' gets a laugh and many film heroes, both good and bad, achieve material gain or hero status through acts of violence. As a result, viewers also are exposed to vicarious reinforcement for aggression.

Figure 2.4 Children imitate the aggressive actions of an adult model

In many classic studies, Bandura demonstrated the powerful effects of aggressive models on children. For example, Bandura *et al.* (1961) showed that children will imitate verbal and physical aggression demonstrated by an adult model towards a 'Bobo doll' (see Figure 2.4). Bandura *et al.* (1963) compared the behaviour of children exposed to different kinds of aggressive modelling, including:

- a real-life aggressive model with a Bobo doll
- the same model performing the same behaviours but recorded on film and projected onto a screen
- a film of an aggressive cartoon character, 'Herman the Cat', presented on a TV – the film looked like a cartoon but was acted by one of the models dressed as a cat, who performed the same sequence of behaviours as in the other conditions
- no film or live model (control group).

In all of the model groups, more aggression was displayed than by the control group, suggesting that on-screen violence is a potent model for aggression.

This effect does not seem to be restricted to the laboratory. In a natural experiment, Joy *et al.* (1986) found that the introduction of transmitted television to a community resulted in an increase in aggressive behaviour.

Applying the behaviourist approach to therapy

The aims of therapies based on the behavioural approach

According to the behaviourist approach, mental disorders develop in the same way as other aspects of our behavioural repertoire: through the processes of classical and operant conditioning and social learning. This suggests that disorders

---

Glossary

natural experiment – a study in which the researcher compares different situations, conditions or groups that already exist (i.e. are 'natural'). These are the different levels of the independent variable.

have arisen because of the effect of the environment, rather than faulty emotions, physiology or cognitions. Behavioural techniques thus attempt to alter associations between stimuli using the principles of classical conditioning. Therapies from the behaviourist approach aim to extinguish maladaptive responses and enable individuals to learn new, more adaptive behaviours to replace them.

Aversion therapy

Some disorders, such as alcoholism, can be controlled using aversion therapy (AT). This uses classical conditioning (see page 24), pairing an unpleasant CS with the maladaptive behaviour that is to be eliminated. This therapy has also been used to help people to stop smoking and is the principle behind the use of nasty-tasting nail varnish to stop nail-biting! The basic action is as follows:

UCS (naturally aversive stimulus) → UCR (unpleasant consequence)
UCS + NS (stimulus relating to the disorder) → UCR (unpleasant consequence)
CS (stimulus relating to the disorder) → CR (unpleasant consequence)

The pairings are repeated and, as a result, an association is built up. The stimulus associated with the disorder (such as the tempting sight of a nail to bite) becomes linked to an unpleasant conditioned response (for example, the nasty taste of the nail treatment).

Box 2.2

Treating alcohol dependence with aversion therapy

Patients with alcohol addiction can be treated with the drug Antabuse, which causes vomiting if it is combined with alcohol. It works like this:

UCS (Antabuse) → UCR (unpleasant sensation of vomiting)
UCS + NS (alcohol) → UCR (expectation of unpleasant sensation of vomiting)
CS (alcohol) → CR (unpleasant expectation)

As the CR is unpleasant (aversive) the drinking of alcohol is deterred.

Aversion therapy is not only used to treat drug addictions. Weinrott *et al.* (1997) used it as a therapy for juvenile sex offenders. An aversive stimulus of videotaped negative consequences of sex offences (UCS) was paired with sexual arousal, produced by playing the offenders an audiotaped scenario of a sexually deviant crime (NS). This created an association between their sexual arousal (CS) and thoughts about the negative effects (CR). Following treatment, they demonstrated significantly less physiological and self-reported arousal.

How does aversion therapy link back to assumptions of the approach?

- Maladaptive behaviours can be acquired through events in the individual's environment, as was shown with the classical conditioning of little Albert's fear (see page 25). It therefore makes sense that changes in the environment – the pairing of coincident appearance of stimuli in aversion therapy – can also change behaviour.
- Two principles of learning also apply to aversion therapy. For therapies such as Antabuse to work effectively, a certain amount of generalisation

must occur – for example, from one or a few types of alcoholic drink to all types. Discrimination is also important, as the aversion must not extend to non-alcoholic drinks.

Systematic desensitisation

Jones (1924) helped a little boy called Peter who, like little Albert, was afraid of small furry animals. She did this by exposing him slowly to a caged rabbit, at first far away, then closer, then on his lap, while keeping him happy with food. This idea forms the basis of systematic desensitisation, a therapy for phobias developed by Wolpe (1958). Like aversion therapy, it is based on the principle of classical conditioning. The therapist initially agrees an anxiety hierarchy with the client. This is a graduated sequence of feared stimuli that rise in terms of subjective discomfort. For example, for a client with a phobia of lifts, this may range from watching other people getting into a lift to being stuck in one themselves. The sequence is a list of increasingly challenging conditioned stimuli. These can be real, imagined or achieved through virtual reality. The aim is to decondition, or desensitise, the client to each of the items on the hierarchy systematically. To achieve this, the therapist must relax the client and preserve this state throughout each level of the hierarchy. A state of relaxation (the unconditioned response) may be induced using a range of techniques – for example, progressive muscle relaxation or hypnosis. The technique used to induce and maintain relaxation is the unconditioned stimulus. As we cannot feel two opposite emotions simultaneously (due to reciprocal inhibition), fear is prevented by the maintenance of relaxation. The therapist works gradually up through the hierarchy, returning to the previous stimulus if the client becomes distressed. The aim is for the client to stay relaxed when confronted with the top of the hierarchy – that is, the feared stimulus itself.

Box 2.3

An anxiety hierarchy for a phobia of illness in others

Note that this hierarchy is for one specific client; another person's hierarchy for the same phobia might differ.
1. Sight of physical deformity
2. Someone in pain
3. Sight of bleeding
4. Sight of somebody seriously ill
5. Automobile accidents
6. Nurses in uniform
7. Wheelchairs
8. Hospitals
9. Ambulances

Source: adapted from Wolpe (1969).

For example, Lang and Lazovik (1963) used systematic desensitisation to help students with snake phobias. Over 11 sessions, they worked through a hierarchy, which included such items as 'writing the word snake' and 'accidentally treading on a dead snake'. Hypnosis was used to assist in the maintenance of relaxation. The participants' fear rating fell between the beginning and end of the sessions. It was found to be effective for most of the treatment group and the improvement was still evident six months later. A different way to present the feared situations on the hierarchy is to use virtual reality, which is especially useful when the situation would be expensive or difficult to create in a consulting room, such as fire or large animals. Rothbaum *et al.* (2000) used virtual reality to help

participants who were afraid of flying, most of whom were willing to take a test flight after treatment and maintained a reduction in phobic symptoms over six months.

How does systematic desensitisation link back to assumptions of the approach?

- Systematic desensitisation works because maladaptive behaviours can be changed by altering the environment – in this case, by pairing pleasant responses (being calm) with feared stimuli to change the individual's responses.
- Two principles of learning apply to systematic desensitisation. Generalisation matters as the client cannot be desensitised to every possible phobic stimulus but the learned relaxation needs to apply across a range of situations. Throughout the course of treatment, the previous response, of fear, undergoes deconditioning. However, between the therapy sessions themselves, the continued absence of phobic responses helps to eliminate the behaviour, so extinction is also important. Conversely, extinction can reduce the long-term effectiveness of the therapy if the new associations are lost and the fear returns.

The methodology of the behaviourist approach

Laboratory studies on animals

Animals offer simple models of learning as their behaviour is less complex than that of humans. They can thus be used to explore the effects of classical and operant conditioning and social learning. In the course of such research, it is possible to use procedures that would not be ethical if conducted with human participants. For example, we do not know what would happen if children were exposed to a 'Bandura-style' aggressive model for a prolonged period of time, such as whether the effects would be long-term. It would be unethical to plan an experiment with the intention of causing a lasting increase in aggressive behaviour in the participants. However, such research has been done with animals. Suzuki and Lucas (2010) showed a group of rats 'aggressive rat models' for ten minutes per day for 23 days. They found that, even 16 days after observations of aggression had stopped, observers who had seen fighting rats were more aggressive than those that had seen non-aggressive encounters or had only watched aggressive rats once.

Animal environments can also be more rigorously controlled than those with human participants, allowing researchers to identify which aspects are the key influences on behaviour. For example:

- Pavlov was able to repeatedly expose animals to pairs of stimuli and precisely record changes in responses (for example, by measuring the volume of saliva produced using a tube inserted through the dog's cheek)
- Skinner systematically varied environmental effects, such as the frequency of rewards, and recorded the effects on behaviour without human interference using Skinner boxes.

Glossary

observer bias – the tendency of a researcher to be subjective when recording behaviour (i.e. to be affected by their personal viewpoint or expectations).

demand characteristics – features of an experimental setting which indicate to the participants the aim of the study so suggest how they are expected to behave, thus altering their responses.

ecological validity – the extent to which a study is a realistic representation, such that the findings will generalise to real-world settings.

social desirability bias – changing one's behaviour to respond in ways that are acceptable to others.

true experiment – a study in which the researcher deliberately manipulates the independent variable to create different conditions.

Evaluation of laboratory studies on animals

As we saw in Chapter 1, animal studies allow more variables to be investigated and controlled than would be possible if human participants were used. Rats in Skinner boxes are typically maintained below their normal body weight to ensure that they are hungry so are motivated to learn to push the bar for food. Many animals can be tested simultaneously in apparatus such as Skinner boxes, which increases the reliability of the findings. The Skinner box collects highly objective data as administration of rewards and the recording of behaviour is automated so there can be no observer bias.

There are ethical as well as practical reasons for using animals. Procedures which contribute to objectivity, such as the surgery needed for direct collection of saliva in Pavlov's studies, can also only be conducted on animals, and studies with unknown but potentially negative consequences, such as the experiment conducted by Suzuki and Lucas (2010), are only possible using animals.

In Chapter 1, we considered whether it is possible to generalise from animals to humans when there are biological differences, such as in the nervous system. There are also important differences in learning processes between animals and humans, which raise doubts about the validity of generalisations in the behaviourist approach too. Although there is no doubt that we, like animals, learn by conditioning and social learning, our ability to acquire new responses is much more complex.

Finally, we can again question whether laboratory animal studies are ethical and consider the extent to which animal suffering is outweighed by benefits to humans. To answer the question, we need to consider two aspects: long-term human gains versus short-term animal suffering and the extent to which, in the case of many learning experiments, the degree of animal suffering is limited. A laboratory rat typically spends only a short time in a Skinner box and, although maintained at a reduced weight (typically 85 per cent), this does not represent an unhealthy weight for a rat.

Natural experiments

Experiments such as Joy *et al.* (1977) are not true experiments because the researcher cannot deliberately manipulate the independent variable. Instead, they make use of naturally occurring differences or changes; hence such studies are called natural experiments. Like other experiments, natural experiments can have different experimental designs. Joy *et al.* (1977) was interested in the effect of introducing transmitted television (the IV) on aggression levels (the DV) in a remote community. They compared behaviour before and after a television transmitter was installed – a repeated measures design – although they also conducted a comparison between towns with differing numbers of TV channels, so this part of the study used an independent groups design.

Evaluation of natural experiments

Unlike laboratory experiments, natural experiments are typically carried out in the participants' normal environment, often with little interference. As a result, the participants are unlikely to be responding to demand characteristics, since there will be little to suggest what the researchers expect to happen in the study.

In addition, the participants may be unaware that they are even involved in a study, unlike being in a lab where it is obvious, so they are less likely to demonstrate a social desirability bias. Together, these mean that the findings are likely to be more ecologically valid than many lab experiments.

However, as the IV is naturally occurring, the researchers cannot randomly allocate participants to conditions. They are therefore less sure that the factor being investigated is indeed the cause of changes in the DV – that is, causal relationships are harder to determine. This is especially so in natural experiments as it is unlikely that the researcher will be able to control possible extraneous variables. For example, Joy *et al.* could not control how much time was spent on other activities (such as 'letting off steam' out of doors or how much parental supervision the children had) before and after TV became available. In this respect, natural experiments have lower validity than their laboratory counterparts. Indeed, Charlton *et al.* (2000), who also explored the effect of the introduction of TV, found contradictory results. Their natural experiment investigating the effect of the introduction of transmitted television to a remote community on St Helena island found that there was no increase in aggressive behaviour.

Evaluation of the behaviourist approach

Strengths

1. Behaviourists focused on observable behaviours occurring in response to known stimuli

The behaviourists deliberately chose to study only observable responses, so the approach is highly objective. For example, the presence or absence of a given response indicates whether learning has occurred and aggressive behaviour can be readily identified. Such measures are less subjective than attempts to investigate cognitive processes, such as those occurring *between* the stimulus and the response.

2. The approach uses scientific methods

Laboratory experiments are often used in this approach, providing a scientific basis for drawing conclusions about cause and effect. Especially in experiments using animals, such as those of Skinner and Pavlov, many extraneous variables can be controlled, so it is more likely that the variable being investigated is responsible for changes in behaviour. In addition, automated equipment, such as Skinner boxes, ensures that data collection is highly objective and reliable.

Weaknesses

1. Focusing on outcomes, not causes

The behaviourist approach is both determinist and reductionist. Its focus is exclusively on the relationship between observable stimuli and responses. In explaining aggression and treating problems such as addictions or phobias, behaviourism therefore considers only a limited range of the influences on

behaviour. For example, if an individual is predisposed to addictive behaviours because of their biology (such as a neurotransmitter imbalance) or an ongoing social problem, it is unlikely that conditioned aversion, which aims to reduce the behaviour but does not explore the reasons behind it, will be successful in the long-term. Similarly, if a phobia stems from an unconscious process (which is not considered by this approach) rather than it being a conditioned maladaptive response, then deconditioning (i.e. tackling only the response not the underlying cause) will probably be ineffective.

2. Generalising from animals to people

While humans undoubtedly can learn in the same ways as animals, we are considerably more sophisticated learners. We have bigger brains, typically learn much faster and are more flexible in our learning than non-human animals. Importantly, we can use cognitive processes to solve problems which animals have to learn by trial and error. Sometimes we find solutions to problems through insight or we can actively use reasoning to work out what new behaviour is required. Animals typically cannot learn new responses in these ways. As a consequence, theories of learning based on animal models are inadequate as explanations of human behaviour.

Box 2.4

Where does the behaviourist approach stand on key issues and debates?

Reductionism

Like the biological approach, the behaviourist approach takes a 'reductionist' stance, focusing on a narrow range of factors (for example, the influence of rewards or of models) to explain phenomena such as aggressive behaviour. This tends to preclude other possible causal factors, such as personality.

Nature–nurture debate

The behaviourist approach occupies an extreme 'nurture' position. It suggests that the development of new behaviours is dependent upon stimuli from the environment and the consequences of differing behaviours within that environment – that is, behavioural change is a result of experience. For example, in the case of mental disorders, this approach suggests they arise because of events in our lives, rather than innately faulty emotions, physiology or cognitions. The approach therefore suggests that such maladaptive responses can be changed through behavioural techniques.

Determinism

The behaviourist approach takes a 'deterministic' view, as can be seen by the inevitability of processes such as generalisation, discrimination, extinction and spontaneous recovery. Such a perspective says that, under a certain set of circumstances (i.e. a particular learning environment), a person will acquire a new behaviour. However, this cannot explain individual differences – why some people learn (or lose) behaviours more readily than others even if they have the same experiences.

Psychology as a science

This is a major strength of the behaviourist approach – since it focuses exclusively on observable events, it is highly testable and very objective. As well as the underlying approach being scientific, the techniques and equipment used in research to support the behaviourist approach, such as Skinner boxes, are typically objective and reliable. However, experiments (whether natural or lab) which use human observers to collect data are less so.

Comparing and contrasting the behaviourist approach

Here we are going to show an example of how to compare and contrast the behaviourist approach with the biological approach.

Exam tip

To get high marks in a compare-and-contrast question, you must refer to the issues and debates.

Table 2.1 A plan for how to compare and contrast behaviourist and biological approaches

CRITERION	BEHAVIOURIST	BIOLOGICAL	SIMILARITY/DIFFERENCE
Assumptions	The environment, observable events and common principles in learning	Neurons, localisation and hormones	Difference
Applications	Aversion therapy and systematic desensitisation	Psychosurgery and chemotherapy	Difference
Methods	Lab studies on animals and natural experiments	Lab experiments using animals and brain scanning	Similarity and difference
Nature–nurture	Mostly nurture	Mostly nature	Difference
Reductionism	Reductionist	Reductionist	Similarity
Determinism	Deterministic	Deterministic	Similarity
Science	Very scientific	Very scientific	Similarity

Summing it up

- Behaviourists focus on observable events, studying the relationship between stimuli and responses.

- The major assumptions of the approach are the importance of the environment, the emphasis of research on observable events and the general principles that underlie all learned behaviours, including generalisation, discrimination, extinction and spontaneous recovery.

- Early behaviourists identified two mechanisms of learning. In classical conditioning, an association is learned between a new stimulus and an existing response. In operant conditioning, new behaviours are acquired because the consequences of an action are pleasant (reinforcement) or unpleasant (punishment). Stimuli and consequences are aspects of the environment.

- In social learning, the learner copies a model, so aggression can be learned through imitation. Models are also a feature of the environment.

- Direct and vicarious reinforcement make behaviours acquired through social learning more likely, as do some features of the model – for example, being the same gender or powerful.

- Aversion therapy uses classical conditioning to treat problems such as alcoholism by associating the to-be-removed behaviour with an unpleasant response (such as vomiting). In relation to the assumptions of the approach, manipulating the environment (the consequences of the unwanted behaviour) allows maladaptive behaviours to be removed. Generalisation must occur, to ensure that the learned association applies to other stimuli (such as other alcoholic drinks), as must discrimination, so that participants do not develop aversion to other stimuli (for example, non-alcoholic drinks).

- Systematic desensitisation is a therapy for phobias based on classical conditioning. It uses an anxiety hierarchy of feared situations and the client is deconditioned to each item by maintaining relaxation throughout exposure. In relation to the assumptions of the approach, the environment is used to create a pleasant response (calmness), which is paired with the feared stimulus to change the individual's behaviour. Generalisation is required to extend the learning to other phobic stimuli, and between therapy sessions the phobic response undergoes extinction.

- Laboratory studies on animals provide simple, testable models of learning and allow testing of variables affecting learning (for example, using Skinner boxes), which can provide objective and reliable data and enable testing of situations which would be impractical with human participants. However, studies on animals raise ethical issues and questions about whether the findings are generalisable to humans.

- Natural experiments utilise existing differences or changes to explore the effects of an independent variable. They are typically highly ecologically valid as demand characteristics and social desirability biases are limited. However, the validity of conclusions about causal relationships is questionable as participants cannot be allocated randomly to conditions and other variables cannot be controlled.

- Overall, the main strength of the behaviourist approach is that it is highly scientific; research is both objective and reliable.

- However, a key weakness is that it is both reductionist and deterministic. By concentrating on observable stimuli and responses, other possible causes of behaviours are ignored.

Consolidate your understanding

The behaviourist approach

Use the following activities to run the information in this chapter through your mind. Each activity is designed to help you process the information in a different way, which should help you ensure you understand it and make it easier to remember.

Wordsearch

E	Y	E	T	G	N	N	I	H	I	N	S	R	E	I	N
T	P	X	C	N	S	L	T	O	T	N	E	E	N	T	S
O	A	T	L	I	S	O	H	N	C	E	E	R	N	N	C
E	R	I	M	N	I	H	R	E	S	P	O	N	S	E	V
G	E	N	E	R	A	L	I	S	A	T	I	O	N	M	N
Y	H	C	R	A	R	E	I	H	Y	T	E	I	X	N	A
I	T	T	N	E	M	H	S	I	N	U	P	N	C	O	N
I	N	I	N	L	N	T	R	T	L	X	U	C	R	R	U
C	O	O	N	L	S	O	S	I	I	T	H	E	E	I	E
L	I	N	Y	A	C	R	A	U	O	M	S	S	S	V	I
G	S	P	Y	I	B	U	S	B	O	U	U	S	X	N	S
C	R	I	X	C	E	C	S	D	C	R	C	L	O	E	I
R	E	E	X	O	B	R	E	N	N	I	K	S	U	T	I
N	V	N	N	S	S	L	R	S	L	T	C	R	N	S	A
R	A	L	S	A	N	I	S	C	O	L	M	L	I	M	I
I	N	N	A	A	N	E	N	O	C	C	B	E	S	C	E

stimulus
response
environment
NS
aversion therapy
generalisation
CS
anxiety hierarchy

extinction
CR
Skinner box
punishment
UCS
social learning
UCR
model

Consolidate your understanding

Crossword

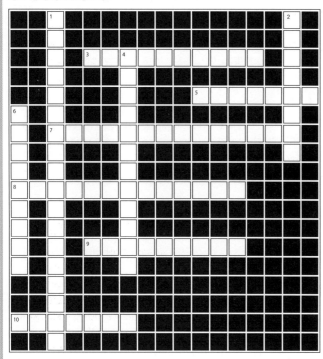

Across

3. A type of validity that indicates the extent to which a study is realistic and the findings will generalise to real-world settings

5. A type of conditioning in which the frequency of a response is altered by its consequences

7. The learned ability to respond differently to similar stimuli

8. Rewards which increase the frequency of the behaviour which they follow

9. A type of conditioning which arises from associations between an old and a new stimulus

10. A type of experiment in which the IV cannot be manipulated by the experimenter

Down

1. A factor which biases our behaviour so we respond in ways that are acceptable to others

2. A relatively permanent change in behavioural potential that arises as a result of experience

4. The subjectivity of researchers when watching behaviour caused by their personal viewpoint or expectations

6. A type of reinforcement arising from seeing a model being rewarded

Wordsearch and crossword solutions begin on page 231.

Consolidate your understanding

Cloze

Behaviourists focus on _____ events, studying the relationship between _____ and responses. The major assumptions of the approach are the importance of the environment, the emphasis of research on observable events and the general principles that underlie all learned behaviours, including _____, discrimination, _____ and spontaneous recovery. Early behaviourists identified two mechanisms of learning. In _____ conditioning, an association is learned between a new stimulus and an existing response. In _____ conditioning, new behaviours are acquired because the consequences of an action are pleasant (_____) or unpleasant (_____). Stimuli and consequences are aspects of the environment. In _____ _____, the learner copies a model, so aggression can be learned through imitation. Models are also a feature of the environment. Direct and vicarious reinforcement make behaviours acquired through social learning more likely, as do some features of the _____ – for example, being the same gender or powerful.

_____ therapy uses classical conditioning to treat problems such as alcoholism by associating the to-be-removed behaviour with an _____ response (such as vomiting). In relation to the assumptions of the approach, manipulating the environment (the consequences of the unwanted behaviour) allows maladaptive behaviours to be removed. Generalisation must occur, to ensure that the learned association applies to other stimuli (such as other _____ drinks), as must _____, so that they do not develop aversion to other stimuli (for example, non-alcoholic drinks). _____ _____ is a therapy for phobias based on classical conditioning. It uses an anxiety hierarchy of feared situations and the client is deconditioned to each item by maintaining _____ throughout exposure. In relation to the assumptions of the approach, the environment provides a pleasant response (calmness), which is paired with the feared stimulus to change the individual's behaviour. Generalisation is required to extend the learning to other phobic stimuli, and between therapy sessions the phobic response undergoes _____.

Laboratory studies on animals provide simple, _____ models of learning and allow testing of variables affecting learning (for example, using _____ boxes), which can provide _____ and reliable data and enable testing of situations which would be impractical with human participants. However, studies on animals raise ethical issues and questions about whether the findings are _____ to humans. Natural experiments utilise existing differences or changes to explore the effects of an _____ variable. They are typically highly ecologically valid as _____ _____ and social desirability biases are limited. However, the validity of conclusions about causal relationships is questionable as participants cannot randomly be allocated to conditions and other variables cannot be controlled.

Overall, the main strength of the behaviourist approach is that it is highly scientific; research is both objective and _____. However, a key weakness is that it is both reductionist and _____. By concentrating on observable stimuli and responses, other possible causes of behaviours are ignored.

For help completing the cloze activity, see the 'Summing it up' section for this chapter.

Consolidate your understanding

Concept map

Complete the empty boxes and you will have a visual revision plan.

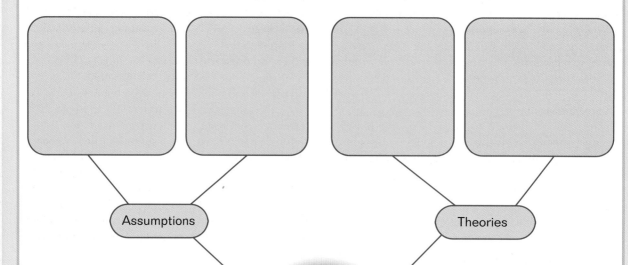

Assumptions

Theories

Applications

Behaviourist approach

Methods

Evaluation

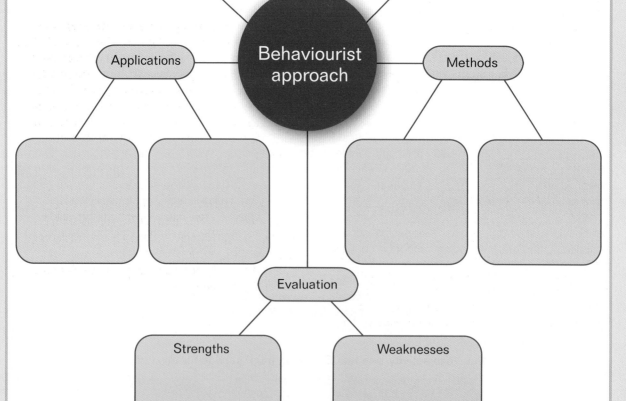

Strengths

Weaknesses

Exam focus

The behaviourist approach

Probably the most straightforward approach to understand, learn, apply to real life and also memorise for the exam.

Assumptions

As with all the approaches you will need two assumptions here. Some teachers use classical and operant conditioning as assumptions, and these are credited in the mark scheme. They are elaborations of the basic assumption that, apart from some reflexes, all behaviour is learnt. Another assumption is that only observable behaviour can be measured and is therefore scientific.

Theory

If there ever was a great theory to discuss and investigate in class, this is it. It's the one all students remember in detail. But it's only worth 8 marks, and the temptation is to write all about Bandura in great detail. However, the question is about SLT of aggression, not Bandura – his work provides the central evidence for your answer, but you need to mention the processes of imitation and modelling, and how the family and the peer group are key models.

Therapy

Don't forget **the link** here – it's with the fundamental processes of learning. Aversion therapy features classical conditioning specifically, but systematic desensitisation features both classical and operant conditioning. Remember too the wide use of desensitisation as a therapy for phobias in the NHS and private clinics in the UK (a statement of fact, not an evaluation). In both cases, the link is followed by the learning processes and then by a description of the course of therapy. **Don't evaluate – there are no marks for it**.

Strengths and weaknesses

Remember that strengths and weaknesses will be asked about separately with part a) of the question asking about strengths and part b) about weaknesses. This approach has tightened up the scientific methodology of psychology but has been superseded in general by cognitive approaches, so your answer should reflect that historical change, perhaps saying as a weakness: 'In failing to account for so many psychological phenomena, and with its very narrow approach to explanation, the main weakness was its failure to develop as an approach and remain relevant to twenty-first century psychological science.' Most people write about determinism and reductionism; have one of them but then be different. Being able to show that you can think for yourself, explain, understand and give a relevant answer will always gain good marks.

Compare and contrast

This approach is **very easy to contrast** with any of the other approaches as it has such obvious differences: the **non-invasive contrast with biological**, the **non-mental in contrast to both cognitive and psychodynamic**, and the resolutely **unimaginative in contrast to psychodynamic** (and to be honest, cognitive too!). Use the therapy material as an important contrast (especially with biological).

Explain and evaluate method

Very much the same as other approaches as far as experiments go, so there will be some overlap with biological and cognitive. Remember to make any examples (always a good idea to use examples!) relevant to that approach – in this case Bandura, Skinner and Pavlov.

3 The psychodynamic approach

This chapter includes:

I should be able to:

- outline two assumptions of the psychodynamic approach
- describe Freud's theory of personality development
- describe how the psychodynamic approach has been used in therapy with particular reference to dream analysis or free association
- describe and evaluate the research methodology used in the psychodynamic approach
- evaluate the psychodynamic approach, including two strengths and two weaknesses
- compare and contrast the psychodynamic approach to other approaches to psychology.

What could I be asked?

There is no guarantee that future exams will keep precisely to this wording or mark allocation. However, it is likely that any questions you are asked about the approach will be much like the following:

1. (a) Outline **two** assumptions of the psychodynamic approach. [4]

   (b) **Describe** Freud's theory of personality development. [8]

2. **Describe** how the psychodynamic approach has been applied in **either** free association or dream analysis. [12]

3. (a) Evaluate **two** strengths of the psychodynamic approach. [6]

   (b) Evaluate **two** weaknesses of the psychodynamic approach. [6]

4. **Compare and contrast** the biological and psychodynamic approaches in terms of similarities and differences. [12]

5. **Explain and evaluate** the methodology used by the psychodynamic approach. [12]

The psychodynamic approach is one of the older approaches to psychology, originating at the end of the nineteenth century. The most famous and historically important person in this approach was Sigmund Freud. Freud was a medical doctor who had a particular interest in using psychology to treat patients, including those whose symptoms were apparently medical rather than psychological. Freud's ideas come largely from his work with patients. From listening to and observing his patients, Freud concluded the following principles of psychology, which continue to underlie the psychodynamic approach.

Assumptions of the psychodynamic approach

The main assumptions of the psychodynamic approach include the following ideas:

- the importance of the unconscious mind – that is, mental processes we are not aware of
- the importance of early relationships to later psychological functioning.

The importance of the unconscious mind

One of the central ideas of the psychodynamic approach to psychology is that our emotions, motivations and behaviour are constantly affected by the unconscious mind. In the broad sense, the unconscious mind includes any mental activity we are not aware of. However, Freud (1915) proposed that the unconscious works in particular ways, quite differently from the conscious. It is not logical, and makes no distinction between real external events and internal ones, such as dreams. The unconscious seeks pleasure (what Freud called *lust*) and avoids displeasure (or, as Freud called it, *unlust*). The unconscious mind constantly influences our behaviour, urging us towards pleasure and away from displeasure. Thus we might dream of something that would give us pleasure, commit a slip of the tongue that might reveal something we really want or forget something unpleasant. To Freud, most mental activity is unconscious. He illustrated this by comparing the mind to an iceberg, most of which is under the surface (see Figure 3.1).

The importance of early relationships

In psychodynamic theory, there is a close connection between childhood experiences and adult functioning. Many aspects of adult thinking, emotion and behaviour can be linked to particular childhood experiences. Relationships with parents are particularly important. Freud believed that the quality of the relationship with parents is reflected in how well the child progresses through each stage of childhood development. As adults, the ways we respond to people are affected by our relationships to our parents. If we do/did not get on with our mother, for example, we may find getting on with women difficult. This is called *transference* because emotions from one relationship are *transferred* onto new ones.

Freud's theory of personality development

Freud's collection of ideas is vast (the Collected Works include 26 books). Here we are interested in Freud's ideas about the personality and how it develops through childhood. Personality can be defined as the aspects of human behaviour that vary from one person to another but which remain fairly consistent within the individual.

Glossary

lust – pleasure.
psychodynamic – refers to a set of theories, concepts and therapies that depend on the importance of the unconscious mind and early experience of relationships.
transference – transferring emotions from one relationship onto another.
unconscious – mental processes of which the thinker is unaware.
unlust – displeasure.

Figure 3.1 Freud believed that most mental activity is 'below the surface', like an iceberg

What did Freud mean by personality?

Freud (1923) suggested that we think of the personality as having three aspects: an instinctive part, a logical part and a moral part. We are thus influenced by instinct and morality but have the ability as well to make logical decisions that satisfy our instincts to seek pleasure and avoid displeasure, while not falling foul of our conscience. These three parts to the personality are known as the id, ego and superego.

- The *id* is the instinctive aspect of the personality. It seeks purely to receive pleasure and avoid displeasure. It is thus said to operate on the pleasure principle. We are born without logic or morality, and Freud thus described babies as 'bundles of id'.
- The *ego* is the logical part of the personality that can make conscious and logical decisions that reflect the demands of instinct, morality and external reality. The ego is thus said to operate on the reality principle. Freud believed the ego was part of the personality by around one year of age.
- The *superego* is the moral aspect of the personality. It is formed when an image of the same-sex parent is internalised and it functions as a mental representation of that parent, internally punishing and rewarding us according to the morality of our actions.

Figure 3.2 The id is sometimes pictured as a devil and the superego as an angel

We constantly have to make decisions. How we go about this and how we then respond to the decisions we make can form an important part of our personality. We might, for example, find ourselves in the position of finding a wallet in the street. Our id will push us towards taking it and keeping any money in it. Our superego, on the other hand, will influence us in a more moral direction, perhaps leading us to hand it in at a police station. If we give in to our id and take the money, our superego will probably punish us with guilt and shame later. It is the ego that has the final say in a situation like this, and a successful decision will satisfy our pleasure-seeking id and our moral superego *and* make sense in the light of circumstances. We might, for example, hand the wallet in but hope to receive a reward for doing so. This should satisfy the superego, because it is the 'right' course of action, and the id, because there is a selfish motive.

How personality develops: psychosexual stages

Freud (1905) suggested that our personality develops through our childhood and that particular aspects of our personality are rooted in the experiences we have at particular stages of development. He identified five stages of development, but proposed that the adult personality is largely formed by the end of the third stage. The stages are shown in Table 3.1.

Table 3.1 Freud's stages of development

STAGE	AGE
Oral	0–1 year
Anal	1–3 years
Phallic	3–6 years
Latency	7 years–puberty
Genital	Puberty and adolescence

At each of the first three stages of development, a region of the body has particular significance because psychic energy or *libido* is concentrated there.

The oral stage (0–1 year)

From birth, a baby is pleasure-seeking but at first has no logic or morality. In the oral stage, the child's pleasure-seeking largely revolves around the mouth, as the child is breast-feeding and being weaned. As well as nourishment, children in the oral stage take comfort and information via the mouth (hence babies suck objects to calm themselves and put objects they are investigating in the mouth). From the first year of life, we take away to adulthood a number of 'oral' characteristics. These can include an enjoyment of food and drink, and other mouth-related pleasure-seeking behaviour, such as smoking. We also take away aspects of the infant's relationship with the world, including the capacity for dependence on another person and acceptance of nurture.

If our oral stage goes smoothly, we take away from it the capacity to have an adult enjoyment of food and drink and to have close relationships. However, if a person experiences a trauma in their first year, such as being separated from their primary carer or having a feeding difficulty, they can go on to experience psychological problems centred around eating or drinking, and may be excessively dependent on others or highly gullible. These attitudes of dependence and gullibility represent the infant's attitudes of dependence on their primary carer and unconditional acceptance of nurture.

The anal stage (1–3 years)

To Freud, the next stage of development is centred on the development of bowel control and potty training, hence the term 'anal'. In this stage, the focus of libido thus shifts from the mouth to the anus. By this stage, children have an ego; therefore, they are aware that they are separate from other people and that their own wishes can bring them into conflict with others. This type of conflict typically comes to a head in potty training, when adults impose restrictions on when and where the child can poo.

If the anal stage goes smoothly, we take away from it the ability to deal with authority, to assert our wishes appropriately and to maintain a balance between being ordered and being able to tolerate mess. However, excessively early or harsh potty training can lead to an adult personality dominated by the anal triad of personality characteristics:

Figure 3.3 How the anal stage is managed by parents affects the child's relationship with authority

- stubbornness – this represents the failure to resolve appropriate relationships with authority
- orderliness – this represents the intolerance of mess
- stinginess – this represents the refusal to give parents the bowel movement they want.

The phallic stage (3–6 years)

In this stage, the child's focus is on gender and gendered relationships, in particular the triangular relationship between themselves and each parent and the parents with each other. The focus of libido now shifts from anus to genitals (the word 'phallus' means penis). Initially this may manifest itself as *scopophilia*, a type of infantile voyeurism in which children are fascinated by adult genitals and may attempt to see them – for example, by following adults into the toilet.

This awareness of gender and concentration of libido on the genitals coincides with the child's growing awareness of their being left out of some aspects of their parents' lives. For example, parents at this stage may become less happy with a child climbing into bed with them. The resulting three-way relationship is known as the *Oedipus complex*, named after Oedipus, a character in a play based on a Greek legend. Through a series of unhappy coincidences, Oedipus came to kill his father and marry his mother, not realising who they were. In the Oedipus complex, a rivalry relationship develops between the child and the same-sex parent for the affection of the opposite-sex parent. On an unconscious

Box 3.1

The case of Little Hans (Freud, 1909)

Freud used the case of Little Hans to illustrate his ideas about the Oedipus complex. At the age of five, Hans was brought to Freud suffering from generalised anxiety, a phobia of horses (in particular, white horses with black nose bands) and anxiety about his mother leaving him. At the time, Hans' father had begun to object to Hans' habit of getting into his parents' bed in the mornings. Freud interpreted Hans' symptoms as being due to his struggle with the Oedipus complex. Horses, with their large penises, symbolised Hans' father; in particular, the nose bands reminded him of his father's moustache. Hans' symptoms improved after two daydreams. In one of these, a plumber fitted him with a big penis like his father's, and in the second Hans was married to his mother and his father took the role of grandfather. Freud interpreted this as Hans having resolved the Oedipus complex.

Figure 3.4 White horses may have represented Hans' father

level, the child is expressing instinctive wishes to have sex with his mother and kill his father.

To Freud, the resolution of the Oedipus complex is an essential part of a child's personality development. The superego, the moral aspect of the personality, is formed at this point as the child's same-sex parent is internalised or *introjected* into the personality. To Freud, our conscience is literally the mental representation of our same-sex parent telling us what is right and wrong and rewarding and punishing us for our actions. How the Oedipus complex is handled has implications then for our moral development; parents who brutally suppress their children's desire for the opposite-sex parent risk leaving the child with a harsh, punitive superego, thus they may experience excessive guilt and shame. Failure to sensitively parent children through their Oedipus complex can also affect their sexual development, leaving them sexually over- or under-confident. By the end of the phallic stage, the adult personality is largely formed. This is summarised in Table 3.2.

Table 3.2 The formation of personality in the first three stages

STAGE	ASPECT OF PERSONALITY
Oral	Begins with id only. Ego forms by end of stage.
Anal	Id and ego in conflict.
Phallic	Superego forms during this stage.

Latency (7 years–puberty)

To Freud, this period of middle childhood is not particularly important in the development of the personality. By now, the child has a well-developed id, ego and superego, and the focus of their general development is very much on external factors, like school and peer relationships. Technically, this is not a 'psychosexual' stage, but a gap between psychosexual stages.

The genital stage (puberty and adolescence)

Although the three aspects of the Freudian personality are largely formed by the end of the phallic stage, the earlier stages are revisited in adolescence. The more that goes wrong in the relationships with parents in the first three stages, the more difficult adolescence can be. This is because the adolescent and their parents have to deal with some of the same issues again. The issues of the anal stage can resurface as the young person once again asserts their independence and parents exert control. This is an opportunity to improve the person's relationship to authority if the anal stage went wrong. In particular, as the young person begins having sexual relationships, the emphasis on gender and relationships resurfaces and the Oedipus complex is revisited. Although adolescence can be a difficult time as early conflicts are worked through again, it is also an opportunity to reconcile these difficulties and get the adult personality 'right'.

Applying the psychodynamic approach to therapy

Probably the most important application of psychodynamic ideas is in understanding and treating people suffering from psychological distress and/or mental health problems. Psychodynamic therapies come in various forms. Classical psychoanalysis is a very intensive and long-term therapy. It takes place four or five times per week and can last for several years. Sessions normally last exactly 50 minutes. The patient often lies on a couch. Psychoanalytic psychotherapy is a less intensive but still usually long-term therapy. Sessions take place one to three times per week. The patient may lie on a couch or face the therapist. Brief dynamic therapy is generally a less intensive and more short-term therapy. It may focus on a single problem rather than the very broad approach to the patient's mental functioning in psychoanalysis.

The aims of psychodynamic therapies

Psychodynamic therapies work by helping patients remember and talk about early experiences (often of relationships with parents) and helping them make the links between these experiences and their current problems. There are two reasons why this is therapeutic.

1. **Catharsis**: negative emotions stored up from early experiences are discharged as they are remembered and talked about. This is what we mean when we talk about people 'getting something off their chest'.

2. **Insight**: once we have more of an idea *why* we are feeling or acting as we are, we have a better chance of changing that feeling or behaviour. This understanding is called insight.

Glossary

catharsis – discharging of built-up emotion.
free association – saying whatever comes into the mind.

Exam tip

The background material on general aims and varieties of psychodynamic therapy is here to give you a better overall understanding. In the exam, you will just have to describe **either** free association **or** dream analysis.
However, to gain full marks in a question about psychodynamic therapy you must link dream analysis or free association back to the assumptions of the approach.

Free association

In free association, the patient makes no conscious effort to recall or focus on anything specific but simply allows their thoughts to drift and says whatever comes into their mind. The idea behind this is that it creates the best possible conditions for important unconscious material to come to mind. Thus, even if we had only a vague idea of what our problem really was and no idea where it came from, if we were to lie on the couch and free-associate, we would expect sooner or later to start talking about both the problem and its origins.

The first benefit of free association would probably be catharsis. Often when free-associating, patients talk about painful things that they do not discuss in everyday life, and this gives them a chance to 'get things off their chest'. A therapist could then feed back to the patient the possible links between the problem and its origin. This should give the patient insight into their problem and help them think about it and deal with it consciously. Some free associations just allow a patient to communicate something to the therapist that they would not have thought consciously to say. An example of this is shown in Box 3.3.

Figure 3.5 In free association, patients say whatever comes into their mind

Box 3.2

Free association in the case of Anna O (Breuer and Freud, 1895)

The first recorded case of the benefits of free association was that of Anna O (Breuer and Freud, 1895). Anna O suffered a range of odd symptoms, including paralysis, deafness and inability to recognise faces before and, in particular, just after the death of her father. Breuer, who was treating Anna, noticed that when he let her talk she often made connections between a symptom and a childhood event. Sometimes this was followed by the easing of her symptoms. For example, Anna's deafness at first worsened as she and Breuer discussed it but disappeared completely after she recalled the shameful memory of being caught as a child listening outside her parents' bedroom door.

How does free association link back to assumptions of the approach?

- Free association is a way of allowing **unconscious** material that we would not normally be aware of come to the surface so that we can consciously think about it.
- Very often when patients free-associate, they begin talking about childhood events, frequently involving their **early relationships**.

Dream analysis

Freud (1900) famously called dreams 'the royal road to a knowledge of the activities of the unconscious mind' (page 769). He believed that dreams perform psychological functions – the most important being the satisfaction of wishes. Freud suggested that behind the scene and story of a dream (this is called the *manifest content*), there is likely to be a hidden wish or *latent content*. The processes in which the underlying wish is transformed into the manifest content are called *dreamwork*. Dreamwork is important because it allows us to continue to sleep while dreaming about the sort of latent content that would be extremely exciting (in a good or bad way) and so probably wake us up. Freud identified four processes in dreamwork:

1   Displacement takes place when we change one person or object into another.

2   Condensation takes place when we combine the features of two or more people or objects into one.

3   Symbolisation takes place when an object or action serves as a symbol for another. Thus if we dream about phallic objects like pens, swords, etc., Freud might suggest these are penis symbols.

4   Secondary elaboration is the final part of dreamwork and takes place as the unconscious mind strings together images into a logical storyline. This further disguises the latent content.

Dream interpretation can be an important technique in psychodynamic therapy. Of course not all patients remember their dreams or choose to bring them to therapy. However, on occasion, dreams can reveal things about the mental state of the patient – for example, what they want or what is worrying them. In particular, dreams can represent socially unacceptable sexual or aggressive desires. We will look briefly at two examples of this in Boxes 3.4 and 3.5.

Box 3.3

Dora's dream (Freud, 1905)

At the age of 16, Dora had had a friend of her father make sexual advances towards her. Her father refused to believe her. She began to have a recurring dream in which her father woke her in the night, telling her that the house was on fire and that they had to get out. Her mother wanted to stop for a jewel-case but her father refused. In those days, the term 'jewel-case' was sometimes used to mean female genitals. Freud's interpretation was that Dora felt that her own 'jewel-case' was in danger but that her father had failed her by refusing to help. More controversially, Freud also believed that the dream was a result of the conflict between her revulsion at being molested and the expression of her sexual instincts.

Box 3.4

The Wolf Man's dream (Freud, 1918)

Between 1910 and 1914, Freud treated Sergei Pankejeff for depression and psychological dependency on enemas. In therapy, he reported a dream he had had at the age of four in which he awoke terrified to see white wolves with fluffy tails in a tree outside his window staring at him. As a toddler, he had awoken at 5pm and looked through the bars of his cot and watched his parents having sex 'doggy-style'. The time was significant as in adulthood his depression was generally worst at that time. Freud's interpretation was that the wolves represented Pankejeff's parents, while the window represented the bars of the cot. Wolves made good symbols of his parents because of the linguistic association between wolves and 'doggy-style'. Freud further interpreted that the Wolf Man was gay and that the dream expressed his wish to perform a sex act in that position.

How does dream analysis link back to the assumptions of the approach?

- To Freud, dreams often represent unfulfilled wishes. These wishes are in turn influenced by instincts, which are an important part of the unconscious mind. Both the famous dreams of Dora and the Wolf Man were interpreted as expressions of sexual instincts.

- Dreams often feature family members, either in the manifest or latent content. For example, Dora's dream featured her father, and the wolves in the Wolf Man's dream represented his parents.

Figure 3.6 The wolves in the tree, as dreamed by the Wolf Man

The methodology of the psychodynamic approach

Clinical case studies

Freud's principal method of research was the clinical case study, and later psychologists and therapists adopting a psychodynamic approach have largely stuck to this tradition. There are now thousands of clinical case studies recorded in psychodynamic books and journals. These are used for several purposes:

- to give an insight into the experience of people in particular situations or suffering particular conditions
- to help train and prepare new therapists for the experience of working with patients
- to provide evidence for psychodynamic ideas and techniques, and for the effectiveness of psychodynamic therapy.

A case study is an in-depth study of one person or small group in a particular situation. A clinical case study is an in-depth study of a patient in therapy. Freud referred to a total of 119 cases in his writing. Twelve of these were written up in detail. We have already touched on four of these in this chapter:

- Little Hans (Freud, 1909) was treated for anxiety and a phobia of horses at a time when his father started to object to him getting into the parents' bed.
- Anna O (Breuer and Freud, 1895) was treated for a range of symptoms before and following the death of her father.
- Dora (Freud, 1905) was treated for anxiety after being molested by a friend of her father's.
- The Wolf Man (Freud, 1918) was treated for depression and psychological dependence on enemas.

Case studies generally begin with details of the patient's background, age, sex and any other relevant details. There is normally a detailed description of the patient's symptoms and the circumstances in which they appear. The case study then describes the treatment, generally in order from beginning to end. Sometimes this is divided into chapters, each of which describes a significant event – for example, a dream. The case study will normally end with an assessment of the patient's state following therapy and an evaluation of the success

of the treatment. Case studies carried out from a psychodynamic perspective will include the therapist's interpretation of the patient's symptoms, dreams and free associations.

The data gathered in a clinical case study are derived from conversations between the therapist and the patient, and the therapist's interpretations of what is reported by the patient. These data are generally qualitative, in the form of what is said, along with observations of non-verbal communication.

Evaluation of clinical case studies

Clinical case studies have strengths and weaknesses. One strength is that they provide rich qualitative data. Psychodynamic psychology is concerned largely with complex motives, of which the individual being studied is often not aware. Other research methods do not usually gather enough detail on any individual to be able to get an insight into these motives. Clinical case studies also have practical value because they give us an idea of how patients may respond in therapy and what a therapist can expect to experience when treating psychological conditions. This means that clinical case studies are useful for therapists, particularly those in training.

Sometimes case studies are the only way to get information on a condition because it is uncommon and socially undesirable. In this sort of case, we are unlikely to be able to study a large group of people, yet when individuals come for psychological help for such conditions they present the opportunity for in-depth study. A case study therefore becomes the only practical solution. An example of such a condition is adult baby syndrome (Pate and Gabbard, 2003). Adult baby syndrome is an uncommon condition in which adults dress up as babies and get pleasure from being treated as babies – for example, drinking milk from the breast or baby bottle and having their nappies changed. As an uncommon and largely socially unacceptable condition, adult baby syndrome is a very difficult topic to investigate any way other than by case studies. In fact, there has never been a paper published on adult baby syndrome that used any method other than a clinical case study.

The problems of clinical case studies really begin when we start to think of them as evidence for psychodynamic ideas or for the effectiveness of psychodynamic techniques. This is for two main reasons:

1. Because most people do not have psychotherapy or the kind of symptoms that would lead them to have therapy, case studies are always one-off studies of unrepresentative individuals. This makes it very difficult to generalise conclusions to other people. The one-off nature of clinical case studies also means that we cannot use them to answer questions that would require comparison of two or more groups. For example, do people who have psychodynamic therapy get better? To answer this question scientifically, we would need to compare how many people who did and did not have therapy showed improvement to their symptoms. We cannot rely on case studies of people who did improve because we have no idea of how many of them would have got better anyway or how many cases of unsuccessful therapy were carried out and not published.

2. It is hard for a therapist who gets to know their patients well, and who

probably has a loyalty to the psychodynamic approach, to be objective as a researcher. They may, for example, selectively focus on aspects of the case that fit in with psychodynamic theory or over-estimate how successful the therapy has been. Freud certainly did this. He pronounced Anna O and the Wolf Man cured, although a range of other professionals who evaluated them later disagreed.

Exam tip

Make sure you illustrate these methods with examples. For example, you could use Anna O, Little Hans, Dora and the Wolf Man to illustrate the clinical case study method. The Harris and Campbell study could be used to illustrate the clinical interview method.

Clinical interviews

All approaches to psychological therapy will include a clinical interview as the therapist needs to get to know their patient well and understand their symptoms. However, the interview method has also been used to research psychodynamic ideas on a larger scale. An example is shown in Box 3.5.

Box 3.5

A clinical interview research study

In an interview study, Harris and Campbell (1999) investigated the possible role of unconscious factors in unplanned pregnancy. The researchers interviewed 128 pregnant women about their own pregnancy and their beliefs about pregnancy and what it might mean for them. Those with unplanned pregnancies were significantly more likely than others to believe that pregnancy would benefit them (81 per cent of the unplanned group, as opposed to 16 per cent of the planned group). This suggests that the participants in the unplanned-pregnancy group were unconsciously motivated to get pregnant. This in turn supports Freud's idea of unconscious motivation.

Figure 3.7 Clinical interviews suggest that unplanned pregnancy may be unconsciously motivated

Clinical interviews are conducted individually and face-to-face. When interviews are for research purposes, they are frequently carried out in the home of the interviewee. Typically when they are for the purpose of assessing a patient, they take place in a surgery setting. Clinical interviews have a certain number of predetermined questions, asked in a particular order. These make up the interview *schedule*. This ensures that the interviewer gets the key information they are looking for from each patient. However, participants have the chance to speak freely and the interviewer can ask additional questions in order to follow up on important things the participant has said.

Evaluation of the clinical interview method

One major strength of the clinical interview method is that it can generate rich qualitative data and, in some cases, quantitative data as well. When a large number of participants are interviewed, as in the Harris and Campbell study,

Glossary

confidentiality – the right of participants not to be personally identified when results are published.

schedule – the interview questions and the order in which they are asked.

this adds up to a tremendous volume of information. A skilled interviewer can also get information from participants that would be very difficult using a questionnaire because they have the opportunity to build a relationship with the participant and reassure them about confidentiality. They can also follow up on important things the participant says because not all the questions are predetermined, so the data gathered are not limited to what the researchers thought would be important when they put together the interview schedule.

All interview methods have limitations however. The interview schedules or the interviewers themselves may be biased towards focusing on particular sorts of information and ignoring others. This can lead to a false picture of what participants have actually said. To limit interviewer bias, it is common practice for someone other than the person who designed and carried out the interview to analyse the information gathered.

Interviews are also only valid if participants are honest. Although participants may not set out to lie, they can be affected by social desirability effects. In practice, it can be hard to choose and deliver questions that do not have one answer that is more socially desirable than another. For example, in the Harris and Campbell study, some participants might have found a planned pregnancy more socially acceptable than an unplanned one, and this could potentially have distorted their findings.

Evaluation of the psychodynamic approach

Strengths

1. It has practical value as a therapy

Many people find psychodynamic therapies helpful for a range of symptoms and conditions. This is particularly the case for people who believe that their symptoms are the result of childhood experience, and for people with a number of different symptoms that would be hard to treat using one of the other psychological therapies that aims simply to remove a symptom (for example, behavioural therapies).

There is now strong evidence supporting the idea that psychodynamic therapies are helpful to patients. In one recent study, Lindgren *et al.* (2010) followed up 134 young adults who had long-term psychodynamic psychotherapy for depression, anxiety or low self-esteem. At the end of the therapy and 18 months later, patients were assessed as having significantly reduced levels of symptoms. This showed that the therapy worked. Because psychodynamic therapies tend to be long-term, and therefore expensive, their use has declined in public healthcare systems like the National Health Service. However, they are still recommended in government guidelines in some cases – for example, complex cases of depression accompanied by other symptoms (NICE, 2004).

2. It has good explanatory power

The psychodynamic approach is well-suited to explaining real-life situations. This is important because it makes the approach highly relevant to the layperson.

Often more scientific approaches to psychology can seem quite remote from the sorts of things ordinary people want from psychology, but this is not true of the psychodynamic approach. Some questions people ask of psychologists might include:

- Why did I dream about that?
- Why does that very ordinary man make me nervous?
- Why is he so uptight?

Questions like these are quite hard to answer using most approaches to psychology, but after reading this chapter you can probably have a go at answering them yourself. You might dream about something because it represents an unfulfilled wish. Someone might make you nervous because they remind you of a parent and trigger memories of your Oedipus complex. According to Freud, someone who we might describe as 'uptight' might be seen as having an anal retentive personality, so the answer to the question lies in the person's potty training. Of course these explanations might not be correct! This brings us neatly to the weaknesses of the approach.

Weaknesses

1. It is based on questionable methods

Most approaches to psychology have developed through a process of systematic research and theory designed to explain research findings. Freud, by contrast, got a lot of his ideas from self-analysis and later used clinical case studies of patients for his evidence. For example, his ideas about dream analysis largely came from a dream of his own and the idea of the Oedipus complex came from Freud's memories of his own childhood.

This process of developing theory would not generally be considered acceptable in modern psychology, which prides itself on systematic and scientific research. Freud's patients, being by-and-large neurotic members of the Austrian middle class, were an unrepresentative group of people on whom to base a theory intended to apply to everyone. Furthermore, Freud tended to ignore aspects of these cases that did not fit with his ideas and often made quite contrived links between theory and case study. Think back to the Wolf Man. The whole case really depends on Freud being right that wolves represented his parents having sex, yet to most modern psychologists that is quite a big leap!

2. Many psychodynamic ideas are hard to test

Although some psychodynamic concepts are supported by solid evidence, many of Freud's ideas are extremely hard to investigate scientifically. For example, there is plenty of evidence to show that, in general terms, the quality of early relationships is important in influencing later development. However, it is extremely difficult to investigate ideas like the oral stage or the Oedipus complex more closely. We would have to say, therefore, that these ideas lack supporting evidence. Similarly, although there is some evidence supporting a link between wishes and dream content, it has turned out to be impossible to investigate whether Freud was correct to say we use processes like displacement or symbolisation to disguise wishes.

To understand why this is such a problem, let us take a moment to look at some philosophy of science. Karl Popper claimed that a theory is only 'good science' if it can be proved wrong. Freud's ideas, however, are very hard to disprove. Take the idea of dreams and wish fulfilment. Some modern findings are consistent with Freud's idea that dreams express wishes. For example, Solms (2000) reports that people with brain injury dream a lot about the abilities they have lost – for example, people suffering paralysis dream more about sport, dancing, etc., than others. If we could find a single dream that definitely did not represent a wish, we could make a case for having disproved Freud's idea. However, that is impossible. Because dream content is supposed to be disguised by dreamwork, it is impossible to say that a particular dream does not represent a wish. Even a nightmare might represent a wish for something *not* to happen.

Box 3.6

Where does the psychodynamic approach stand on key issues and debates?

Nature–nurture debate

The position taken on the nature–nurture debate in the psychodynamic approach is quite balanced and sophisticated. Freud suggested that we are born with a set of biological instincts (nature), but that how these express themselves depends on childhood experience – in particular, the quality of relationships with parents at key stages of development (nurture). Freud tried to explain not just that nature and nurture are both important, but how they interact.

Reductionism

This is also a strength of the approach. Some approaches to psychology reduce complex phenomena to simple ones. For example, the behaviourist approach looks purely at learning of observable behaviour. However, the psychodynamic approach takes a much more holistic approach, looking at human behaviour, thinking, emotion and experience.

Determinism

This can be considered a weakness of the approach because Freud believed our behaviour is determined by unconscious influences. However, Freud also believed that we can become more aware of these influences – for example, in psychotherapy – and that once we are aware of the things influencing us we can take more conscious control of our lives. He was not therefore entirely deterministic in his view.

Psychology as a science

This is a big weakness of the approach. Freud based his ideas on questionable methods, including self-analysis and case studies. In addition, many of his ideas are hard to investigate, meaning they cannot be disproved and lack direct supporting evidence.

Exam tip

To get high marks in a compare-and-contrast question, refer to the issues and debates.

Comparing and contrasting the psychodynamic approach

Here we are going to show an example of how to compare and contrast the psychodynamic approach with the behaviourist approach.

Table 3.3 A plan for how to compare and contrast behaviourist and psychodynamic approaches

CRITERION	BEHAVIOURIST	PSYCHODYNAMIC	SIMILARITY/DIFFERENCE
Assumptions	Importance of learning	Unconscious mind and early relationships	Difference
Applications	Therapy	Therapy	Similarity
Methods	Lab experiments and animal studies	Clinical case studies and interviews	Difference
Nature–nurture	Mostly nurture	Balance of nature and nurture	Difference
Reductionism	Reductionist	More holistic	Difference
Determinism	Deterministic	Deterministic	Similarity
Science	Very scientific	Not scientific	Difference

Summing it up

- The major assumptions underlying the psychodynamic approach are the importance of the unconscious mind and the importance of early relationships in psychological development.

- Freud saw the personality in terms of an instinctive aspect (the id), a logical aspect (the ego) and a moral aspect (the superego).

- Freud saw the personality developing in childhood through a series of stages. Events in the oral, anal and phallic stages are associated with particular personality characteristics.

- Freud used the case of Little Hans to illustrate his ideas about the Oedipus complex.

- Psychodynamic therapies work on the basis that psychological distress and other symptoms of mental health difficulties result at least in part from unconscious influences, early experience and relationships.

- Free association takes place when a patient tries to empty their mind and say whatever comes into it. This is seen in Freud's case of Anna O.

- Dream analysis takes place when a patient brings their dreams to therapy and the therapist suggests hidden meanings behind the content of the dream. This is seen in Freud's cases of Dora and the Wolf Man.

- The major research method used in the psychodynamic approach is the clinical case study. This is an in-depth study of a patient in therapy.

- Case studies gather in-depth information and have practical applications but are poor evidence for psychodynamic ideas because they are biased accounts of unrepresentative cases.

- Another method used in the psychodynamic approach is the clinical interview. This can provide stronger evidence for psychodynamic ideas but is limited by the accuracy of what participants say and the risk of bias in focusing on particular things the participants say.

- Overall, the key strengths of the psychodynamic approach are its good explanatory power and practical application as a therapy.

- Key weaknesses centre on the approach's scientific status. Freud based his ideas on self-analysis and a small number of case studies, rather than systematic research. Some of his ideas are also hard to test scientifically and so lack direct supporting evidence.

Consolidate your understanding

The psychodynamic approach

Use the following activities to run the information in this chapter through your mind. Each activity is designed to help you process the information in a different way, which should help you ensure you understand it and make it easier to remember.

Wordsearch

S	N	R	D	T	F	N	R	D	W	R	A	E	N	P
C	U	U	O	R	R	R	O	E	C	N	P	P	O	E
S	T	O	S	S	E	L	R	T	L	L	H	C	I	R
L	O	N	I	N	U	A	N	A	L	A	R	O	T	D
E	R	P	E	C	D	T	M	N	L	I	D	G	A	E
I	S	M	N	M	S	E	N	L	R	T	E	E	T	L
U	T	S	R	R	E	N	I	D	E	T	T	R	E	F
N	O	I	T	A	I	C	O	S	S	A	E	E	R	F
D	E	E	O	T	E	Y	A	C	I	C	R	P	P	S
C	E	O	E	V	S	C	D	L	N	E	M	U	R	R
M	T	T	A	M	N	D	A	O	P	U	I	S	E	N
E	U	E	E	R	A	A	E	P	D	S	N	F	T	P
S	T	E	P	T	E	G	O	S	I	R	I	C	N	I
R	O	N	M	I	O	P	I	E	I	T	S	D	I	O
A	E	P	S	O	W	E	I	V	R	E	T	N	I	O

oral
anal
phallic
id
ego
superego
latency
unconscious
free association

displacement
interpretation
dream
interview
Freud
Popper
determinist

Crossword

Across

4. A problem for case study and interview evidence
5. You might get this interpreted in therapy
6. Had a famous dream
9. First recorded case of free association
10. The moral part of personality

Down

1. A possible issue for the psychodynamic approach
2. Part of dreamwork
3. An assumption of this approach
7. All the world has them
8. Critic of Freud – sounds like a party animal

Wordsearch and crossword solutions begin on page 231.

Consolidate your understanding

Cloze

The major assumptions underlying the psychodynamic approach are the importance of the
_____ mind and the importance of early _____ in psychological development.
Freud saw the personality in terms of an instinctive aspect (the _____), a logical aspect (the _____)
and a moral aspect (the _____). Freud saw the personality developing in childhood
through a series of stages. Events in the oral, anal and phallic stages are associated with particular
_____ characteristics. Freud used the case of Little _____ to illustrate his ideas about
the Oedipus complex. Psychodynamic therapies work on the basis that psychological distress and other
symptoms of mental health difficulties result at least in part from unconscious influences, early experience
and relationships. Free _____ takes place when a patient tries to empty their mind and say
whatever comes into it. This is seen in Freud's case of _____. Dream _____ takes
place when a patient brings their dreams to therapy and the therapist suggests hidden meanings behind
the content of the dream. This is seen in Freud's cases of Dora and the _____ Man. The major
research method used in the psychodynamic approach is the _____ case _____.
This is an in-depth study of a patient in therapy.

Case studies gather in-depth information and have practical applications but are poor evidence for
psychodynamic ideas because they are biased accounts of _____ cases. Another method
used in the psychodynamic approach is the clinical _____. This can provide stronger
evidence for psychodynamic ideas but is limited by the accuracy of what participants say and the risk of
_____ in focusing on particular things the participants say.

Overall, the key strengths of the psychodynamic approach are its good _____ power
and practical application as a therapy. Key weaknesses centre on the approach's _____
status. Freud based his ideas on self-analysis and a small number of case studies, rather than
systematic research. Some of his ideas are also hard to test scientifically and so lack direct supporting
_____.

For help completing the cloze activity, see the 'Summing it up' section for this chapter.

Consolidate your understanding

Concept map

Complete the empty boxes and you will have a visual revision plan.

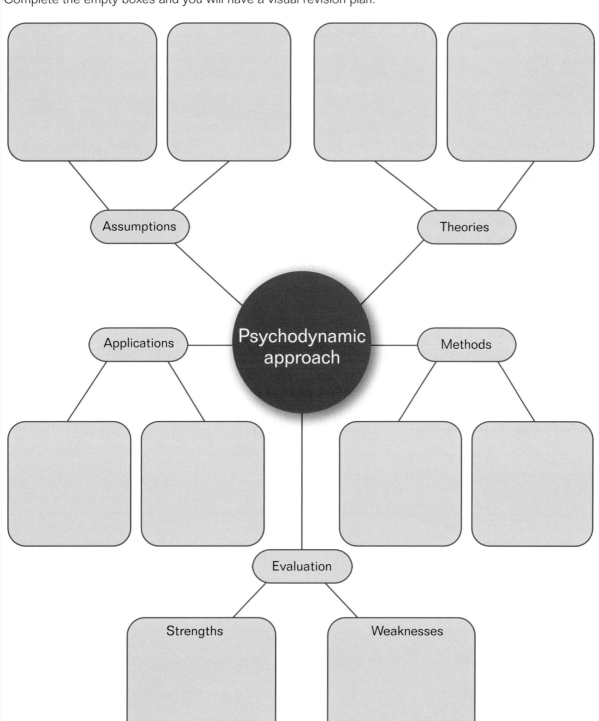

Exam focus

The psychodynamic approach

The difficult approach in terms of understanding, and the most technically difficult to write about, this requires some learning of terms – but not as much as you might think.

Assumptions

As with all the approaches you will need two assumptions here. Remember that the 'Unconscious' is a central assumption; the existence of a realm of memories (that you are unaware of) that drive behaviour. This is the assumption that makes sense of all the others like the effect of psychosexual stages on personality or the operation of defence mechanisms.

Theory

This is a real problem for many students! The question asks for a description of **Freudian personality theory**. This is NOT the description of the structure of personality or the psychosexual stages, but what occurs to an adult personality as a result of things going wrong (or right) in those stages. What happens when an id remains dominant? What happens if a superego becomes dominant?

Here is an example of part of an answer:

'People fixated in the anal stage can form personalities in two main categories. Those who withheld faeces, the anal-retentive type, become miserly, tight-fisted, hoarders and collectors, and like everything neat and orderly. Those who had uncontrolled defecation, the anal-expulsive type, are messy, emotional people, prone to crises where others have to pick up the pieces (literally clean up their mess).'

Now this is easier to write than a description of the psychosexual stages, and it leads towards top marks! However, you do need to carefully prepare a short (8 minutes writing) half-page or so with help from your teacher.

Therapy

You must not forget the **link with the approach** here. This should be something to do with **the Unconscious**, as this is a key feature of the therapy. You can develop this via the basis for interpreting either verbal output or dream descriptions, and then move on to a blow-by-blow account of the course of therapy. Never forget that any therapy has the purpose of restoring control, and therefore **free will**, to the person, no matter how deterministic the approach may be.

Strengths and weaknesses

Remember that strengths and weaknesses will be asked about separately with part a) of the question asking about strengths and part b) about weaknesses. Don't forget the **massive social impact** that Freudian ideas had on society and the arts, and how they created a view of human motivation that still fuels arguments today. Also remember that some Freudian ideas are questionable, and some are very insightful – and some are being revived by scientific studies, especially using fMRI. Not all Freudian hypotheses are unfalsifiable! This is very much 'on the one hand….this is a strength, on the other….'.

Compare and contrast

This is the easiest approach to contrast with the other approaches, as the **methodology** is quite different. It is a contrast between the nomothetic and the ideographic, the experiment and the case study. But you need to note, if contrasting with either the cognitive or the biological approach, that they too use case studies as the starting point for theorising. You can also make some mileage from the theatrical superstructure of theory, especially the ludicrous Oedipus complex, where Freud's exceptional eye for detail and incisive mind get swamped and eventually befuddled. Compare that to the simple models of the cognitive approach or the resolutely unimaginative behavioural approach.

Explain and evaluate method

You should not have any problems here; indeed you should have learnt all this stuff as material from Q4 'Compare and contrast'. Case studies are clearly a main method. If you feel a struggle to distinguish between case study and clinical interview, one of the projective tests, Thematic Apperception Tests or ink blot (Rorschach) tests could be used as a second method.

4 The cognitive approach

I should be able to:

- outline two assumptions of the cognitive approach
- describe attribution theory
- describe how the cognitive approach has been used in therapy with particular reference to CBT or REBT
- describe and evaluate the research methodology used in the cognitive approach
- evaluate the cognitive approach, including two strengths and two weaknesses
- compare and contrast the cognitive approach to other approaches to psychology.

What could I be asked?

There is no guarantee that future exams will keep precisely to this wording or mark allocation. However, it is likely that any questions you are asked about the approach will be much like the following:

1. **(a)** Outline **two** assumptions of the cognitive approach. [4]

   (b) Describe attribution theory. [8]

2. **Describe** how the cognitive approach has been applied in **either** CBT or REBT. [12]

3. **(a)** Evaluate **two** strengths of the cognitive approach. [6]

   (b) Evaluate **two** weaknesses of the cognitive approach. [6]

4. **Compare and contrast** the biological and cognitive approaches in terms of similarities and differences. [12]

5. **Explain and evaluate** the methodology used by the cognitive approach. [12]

The cognitive approach originated in the 1950s and has, for the last half century, been the single most popular and influential approach to psychology. Recall the behaviourist approach discussed in Chapter 2. Behaviourism was based on the principle that the mind was simply too difficult to study and explain scientifically. Thus the emphasis of behavioural psychology was on studying and explaining observable behaviour. This is sometimes called 'black box' psychology because the mind was seen as impenetrable. By the 1950s, however, the computer had been invented and this gave psychologists a new way of thinking about the mind. By comparing the way the mind processes information to that of a computer, cognitive psychologists have been able to study the mind as the behaviourists could not.

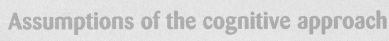

Assumptions of the cognitive approach

The main assumptions of the cognitive approach include the following:

- an emphasis on the internal processes of the mind
- the importance of the ways information is processed in order to make sense of the environment and respond appropriately to it
- the human mind can be understood by comparing it to a computer.

An emphasis on the internal processes of the mind

It might seem obvious that psychology is concerned with the human mind. However, consider the three approaches we have already looked at. Behaviourists essentially ignore the mind, focusing as far as possible on the effects of the environment on behaviour. Biological psychologists are interested primarily in the nervous system and the links between physical mechanisms, particularly in the brain, and psychological functioning. Psychodynamic psychology is concerned with *unconscious* mental processes, a very particular aspect of the mind (see page 43). Cognitive psychologists are concerned with understanding the full range of mental processes, including the following:

- **perception**: the processes by which we take in and make sense of information from the environment
- **attention**: the processes by which we focus on particular sources of information rather than others and maintain this focus over time
- **memory**: the processes by which we retain and recall information
- **language**: the use of mental symbols to represent information in the mind, helping thinking and communication between people
- **thinking**: the processes by which we manipulate information in the mind in order to reason, solve problems, make decisions and otherwise make judgements.

The importance of information processing

Most cognitive psychologists have adopted an information processing approach to understand the mind. This means that the cognitive processes of perception, attention, memory, etc., can be seen as a series of processing systems. Working together, these processing systems allow us to make sense of and respond to the world. For example, when we look at an orange (attention), we perceive a distinctive shape, texture and colour (perception), we recognise it (memory) and name it an orange (language). Once we have identified it as an orange, we can think about it. We might, for example, analyse whether it looks like a tasty orange, consider whether we are hungry, etc. We can also make the decision to eat it!

The computer analogy

Many cognitive psychologists find it useful to think of the ways in which the mind processes information as similar to the processing taking place in a computer. Like a computer, the mind has an input of information from the senses, throughput in the form of memory, thinking and language, and output in the form of decision-making, speech and action. Like a modern computer, we process information in parallel – that is, we perform different cognitive tasks at the same time. In some ways of course, the mind is *not* like a computer. We are slower at processing information and make more mistakes; we are, however, much better than a computer at making guesses. Nonetheless, we can think of the brain as a piece of hardware and our experiences and learned responses as software. One branch of cognitive psychology, known as computational cognitive science, focuses on modelling cognitive processes as we believe they take place in the mind, on a computer.

Figure 4.1 In some ways, the human mind works like a computer

Box 4.1

Pure and applied cognitive psychology

The cognitive approach dominates modern psychology, in the form of both pure and applied cognitive psychology. Pure cognitive psychology is a huge area of theory and research in itself. This involves achieving a better understanding of how we perceive, remember and think, etc. However, the cognitive approach can also be applied to understanding other areas of psychology. For example, in this chapter, we consider attribution theory, a cognitive approach to understanding an important social process. Cognitive principles have also been applied to understanding and treating mental disorder. We know, for example, that people suffering from depression tend to attend to the negative aspects of a situation and remember unhappy events much more than do the rest of us. Cognitive therapies work by altering these patterns of information processing.

Attribution theory

Whenever we interact with other people, we constantly process information about their behaviour. According to German psychologist Fritz Heider (1958), one of the key things we are looking for when we analyse this information is why people behave as they do. The cognitive processes whereby we try to judge why people behave as they do are called *attribution*. *Attribution theory* is the general term used to describe a group of explanations for how we make attributions. The most important judgement we have to make in the attribution process is to what extent the person's actions are a direct result of their character and to what extent they are a consequence of the situation. Whenever we judge that a person did something because of the type of person they are, we make an *internal* attribution. Say, for example, we see someone we know behaving in a grumpy manner. We might think that 'Rick really is a crabby chap'. On the other hand, we might make an *external* attribution and judge Rick's grumpiness to be the result of his situation. For example, he might be tired or ill, or the room might be excessively hot. Under some circumstances, we can make attributions based on a single behaviour. However, we can also use information about people's behaviour over time to arrive at more valid conclusions.

Glossary

applied cognitive psychology – using cognitive principles, like information processing, to understand other areas of psychology.
attribution – making judgements about the reasons for behaviour.
attribution theory – a set of ideas aiming to explain how and why we make particular attributions.
pure cognitive psychology – the study of mental processes, such as memory and thinking.

Glossary

correspondent inference – a judgement that a behaviour reflects the character of the person.
covariation – the extent to which behaviour covaries with typical behaviour of that person and with the behaviour of others.

Correspondent inferences

Sometimes we can make judgements about people's characters (i.e. internal attributions) based on a single incident. This process is called *correspondent inference* because we are making an inference (i.e. a judgement) that the behaviour corresponds to the person's character. Jones and Davis (1965) suggested that in order to make an internal attribution from a single behaviour, three criteria must be met.

1. The behaviour must be deliberate; if it is accidental, we cannot use it as a basis to judge someone's character.

2. The behaviour must have distinctive effects; if a behaviour has several possible consequences, then it becomes unclear why it might have been done.

3. The behaviour should be low in social desirability; behaviour that simply follows social norms reveals little about a person's character.

Covariation theory

Correspondent inference theory provides a partial explanation for when we make internal attributions based on single behaviours. However, when we are judging someone we know in a situation we are familiar with, we generally have the opportunity to make use of rather more information than a single behaviour. Kelley (1967) proposed a model of how we make attributions when we have information about the person's past behaviour and about other people's behaviour in the same situation. Given this sort of information, we can judge how an action *covaries* with their own and others' behaviour based on three criteria.

1. Consensus: whether other people also act in the same way in the same situation.

2. Consistency: whether the person we are judging always acts that way given the same situation.

3. Distinctiveness: whether the person behaves similarly across a range of situations.

The way this information can be used to make an attribution is shown in Table 4.1.

Table 4.1 The covariation model

	CONSENSUS	CONSISTENCY	DISTINCTIVENESS
Internal attribution	Low	High	Low
External attribution	High	High	High

Note that consistency of behaviour has to be high before any sort of attribution can be made. In other words, we cannot make good use of behaviour that takes place irregularly and unpredictably to make any sort of judgement. Where consensus and distinctiveness are low – that is, the behaviour is unusual and takes place in a range of situations – then we can make an internal attribution. If it only takes place in a particular situation or it is common behaviour among

other people as well, then we cannot attribute the behaviour to the character of the person.

As a psychology student, you may have had the experience of being late for lessons. This is a real-life example of where the covariation process is likely to be used by your teachers! For example, if Lana is always late (high consistency) to all lessons (low distinctiveness), and other students are generally on time (low consensus), then a teacher is likely to attribute the lateness to her character. If, however, all students are late to their lessons (high consensus) but on time to other teachers' lessons (high distinctiveness), then it is likely to be the situation (i.e. psychology lessons!) that is the problem.

Figure 4.2 According to the covariation principle, we can make judgements about a student's character based on their behaviour if the behaviour is consistent, low in distinctiveness and low in consensus

Box 4.2

Attribution biases

One of the limitations of correspondent inference and covariation theories is that they assume we are fairly logical in our judgements about people. Of course in reality this is not entirely true. There are a number of common errors or biases in the attribution process. Perhaps the most obvious and important is the *fundamental attribution error* (or FAE). This is our tendency to overemphasise the character of the person and de-emphasise the situation, meaning that we tend to make incorrect internal attributions. A topical example of the FAE at work is in attribution of obesity. In reality, a range of factors, including genetic predisposition, affect body type. However, there is a strong tendency to attribute obesity to character flaws in the individual. This effect can be seen even in young children. Musher-Eizenman *et al.* (2004) asked 42 children of an average age of five years to describe other children of different body types and about their beliefs of the explanations for different body

types. The children tended to make internal attributions for being overweight; the most negative descriptions of overweight children being from the children making internal attributions.

Another attribution bias is the actor–observer effect. This takes place when the person exhibiting a behaviour makes a different attribution from that made by people who observe it. Usually the actor tends to make external attributions for socially undesirable behaviour and internal attributions for desirable behaviour. Observers tend to do the reverse. Stewart (2005) demonstrated the actor–observer effect in a study of 321 car crash survivors. When surveyed, the survivors overwhelmingly attributed accidents to the behaviour of other drivers. In other words, when it came to judging their own driving, they made external attributions, but when it came to the behaviour of other drivers, their attributions tended to be internal.

Applying the cognitive approach to therapy

The cognitive approach to psychology has a number of practical applications. One of the most important is in understanding and treating mental health problems. Cognitive therapies are now the most commonly used in clinical psychology. Two approaches to cognitive therapy are rational emotive behaviour therapy (REBT) and cognitive behaviour therapy (CBT).

The aims of cognitive therapies

All therapies have the ultimate aim of making patients feel and function better. However, different therapies have different *mediating aims* – that is, what they seek to directly alter. Whereas behavioural therapies have the mediating aim of changing behaviour and psychodynamic therapies have the mediating aim of improving emotional state, the mediating aim of CBT is to alter the ways in which people think. This is based on the idea that how we think affects our emotional state and our behaviour.

Rational emotional behaviour therapy

Albert Ellis (1977) applied cognitive principles to understanding how people respond to negative events. Specifically, he believed that how we respond emotionally when something goes wrong is based on the beliefs we have about such events. To Ellis, mental health is dependent on stoicism. Stoicism is the ability to remain emotionally stable in the face of difficulty. Ellis believed that stoicism stems from a healthy set of beliefs about the world. Beliefs that are overly negative or that put pressure on us to function perfectly at all times predispose us to over-react when something goes wrong. This in turn leads to anxiety and depression. This idea was crystallised in the ABC model. In this model, A = the activating event, B = beliefs and C = (emotional) consequences. The following example shows the ABC model applied to understanding the effects of failing an exam (from Palmer and Dryden, 1995).

Table 4.2 An example of the ABC sequence (after Palmer and Dryden, 1995)

A	Activating event	Failing an exam
B	Beliefs	'I should have passed' 'There shouldn't be exams like this' 'I can't bear not passing'
C	Consequences	Depression

Glossary

I-can't-stand-it-itis – beliefs that difficulty or discomfort is unbearable.
musturbation – beliefs phrased in musts (e.g. 'I must be perfect').
outcome study – study into the effectiveness of a therapy.
utopianism – belief that world should be a perfect place.

Although Ellis originally trained in psychodynamic therapy, he came to believe that it was quicker and more efficient to tackle the symptoms of mental disorder by challenging people's irrational beliefs and so make them more stoical. He called this rational emotive behaviour therapy (or REBT). The name comes from the idea that if people can be made more rational in their thinking, then their emotional state and behaviour will also normalise. Two types of irrational belief are particularly challenged in REBT.

- *Musturbation* is the belief that we *must* be perfect and successful at all times.
- *I-can't-stand-it-itis* is the belief that we cannot cope when something does not go smoothly.

Musturbation makes us extremely sensitive to any kind of failure. I-can't-stand-it-itis makes even the most minor problems and setbacks seem disastrous. Musturbation and I-can't-stand-it-itis refer to beliefs we might have about ourselves. But what about our beliefs about the world? REBT therapists use the term 'utopian' beliefs to describe the belief that the world is meant to be fair and easy to live in.

REBT involves vigorous argument with the patient in order to challenge irrational beliefs like musturbation, I-can't-stand-it-itis and utopianism. REBT therapists may also ask patients to keep diaries of thoughts and events so that the therapist can show them evidence of how irrational their beliefs were. If patients are to tolerate this sort of attack on their beliefs, it is essential for them to trust and respect the therapist. In order to be successful, a therapist using REBT must be able to quickly form a good relationship with the patient.

How does REBT link back to the assumptions of the cognitive approach?

- REBT focuses on identifying and altering unhelpful beliefs. A belief is an aspect of thinking, which is a mental process.
- REBT aims to alter information processing; the idea is that incoming information about an event is interpreted in the light of existing beliefs. Altering those beliefs will lead to a healthier interpretation.

> ### Exam tip
>
> In the exam, you will have to describe **either** CBT or REBT. However, to gain full marks in a question about a cognitive therapy, you must link CBT or REBT back to the assumptions of the approach.

Cognitive behaviour therapy

Cognitive behaviour therapy is not a pure therapy in itself but a blend of techniques from different cognitive therapies, including REBT. It is described as cognitive-*behavioural* rather than just cognitive for two reasons. First, as in REBT, there is an assumption that if we alter cognition this will result in a change to patients' behaviour. Second, cognitive techniques are often used alongside the behavioural techniques discussed in Chapter 2.

Many of the ideas in modern CBT come from the work of Aaron Beck. Whereas Ellis was particularly interested in the role of irrational beliefs in stress, Beck was more concerned with the role of negative thinking in depression. Beck (1976) identified three types of negative thinking that characterised depression. The first of these is negative automatic thinking. This comes in the form of the *cognitive triad* of a negative view of self, negative view of the world and negative view of the future.

The second type of negativity identified by Beck results from a distinctive pattern of selective attention. He noted that depressed people tend to attend to the negative aspects of a situation and ignore the positive aspects. This leads them to overestimate the 'downside' of any situation. Beck's final form of negative thinking involves the activation of *negative self-schemas*. Cognitive psychologists use the term 'schemas' to describe packets of information in which our knowledge of each aspect of the world is contained. Our self-schema contains all the information, beliefs, etc., we have that relate to ourselves.

Like REBT, cognitive therapy aims to change the sort of cognitions that predispose us to psychological problems. In CBT, however, there is less emphasis on aggressive argument against negative beliefs and more emphasis on testing and disproving them. Patients in CBT are thus given tasks to carry out. For example, a depressed patient might typically say that they have not been going out lately because there was no point as they would not enjoy it. A cognitive

Figure 4.3 CBT might involve recording enjoyable events and discussing them at the next session

therapist might respond to this by setting them the task of going out with friends and recording whether they had enjoyed it. In the next session, they would have to admit they had enjoyed going out, and this would help change their negative beliefs about the world.

How does CBT link back to the assumptions of the cognitive approach?

- CBT is concerned with a range of mental processes, including thinking (e.g. negative thinking in depression) but also attention (e.g. to negative aspects of a situation) and memory (e.g. recalling unhappy events rather than happy).
- CBT seeks to alter the ways we process information; so, for example, people are taught to process information differently by attending to the positives or trying to recall happy memories.

The methodology of the cognitive approach

Laboratory experiments

Although many methods have been used to study cognitive processes, perhaps the single most important method is the lab experiment. An experiment is a study that tests the effect of one variable (called the independent variable) on another (the dependent variable). An example of a lab experiment you will cover in this course is Loftus and Palmer's study of the effect of leading questions (the independent variable) on the accuracy of eyewitness memory (the dependent variable). You will look at this study in some depth in Unit 2 of your AS level, and you can read about it on page 125.

Figure 4.4 A classic cognitive experiment is Loftus and Palmer's study of witness memory for car accidents

Box 4.3

What lab experiments tell us about cognitive processes

In the cognitive approach, we conduct experiments to give us an idea about mental processes like memory or attribution. Take the Loftus and Palmer example. The mental process they were interested

in was memory, specifically recall of visual information about a witnessed car accident. They found that participants frequently made errors when asked leading questions. This behaviour allowed the researchers to make the judgement that memory for events can be altered after the event by information like questions.

A lab experiment takes place in a laboratory as opposed to more natural surroundings (that would be a *field* experiment). A laboratory is simply a controlled environment. It may or may not have specialist equipment, depending on the nature of the experiment. The purpose of the controlled environment

is to make as sure as possible that only the independent variable being varied in the experiment causes changes to the dependent variable. This helps eliminate the effects of extraneous variables like temperature, sound and distracting visual stimuli.

Evaluation of the laboratory experiment

The major advantage of laboratory experiments is that they can be controlled. This means that we can reduce or eliminate the effect of extraneous variables and so be reasonably certain that our independent variable is the main thing affecting our dependent variable. This allows us to study cause-and-effect relationships. Lab experiments are also easy to replicate – that is, to repeat the procedure in order to see whether we obtain the same results. This means that laboratory experiments tend to have good reliability.

A common problem with laboratory experiments is their ecological validity. This is the extent to which the procedure is a valid representation of what happens in real life. Lab experiments are at a disadvantage here because they take place in controlled and therefore, probably artificial surroundings where people may not act as they would in their natural surroundings. This is made worse if participants are given tasks that differ from those they are meant to represent in real life. To return to our Loftus and Palmer example, participants sat in a lecture theatre and watched a film of a car accident. Ecological validity is a problem here because they are not in the sort of environment where they would see a real car crash and because the task of watching a film is quite different from unexpectedly seeing an accident.

There are other potential problems with laboratory experiments. One such problem is bias. Experimenters know what they expect to find and they may accidentally communicate their expectations to participants through subtle cues called demand characteristics. Once participants get an idea of what 'should' happen or what the experimenter wants, their own biases come into play and these may affect the results of the experiment.

Case studies of people with brain injury

Case studies are in-depth studies of individuals or small groups of people in particular circumstances. One way to study normal cognitive processes is to look at how they are disrupted by injury to the brain. The brain may be injured by strokes, tumours, physical trauma or the side effects of surgery. Some people who have suffered brain injury are willing to help psychologists by being studied.

Cognitive psychologists are interested in *dissociations* in brain injury. A dissociation between two cognitive processes is shown when one is badly damaged and the other undamaged, or much less so by brain injury. This tells us that the two processes are separate. Say, for example, we are interested in whether long-term memory is a separate cognitive process from short-term memory. A case study of a person whose brain injury affects long-term memory and not short-term memory is evidence that the two processes are separate. Even stronger evidence comes from a *double dissociation* – that is, one person has a brain injury that affects long-term memory but not short-term and another has a different injury that affects short-term memory but not long-term. Such cases do exist and this is one

Glossary

dissociation – brain injury affecting one cognitive process and not another, showing their separateness.
double dissociation – brain injuries in at least two patients, such that each has one process intact and the other damaged (e.g. one patient has damaged short-term memory alone and the other has damaged long-term memory alone).

reason why cognitive psychologists believe short-term and long-term memory are separate, though closely connected, processes.

Evaluation of case studies of brain injury

Brain injury gives us a unique opportunity to separate out mental processes that normally work together. This is not possible in laboratory experiments on neurotypical participants (i.e. those with normal brain function) and allows us to better understand the relationship between one process and another (e.g. short- and long-term memory). Another strength is that, like all case studies, this type of study generates large amounts of qualitative data. Some patients are willing to be studied over several decades, so providing enormous volumes of information.

The major weakness of case studies of this type is the same for any case study: the sample. We are always looking at a single person who is, by definition, not typical of the population because of their brain injury. Because the individual must volunteer to be studied, they may in fact not even be representative of people with brain injury. There are also serious ethical issues associated with this type of study. Most seriously, how does a researcher get real consent from someone with a serious cognitive problem? HM was studied from 1953 until his death in 2008 by a range of memory researchers after his long-term memory was severely damaged by an operation to relieve the effects of epilepsy. HM was apparently happy to participate in research, but consider the nature of his injury: He was not able to form any new memories and forgot what he was doing every few minutes. Although he gave consent to be studied, he would not remember doing so by the time a procedure was completed. Under those circumstances, could he give real consent?

Evaluating the cognitive approach

Strengths

1. It is good science

There is a long-running debate concerning the extent to which psychology is a science. Generally, psychologists say that it is but some scientists of other flavours are less convinced (try asking a chemistry teacher)! The problem for psychologists is that we have to study and explain a tremendous range of human characteristics, abilities and experiences. Some of these are easier than others to study using the scientific method, and some approaches, such as the psychodynamic approach (see Chapter 3), are open to accusations of poor science. However, this cannot be said of the cognitive approach. Its major research method is the laboratory experiment, the preferred method for scientists from other disciplines. Theories are largely testable, often, though not always, by means of experiments.

2. It has many practical applications

The cognitive approach has many applications in real life. Following the work of researchers like Elizabeth Loftus, psychologists have informed courts about the accuracy of eyewitness memory, and the questioning procedures used by police officers and lawyers have been improved as a result. CBT and REBT are

used successfully on a wide scale to relieve psychological distress associated with depression and anxiety. Our understanding of attribution biases helps us understand how people respond to health problems like obesity and to difficult and unexpected situations like accidents.

Weaknesses

1. Cognitive reductionism

The cognitive approach explains human behaviour and experience in terms of cognitive processes. So in looking at how we respond to any situation, the ways we process information are of prime importance. According to a cognitive account, we blame someone for being overweight because we tend to make internal attributions and we get depressed because we attend to negative aspects of a situation. However, humans are more complex than this, and we cannot always explain our behaviour or experience by reference to cognition alone. We are, for example, emotional and instinctive beings, as well as cognitive ones. There are non-cognitive factors that may well affect our responses in the above situations. Our tendency to blame someone for being overweight may be instinctive, hard-wired into us as a mechanism to ensure the physical fitness of our group. It may also be a defensive emotional response to fears about our own fitness and mortality. The tendency of cognitive psychologists to ignore these things and just focus on the role of cognitions is called cognitive reductionism.

2. Limitations of the computer analogy

Recall one of the assumptions of the cognitive approach – that the mind can be understood by likening it to a computer. In some ways, the human mind does function in this way – certainly we input information through our senses and output it in the form of decisions and behaviour. In other ways, however, our minds work very differently from computers. We process information much more slowly than a computer but we are much better at using mental tricks and shortcuts. Unlike computers, we have motivations and emotions. This makes our responses much more irrational and unpredictable than would be the case if

---

Box 4.4

Where does the cognitive approach stand on key issues and debates?

Nature–nurture debate

The cognitive approach as a whole does not really take a position on the nature–nurture debate. This can be seen as a weakness of the approach. The cognitive approach is generally concerned with current information processing; where that information processing comes from is simply not the main issue.

Reductionism

Cognitive psychology is guilty of reductionism because cognitive psychologists rely on explaining a huge range of human behaviours and characteristics by means of how we process information. Actually, people are subject to a wide range of influences (e.g. instinct, motivation, emotion), not all of which can be explained this way.

Psychology as a science

This is a major strength of the approach. Cognitive psychologists generally function as classic 'good scientists', carrying out experiments and developing testable theories to explain their findings.

we were really like computers. This is one reason why we cannot be explained by cognitive processes alone and why cognitive reductionism is such a problem.

Exam tip

To get high marks in a compare-and-contrast question, you must refer to the issues and debates.

Comparing and contrasting the cognitive approach

Here we are going to show an example of how to compare and contrast the cognitive approach with the psychodynamic approach.

Table 4.3 A plan for how to compare and contrast cognitive and psychodynamic approaches

CRITERION	COGNITIVE	PSYCHODYNAMIC	SIMILARITY/DIFFERENCE
Assumptions	Importance of information processing	Unconscious mind and early relationships	Difference
Applications	Therapy	Therapy	Similarity
Methods	Lab experiments and case studies	Interviews and case studies	Difference and similarity
Nature–nurture	Does not take a position	Balance of nature and nurture	Difference
Reductionism	Reductionist	More holistic	Difference
Determinism	Deterministic	Deterministic	Similarity
Science	Very scientific	Not scientific	Difference

Summing it up

- ➡ The major assumptions of the cognitive approach are an emphasis on mental processes, seeing the mind in terms of its processing of information and an understanding of the mind by comparison with a computer.

- ➡ How the mind processes information is important in its own right, and is studied within the field of pure cognitive psychology. However, the cognitive approach can also be applied to understanding other areas of psychology. This is applied cognitive psychology.

- ➡ An important area of applied cognitive psychology is attribution theory. We make attributions when we decide why someone behaved as they did. In particular, attribution theorists are concerned with how and when we make judgements about someone's character based on their behaviour.

- ➡ We can make correspondent inferences about someone (i.e. judgements about their character) based on a single behaviour. This, however, requires that the behaviour is deliberate, socially undesirable and has a single distinctive effect.

- ➡ When we have access to information about multiple behaviours by different people in a variety of situations, we can make attributions by the covariation principle. This states that we can make an internal attribution when someone consistently acts differently from others across a range of situations.

- ➡ Both correspondent inference and covariation models represent ways we can make judgements about people based on their behaviour. However, research shows that in reality we also use other sources of information.

- ➡ We can apply the emphasis on mental processes and how the mind processes information to understanding mental health problems. Cognitive behavioural therapies aim to alter faulty or unhelpful cognitions.

- ➡ REBT does this by vigorous argument – in particular, challenging beliefs that make us more sensitive to failure or difficulty. CBT focuses more on testing and disproving patterns of negative thinking.

- ➡ Cognitive therapies are very popular at present and have a large body of evidence to support their effectiveness.

- ➡ The most important research method used in the cognitive approach is the laboratory experiment. This has the advantage of good control over variables but can lack ecological validity and is open to bias.

- ➡ Case studies of brain injury are also used to study cognitive processes. These can be useful because they give us the opportunity to study cognitive processes in isolation, but they depend on a small unrepresentative group of participants.

- ➡ The cognitive approach has good scientific status and many practical applications. However, it can be guilty of cognitive reductionism and the assumption of many cognitive psychologists that the mind can be compared to a computer is flawed.

Consolidate your understanding

The cognitive approach

Use the following activities to run the information in this chapter through your mind. Each activity is designed to help you process the information in a different way, which should help you ensure you understand it and make it easier to remember.

Wordsearch

E	X	P	E	R	I	M	E	N	T	M	O	A
N	C	E	N	A	O	C	U	O	S	P	L	L
O	O	N	O	I	T	U	B	I	R	T	T	A
I	G	I	I	C	T	C	L	T	A	I	P	B
T	N	R	T	R	O	L	D	A	I	R	T	O
A	I	E	A	A	E	M	O	B	M	D	R	R
I	T	L	M	I	I	D	P	R	T	O	E	A
R	I	I	R	T	B	C	T	U	L	B	O	T
A	V	A	O	E	T	R	O	T	T	I	A	O
V	E	B	F	I	T	I	I	S	A	E	D	R
O	O	L	N	R	I	U	U	U	S	T	R	Y
C	H	E	I	D	E	R	D	M	N	I	T	I
E	C	O	L	O	G	I	C	A	L	B	D	L

information	cognitive
attribution	Ellis
REBT	triad
experiment	reliable
computer	Heider
covariation	CBT
musturbation	laboratory
ecological	dissociation

Crossword

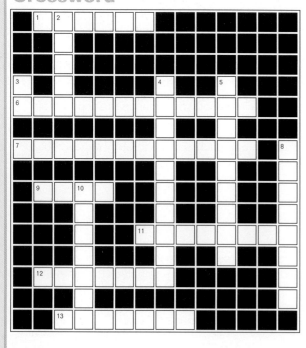

Across

1. Developed attribution theory
6. Thinking we must be perfect at all times
7. Weakness of the cognitive approach
9. Developed a model of cognitive therapy
11. What do cognitive psychologists compare the mind to?
12. One health problem we tend to make internal attributions about
13. Beliefs that the world should be perfect

Down

2. Developed REBT
3. Famous cognitive case study
4. Where a lot of cognitive psychology is studied
5. One factor affecting covariation
8. An attribution to the character of the individual
10. Ethical issue for researchers into brain injury

Wordsearch and crossword solutions begin on page 231.

Consolidate your understanding

Cloze

The major assumptions of the cognitive approach are an emphasis on _____ processes and an understanding of the mind by comparison with a _____. How the mind processes information is important in its own right, and is studied within the field of pure cognitive psychology. However, the cognitive approach can also be applied to understanding other areas of psychology. This is _____ cognitive psychology. An important area of applied cognitive psychology is attribution theory. We make attributions when we decide why someone behaved as they did. In particular, attribution theorists are concerned with how and when we make judgements about someone's _____ based on their behaviour. We can make correspondent inferences about someone (i.e. judgements about their character) based on a single behaviour. This, however, requires that the behaviour is deliberate, socially _____ and has a single distinctive effect. When we have access to information about multiple behaviours by different people in a variety of situations, we can make attributions by the _____ principle. This states that we can make an internal attribution when someone consistently acts differently from others across a range of situations. Both correspondent inference and covariation models represent ways we can make judgements about people based on their behaviour. However, research shows that in reality we also use other sources of information.

We can apply the emphasis on mental processes and how the mind processes information to understanding mental health problems. Cognitive behavioural therapies aim to alter faulty or unhelpful cognitions. _____ does this by vigorous argument – in particular, challenging beliefs that make us more sensitive to failure or difficulty. CBT focuses more on testing and disproving patterns of negative thinking. Cognitive therapies are very popular at present and have a large body of evidence to support their effectiveness. The most important research method used in the cognitive approach is the laboratory experiment. This has the advantage of good control over variables but can lack _____ validity and is open to bias. Case studies of brain injury are also used to study cognitive processes. These can be useful because they give us the opportunity to study cognitive processes in isolation but they depend on a small unrepresentative group of _____. The cognitive approach has good _____ status and many practical applications. However, it can be guilty of cognitive reductionism and the assumption of many cognitive psychologists that the mind can be compared to a computer is flawed.

For help completing the cloze activity, see the 'Summing it up' section for this chapter.

Consolidate your understanding

Concept map

Complete the empty boxes and you will have a visual revision plan.

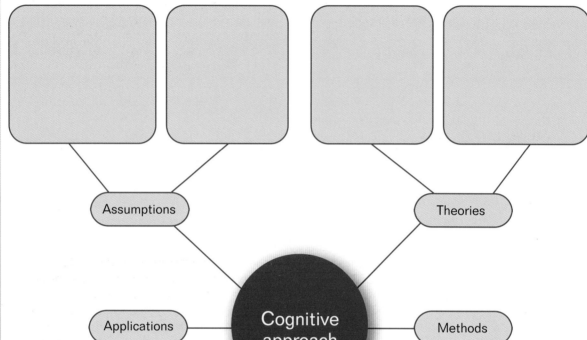

Assumptions

Theories

Applications

Cognitive approach

Methods

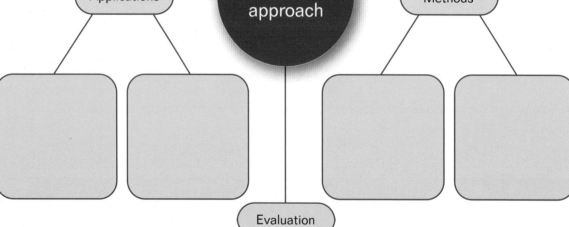

Evaluation

Strengths

Weaknesses

Exam focus

The cognitive approach

Many students find this one the most difficult, as it doesn't seem to have an identity of its own. It is quite difficult to disentangle it from the biological approach (in the real world it is a conjoined twin in neuroscience) and attribution theory in particular can be difficult to grasp.

Assumptions

As with all the approaches you will need two assumptions here. Don't forget the computer analogy. Every approach has its historical and technological context that influences its basic ideas – Freud has the steam era, cognitive has the computer.

Theory

Oh dear, this is never done that well by the majority. It's not really very memorable, it's full of complicated little bits, and it's only worth 8 marks. So what do you do? Get the general idea down (what is attribution?), do a potted theory (Jones and Davis is probably simplest, but don't write too much detail) and then explain the fundamental attribution error and any other **errors and biases** you have time for. This should guarantee 6 out of 8 minimum.

Therapy

Don't forget the link here – the best one being that the way you think determines the way you feel and behave.

- State the general basis for the therapy.
- You should then have a short paragraph about the development of therapies (via Ellis or Beck).
- Outline the technical bits (REBT has some unforgettable terms!).
- Describe a typical passage through therapy.

Strengths and weaknesses

Remember that strengths and weaknesses will be asked about separately with part a) of the question asking about strengths and part b) about weaknesses. 'I am not a computer!' should be the key to the weaknesses, but the computer analogy is also a strength, providing the basis for testable models and hypotheses. The approach can use almost literally the same strengths as behavioural and biological approaches – **you can recycle much of the same material** if you are in need!

'While the computer analogy is largely misleading, and therefore a serious weakness, it has historically also been a strength. It has enabled the construction of understandable models and the generation of testable hypotheses. One example is the working memory model which used a simple computer model in the 1980s and has remained a central model for memory research ever since.'

Compare and contrast

You can **use assumptions here quite effectively as a contrast**. Therapies compare well with non-invasive ones and contrast well with the invasive ones of the biological approach. You can even use relevance – comparison with the cognitive approach in neuroscience, and contrast with the 'has-been' status of either the behavioural or the psychodynamic: 'The cognitive approach is at the forefront of modern psychology whereas the psychodynamic is largely an entertaining footnote in twentieth century history.'

Explain and evaluate method

Recycle, recycle, recycle – experiment and case study could be used in biological and behavioural as well. Remember that your examples distinguish between near identical descriptions and evaluations of the methods, and without them you will not score well. We **call interchangeable descriptions 'generic' ones, and they do not attract many marks.**

5 Core studies in social psychology

This chapter includes:

I should be able to:

- summarise the aims and context of Asch's 1955 study of conformity
- outline the procedure used in Asch's study
- describe Asch's findings and conclusions
- evaluate the methodology of Asch's study
- use alternative evidence to critically assess Asch's research

- summarise the aims and context of Milgram's 1963 study of obedience
- outline the procedure used in Milgram's study
- describe Milgram's findings and conclusions
- evaluate the methodology of Milgram's study
- use alternative evidence to critically assess Milgram's research.

The social approach is concerned with how we interact with one another and how we are affected by the presence and behaviour of others, both individuals and groups. Almost every imaginable way in which people affect or respond to each other has been studied somewhere by social psychologists. Social psychologists use a variety of research methods, including experiments conducted in the laboratory and those under more natural conditions. The two core studies in this section were carried out under controlled conditions.

Figure 5.1 The social approach focuses on how individuals interact with one another

Study 1: Asch (1955) Opinions and social pressure

Asch, S.E. (1955) 'Opinions and social pressure.' *Scientific American*, 193: 31–35.

What could I be asked?

1. **Summarise** the aims **and** context of Asch's (1955) study. [12]

2. **Outline** the procedures of Asch's (1955) study. [12]

3. **Describe** the findings **and** conclusions of Asch's (1955) study. [12]

4. **Evaluate** the methodology of Asch's (1955) study. [12]

5. With reference to **alternative evidence**, critically **assess** Asch's (1955) study. [12]

> To see a hilarious demonstration of the tendency for conformity, look at this clip from the 1970's TV show *Candid Camera*: www.disclose.tv/action/viewvideo/8010/Candid_Camera_proves_the_Sheeple_Theory_correct_/. If this site is blocked, Google 'candid camera elevator'.

Context

As Asch said, it is clear that our beliefs and judgements are influenced by the groups we are in. Asch used the example of cannibalism to illustrate this. To most people reading this, human cannibalism will be disgusting. However, to people growing up in a society where cannibalism is common, it will seem 'fitting and proper' (Asch, 1955: p2). Based on this idea, Asch was interested in investigating the extent to which people conform to social pressure from a group to adopt particular beliefs. Asch believed that it was particularly important to understand the processes of influencing people's beliefs in the 1950s for two reasons:

1. Technology (radio and television) had begun to allow social influence on a mass scale.

2. Nazi Germany had seen a mass-scale 'engineering of consent' (1955: p2), which was a factor in enabling the Holocaust to proceed.

> ### Exam tip
>
> Make sure in a question on aims and context that you cover both. Identify what is the aim and what is the context in your answer.

Asch believed that because of these developments it was important for scientists and good citizens to understand how people's beliefs could be manipulated. Early social experiments had demonstrated that, where there was no clear answer to a question (for example, 'how many beans are there in the jar?'), people's answers would shift towards those of people around them.

Aim

The main aim of the study was to investigate whether an individual would conform to a group belief when that group belief was clearly incorrect. In this case, the task was to identify which of three lines was the same length as another line (Figure 5.2).

This was a departure from early conformity experiments where there was not a clearly correct answer. Asch also aimed to test the effect of several factors on conformity:

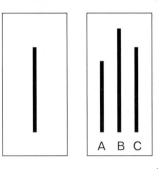

Figure 5.2 The lines in Asch's study

- group size – varied from 1–15 people
- the presence of a 'truthful partner' who did not conform to the group answer
- the presence of a partner who did not conform to the group answer *or* the correct answer
- the presence of a partner who initially gave the correct answer, then began to give the same answer as the group
- the presence of a partner who had to leave part-way through the procedure.

Summary of the study

Aim: To investigate the extent of conformity to an incorrect belief.

Procedure: 123 males volunteered for a perception experiment. They joined a group of stooges and all were asked to choose which of three lines was the same length as a target line. In some trials, the stooges all gave a wrong answer.

Findings: In a third of trials, the participant gave the same incorrect response as the stooges. This effect was reduced when a partner gave the correct answer.

Conclusion: People experience social pressure to conform to the beliefs of those around them. This is reduced when another group member offers a different opinion.

Figure 5.3 A participant and the stooges in the Asch procedure

Procedure

One hundred and twenty-three male student volunteers from four American universities took part in the study. Each participant was told that they were taking part in a psychological experiment but were given no details. They joined a group of six to eight young men sitting around a table. The group was together presented a task in which they had to match the length of a line with one of three alternatives. They were briefed that this was a study of visual perception.

Only one participant in each group was genuine (technically, they are called a naïve participant). The others were stooges working for Asch, the stooges were pretending to be genuine participants but were actually part of the experiment. The naïve participant was seated in order that he was asked last or close to last so that he would hear the answers of the rest of the group before giving his own. Each group member was asked to say in turn which of the three lines matched the length of the target line. This was intended to be a straightforward task.

In a control condition, the stooges always identified the correct lines. This was to ensure that any mistakes made by the naïve participants were due to conformity effects and not difficulty in the task. In the first two trials of the experimental condition, the stooges identified the correct line, as did the naïve participant. However, in the third trial, the stooges all identified the incorrect line. The idea

was to see whether the naïve participant would conform to the majority view or name the correct line in defiance of the group. If the naïve participant turned out at this point to be not so naïve, and realised they were being manipulated, the experiment was stopped. Each participant took part in 18 trials and in 12 of them the stooges named an incorrect line.

Variations from the basic procedure

- Group size was varied so that the naïve participant was with between one and fifteen stooges.
- A 'truthful partner' who did not conform to the group answer was placed among the stooges.
- A partner who did not conform to the group answer *or* the correct answer but gave a different incorrect answer was placed among the stooges.
- A partner was placed among the stooges who initially gave the correct answer but who then began to give the same answer as the rest of group.
- A partner who gave the correct answer was placed among the stooges but he had to leave for an appointment.

Glossary

naïve participant – a participant who has no idea they are being deceived in a study.
stooge (or confederate) – a person appearing to be a participant who is in fact part of the experimental set-up.

Findings

In the control condition in which stooges identified the correct line, each time the naïve participants succeeded in spotting it 98 per cent of the time. In the standard experimental condition where the group identified a different line, this dropped dramatically to 63.2 per cent. In other words, participants conformed to a blatantly wrong group belief over a third of the time.

The size of the majority group also made a difference. In particular, when the group was very small, rates of conformity dropped. Figure 5.4 shows the percentage of participants identifying the wrong line in different sized groups. Once the size of the group reached three, the effects of increasing its size became much more modest.

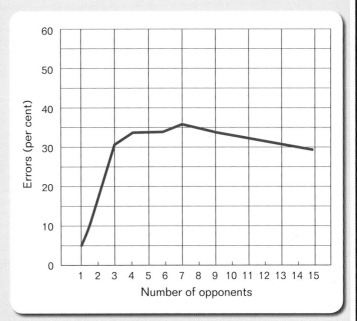

Figure 5.4 Effect of group size from Asch (1955), 'Opinions and social pressure', *Scientific American*, 193: 31–35

The presence of the truthful partner raised the correct responses to 75 per cent. Partners who disagreed with both the majority of the group *and* the correct answer had a more complex effect. When they chose a line slightly different in length to the correct one, they moderately increased the percentage of correct responses from the participant. When, however, they chose the line most obviously different from the correct one, participants chose the correct line 91 per cent of the time.

Having a partner who gradually began to give wrong answers like those of the rest of the group was no different to the basic condition in which they gave the wrong answer all along – around a third of the naïve participant's answers

Exam tip

In a question on findings and conclusions, make sure you cover both. Clearly identify in your answer which are findings and which is the conclusion.

were inaccurate. Where the supportive partner had to leave rather than changing sides, the effect was smaller.

Conclusion

Asch concluded that the tendency for conformity is a powerful influence on our behaviour. As he put it: 'That we have found the tendency to conformity in our society so strong that reasonably intelligent and well-meaning young people are willing to call white black is a matter of concern' (1955: p5). However, he also noted that the majority did not conform to blatantly wrong group beliefs and that people had a tendency to resist conformity, provided they had the support of someone else. In spite of his concern over the findings, Asch thus remained optimistic about human nature. He also noted that all the participants he had questioned believed that independence is more important than conformity.

Tired of reading about studies like this? You can get an audiofile featuring some top psychologists discussing the Asch study at: www.bbc.co.uk/radio4/science/mindchangers1.shtml.
If, on the other hand, this has just whetted your appetite and you want to read about this in more detail, you can read the full text of Asch's 1955 paper here: www.wadsworth.com/psychology_d/templates/student_resources/0155060678_rathus/ps/ps18.html, or here: http://www.columbia.edu/cu/psychology/terrace/w1001/readings/asch.pdf.

Evaluating the Asch study

Strengths of the methodology

This was a **laboratory experiment** and so has the strengths associated with the experimental method and with laboratory procedures. The experiment was carried out under controlled conditions, meaning that the effect of extraneous variables can be kept to a minimum. Each participant had a very similar experience to other participants in the same condition, so the procedure can be said to have good **internal reliability**. The use of a control condition in which stooges gave correct responses means that we can say with confidence that incorrect answers given by the participants were due to conformity, rather than difficulty in perceiving the lines.

Sample size is also a strength. Asch used a sample size of 123 people. This is large for a laboratory experiment of this type. He also took participants from four universities to improve the representativeness of the sample. This also helped to prevent word getting around any one university campus quickly enough for later participants to know what to expect when they arrived for the study.

The study was carried out in a seminar room at the university the participants attended. Thus, although the environment was carefully controlled, it was also quite a natural and familiar environment for participants. **Ecological validity**

is therefore good. Some aspects of the design are also realistic. The fact that the stooges were similar in age, sex and socio-economic status to the naïve participants added realism to the study – in real life, it is our peers with whom we conform.

Weaknesses of the methodology

Although Asch used a reasonably large sample, the **sample characteristics** mean that results may not generalise well. All the participants were young, male, American students. It is unclear from a study of this type to what extent the findings can be applied across ages, sexes, socio-economic groups and nationalities. Like much mid-twentieth century American psychology, this study falls foul of the criticism that it just describes 'the psychology of the middle-class American'. In fairness to Asch, he did acknowledge this and proposed further research to discover to what extent high levels of conformity are a cultural phenomenon.

Validity is a problem in the Asch study. Asch was really interested in social influence on social opinions. Yet what he tested was conformity to perceptions of the length of a line. One is not necessarily a valid representation of the other. Other aspects of the situation are rather different to most real-life situations in which our opinions are manipulated. For instance, each participant in the Asch study was with a group of strangers. In real life, we are probably more influenced by people we know. There are also issues of reliability. Although internal reliability was good because the study took place in a controlled environment, **external reliability** is less good. This is because other people who have replicated the procedure have tended to find lower levels of conformity than those reported by Asch.

The task also raises **ethical issues**. Participants gave consent to take part in a cognitive psychology experiment on perception. They did not consent to take part in a social psychology experiment on conformity and therefore their consent was not *informed* consent. Participants were deceived in key ways, both about the nature of the experiment and about the nature of other people in the room and their responses. Although participants were not harmed by the procedure, they did experience some distress as they struggled to understand why their perception of the lines was so different from those around them.

Exam tip

Evaluation questions may ask you either to evaluate the methodology or to assess using alternative evidence. Be clear what to write for each type of question.

What does alternative evidence tell us?

Modern studies still show that people conform

Modern studies support Asch's basic idea: that people are influenced in their beliefs by the beliefs of those around them. Have you ever watched a show featuring a panel of judges – like *The X-Factor* or *Strictly Come Dancing* – and wondered whether each judge is influenced by the judgements the others have made? A study by Boen *et al.* (2006) may shed some light on this. Twenty-seven judges were divided into panels of up to five and asked to judge the same 30 videotaped skipping performances. In one condition, the judges were aware of

Figure 5.5 Do judges conform to the majority opinion?

each other's judgements and in the other they were not. There was significantly more agreement when they heard each other's feedback, suggesting that they did tend to conform to the judgement of the rest of the panel.

Are people still as conformist as those in 1950s America?

Whenever we look at studies carried out in a particular historical period and one culture, we need to ask ourselves whether similar results would be found in a different time and place. Perrin and Spencer (1980, 1981) repeated Asch's procedure in Britain using science students and youth offenders. They found high levels of conformity in the offenders but not in the students. The results in the offender group support Asch, showing that the same kind of conformity effect could be seen in 1980s Britain as in 1950s America. However, the results in the student group do not support Asch and suggest that his results are tied to 1950s America.

Asch himself posed the question as to whether conformity is culture-specific. This was addressed in a meta-analysis by Bond and Smith (1996). Meta-analysis involves combining the results of smaller studies in order to analyse a large sample size. This particular analysis involved the results of studies comparing conformity in individualist and collectivist societies. Individualist societies are those where the emphasis is on the freedom of the individual, like USA and Britain. Collectivist societies, including China, Japan and Africa, place more emphasis in their culture on people's dependence on and obligations to one another. Bond and Smith concluded that conformity is greater in more collectivist societies. This suggests that, although Asch was correct to identify conformity as part of human nature, there are also cultural differences in the extent to which we conform.

Glossary

meta-analysis – a mathematical procedure in which the results of several studies are combined and analysed together to give an overall result.

Do people really change their mind or just go along with the majority when conforming?

Later interviews with Asch's participants showed that they had not believed the incorrect answers given by stooges in the group. They simply went along with the behaviour of the group. This is called *compliance*. But does conformity ever mean really accepting that the majority are right and we are wrong? This is called *internalisation*. This was tested in a study by Holzhausen and Glyn (2001). They set up a situation similar to the Asch experiment. Three hundred and twenty-one American students were presented with solutions to mathematical problems and told these solutions were the majority view. Participants were asked in front of others (to test compliance) or privately (to test internalisation) if they agreed with the majority answers. It was found that, as long as the problems were easy and the answers correct, the majority of participants both complied and privately agreed. When the problems were more difficult, participants agreed in front of other people but not privately. This suggests that, when the correct answer is clear (like in Asch's study), we just comply with what our group is doing.

However, when the correct answer is unclear, we actually internalise the norms of our group and really believe the incorrect information.

Study 2: Milgram (1963) Obedience to authority

Milgram, S. (1963) 'Behavioural study of obedience.' *Journal of Abnormal and Social Psychology*, 67: 371–378.

What could I be asked?

1. **Summarise** the aims **and** context of Milgram's (1963) study. [12]
2. **Outline** the procedures of Milgram's (1963) study. [12]
3. **Describe** the findings **and** conclusions of Milgram's (1963) study. [12]
4. **Evaluate** the methodology of Milgram's (1963) study. [12]
5. With reference to **alternative evidence**, critically **assess** Milgram's (1963) study. [12]

Context

In his early career, Milgram worked with Asch on his studies of conformity. Milgram maintained this interest in people's responses to social pressure, in particular destructive obedience: the tendency to follow orders to hurt another person. Milgram's family had left Europe for America to escape the Nazis, and Milgram was motivated to help explain the factors underlying the Holocaust, in which millions of Jewish people and other minority groups were systematically murdered. Milgram was particularly fascinated by the role of obedience in the Holocaust. As he put it, 'These inhumane policies might have originated in the mind of a single person, but they could only be carried out on a massive scale if a very large number of people obeyed orders' (Milgram, 1965: p371).

At the Nuremberg trials, where many Nazi war criminals were tried, a common defence was 'I was only obeying orders' (this is now called the Nuremberg defence). In fact, some of those on trial appeared to believe that it would have been more immoral to disobey their orders than to participate in mass murder. Early attempts to apply psychology to explaining the Holocaust centred on the idea that this emphasis on obedience was part of German culture, and that

Glossary

destructive obedience – obeying orders to harm another person or people.

dispositional hypothesis – the idea that behaviour can be explained by the character of the individual rather than the situation; in this case, the disposition is the German personality or culture.

Summary of the study

Aim: To investigate the extent of Americans' destructive obedience.

Procedure: 40 males volunteered for a learning experiment. They took the role of 'teacher', giving simulated electric shocks to a stooge whom they believed to be a fellow participant in the role of learner. Shocks increased by 15V for every wrong answer and went up to 450V.

Findings: All participants gave at least 300V and 65 per cent gave the 450V. Most participants displayed signs of stress.

Conclusion: People are highly obedient to orders from authority figures. However, they get highly distressed when obeying orders to hurt someone.

people in the rest of the world would not have behaved the same way. This idea that there was something different about Germans was known as the 'dispositional hypothesis'. Milgram originally intended to investigate whether this was true by comparing destructive obedience in Germans and Americans; however, this became redundant when Americans turned out to be so obedient.

Aim

Milgram aimed to set up a laboratory situation that recreated some of the characteristics of real-life situations in which people obey orders to commit atrocities. Specifically, he aimed to see how obedient people would be when ordered to give electric shocks increasing in intensity to a helpless victim, apparently causing the victim severe pain and possible harm.

Procedure

Figure 5.6 A participant helps connect the 'learner' to the shock machine

Milgram advertised for male volunteers to take part in an experiment on learning for a fee of $4.50. Forty participants, aged 20–50 took part. They were a mixture of manual workers, white-collar staff and a minority (22 per cent) of professionals. The location of the study was important. Both the reputation and physical environment of Yale University lent the procedure respectability. When they arrived at the university, each participant was told they would be either a teacher or a learner. An apparently random (but manipulated) selection procedure followed so that, in each case, the participant ended up as the teacher. He was then introduced to a mild-mannered and pleasant 47-year-old man as a fellow participant. In fact, this was Mr Wallace, a stooge working for Milgram. He had been chosen for his highly likeable manner.

The stooge-learner was then strapped into a chair and wired up to a shock generator. The generator was demonstrated by giving the participant a mild shock. The stooge and the naïve participant were positioned on either side of a screen so that they could hear but not see each other. An experimenter, played by a 31-year-old male biology teacher, administered the procedure. The participant in their teacher role read out word pairs and tested the learner on their recognition of which words went together. Each time they made a mistake, the experimenter ordered the teacher-participant to give a shock. Following each mistake, the level of the 'shock' appeared to increase by 15 volts. The shock levels on the machine were labelled from 0–450 volts and also had signs saying 'danger – severe shock' and, at 450 volts, 'XXX'.

Figure 5.7 The shock machine

In fact, no real shocks were given. However, the stooge simulated pain and distress. As the voltage increased, he gave a set series of responses. Up to 300V, he was silent, then at 300V and again at 315V, he pounded on the wall. Participants were ordered to keep giving shocks in spite of this. The experimenter, who was in the same room as the participant, gave a series of verbal prods whenever participants protested.

Prod 1: 'Please continue' or 'please go on'
Prod 2: 'The experiment requires that you continue'
Prod 3: 'It is absolutely essential that you continue'
Prod 4: 'You have no choice, you *must* go on'

In answer to any questions about the learner's well-being, participants were informed that the shocks were painful but not capable of causing permanent damage.

When the procedure was completed, the participant was debriefed. During their interview, Milgram asked participants to rate on a 0–14 scale how painful the last few shocks they gave were. This was useful in showing that the participants believed that the shocks were real. Milgram debriefed each participant in depth and introduced them to the stooge. This ensured that they were not distressed when they left.

Figure 5.8 The layout of Milgram's laboratory

Findings

Both quantitative and qualitative data were gathered. Quantitative data came in the form of numbers of participants for whom each voltage was the maximum they would administer under orders. These are shown in Table 5.1.

Table 5.1 Distribution of maximum voltages

VOLTAGE	NUMBER OF PARTICIPANTS GIVING THIS AS A MAXIMUM
15–60V	0
75–120V	0
135–180V	0
195–240V	0
255–300V	5 (at 300V)
315–360V	8
375–420V	1
450V+	26

(*Source*: adapted from Milgram (1963))

A clear majority of participants (65 per cent) administered the whole 450V. One hundred per cent gave at least 300V. Of those who refused to go the whole way, almost all stopped between 300 and 330V. This was the point at which the learner went silent.

From looking simply at the quantitative data, we might be tempted to conclude that the participants were responding in a cold and uncaring manner. However, a look at the observations and transcripts of their speech reveals a very different picture. The majority showed signs of stress: protesting, sweating and striding about the room in agitation. Some became visibly angry, while others wept. This striking contrast between people's actions and their feelings about those actions was very important in helping Milgram put together an explanation for his findings.

Conclusion

Milgram concluded that ordinary people are surprisingly obedient to destructive orders. These results suggested in fact that most people would kill a stranger under orders. Milgram also noted that people were well aware of the significance of their actions and were in no way shielded from their emotional consequences. People apparently obeyed, but not because they wanted to or because they did not care about the consequences. On the contrary, people suffered considerable distress but, crucially, felt that they had no choice but to obey orders.

> You can see footage of Milgram's experiments and various replications online. Try www.youtube.com/watch?v=0PassGyF8X8 or www.psychexchange.co.uk/videos/view/20257/. Note that periodically copyright holders ask for these to be taken down. If this happens, you can see footage of Berger's (2009) replication here: http://thesituationist.wordpress.com/2007/12/22/the-milgram-experiment-today/. Try as well http://home.swbell.net/revscat/perilsOfObedience.html. You can find transcripts here of some of the most interesting conversations Milgram had with his participants over the several studies he ran. The original Milgram paper can be found at www.psychexchange.co.uk//resource/3550/.

Evaluating the Milgram study

Strengths of the methodology

This was a **laboratory** study and so has the strengths associated with laboratory procedures. The procedure was carried out under highly controlled conditions, meaning that the effect of extraneous variables can be kept to a minimum. Each participant had a very similar experience to other participants in the same condition, so the procedure can be said to have good **internal reliability**.

The art of a good laboratory experiment is to create a situation under these controlled conditions that has **validity** as a mirror of a real–life situation. Some aspects of Milgram's procedure were quite effective in achieving this mirroring. The experimenter himself was a figure of legitimate authority, as long as he was in his lab directing an experiment. In keeping with this role, the experimenter wore a scientist's lab coat. This use of a uniform to symbolise legitimate authority mirrors the use of military uniforms to symbolise the legitimate authority of military leaders who give orders during atrocities like the Holocaust. The gradual increase in electric shocks so that participants found themselves on a 'slippery slope' mirrors the typical situation in which communities build up to genocide. This might start by socially excluding a target group, escalating to vandalism and small–scale violence and only then systematic attempts to wipe them out.

A further strength of Milgram's methodology is the gathering of **qualitative** and **quantitative** data. The quantitative data, in the form of the numbers of people giving each level of shock, tell us *how* obedient people were. However,

Glossary

external reliability – the extent to which a procedure can be replicated.

internal reliability – the extent to which each participant in a study has a similar experience.

on its own this might be misleading, suggesting that people *willingly* obeyed. The qualitative data, in the form of observations and transcribed conversations, show clearly that in fact many participants were highly distressed. Having both types of data is useful because it gives us information about both how obedient people are to destructive orders and how they feel about them.

Weaknesses of the methodology

Milgram carried out his study under laboratory conditions and gave his participants a task that they would not normally come across in everyday life. This means that the situation in which Milgram's participants found themselves was in some ways quite artificial, and can be said to lack **ecological validity**. Some features of the methodology lacked realism. For example, the experimenter reassured participants that the shocks were painful but not dangerous, thus the learner would come to no real harm. This is quite different to, say, the position of a Nazi concentration camp guard who could have no doubt that inmates would die as a result of his actions.

The **sample** and **sampling method** used by Milgram are further limitations of his methodology. The volunteer sampling method is usually a poor way of selecting participants because most people do not volunteer and so this method never gives a representative sample. Milgram's sample size of 40 was average, but the fact that all participants were male and from a single geographical area might have made findings hard to generalise. In fact, replications using different populations found similar results, so these potential limitations do not seem to have caused problems.

Psychologists have also criticised Milgram on the basis of the **ethics** of his studies. Participants gave consent to take part in a memory experiment; therefore, they did not give informed consent to take part in a social psychology experiment on obedience. They were deceived in several ways. They believed that the study concerned memory rather than obedience, that the stooge was a fellow participant, that the shocks were real and that they were hurting or even killing the learner. They were also subjected to distress and, most seriously, effectively denied the right to withdraw from the study by the final prod: 'you have no choice, you must continue'. In response to these criticisms, Milgram's membership application to the American Psychological Association was suspended. However, he was cleared after an investigation. This concluded that he had taken great care to check the welfare of each participant following the procedure, and that his work was sufficiently important to justify his methods.

What does alternative evidence tell us?

Modern replications still show high levels of destructive obedience

Since Milgram's classic study, destructive obedience has been investigated in a number of ways. It is not considered ethically acceptable to replicate Milgram's procedure in full; however, two partial replications have been published recently. Slater *et al.* (2006) recreated the Milgram scenario in virtual reality. Thirty-four volunteers from an English university were ordered to shock an avatar (see Figure 5.9). Seventy-four per cent of participants obeyed the orders and gave all the shocks; however, physiological measures showed signs of stress. Burger (2009)

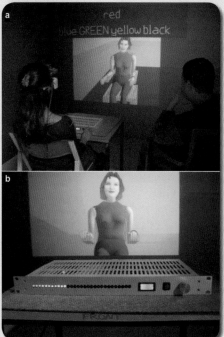

Figure 5.9 The avatar used in the Slater *et al.* (2006) study

replicated Milgram's procedure with 70 American volunteers, but in order to minimise distress for the participants, he stopped the procedure at 150V. Burger reported that 66.7 per cent of men and 72.7 per cent of women obeyed up to the 150V point. Remember that 100 per cent of Milgram's participants went to 300V. So what do these findings suggest in terms of Milgram's study? Like Milgram, both recent studies show high rates of destructive obedience, somewhat higher in the Slater study and somewhat lower in the Burger study. It seems then that the high levels of obedience Milgram found still hold true today.

People are obedient in real-life settings as well as the laboratory

A number of studies have investigated obedience in real–life settings, including destructive obedience. Hofling *et al.* (1966) carried out a field study of obedience in 22 American hospitals. Boxes of capsules labelled 'Astroten' were placed in the medicine cabinets of different wards. These contained sugar, but had a label identifying a maximum safe daily dose of 10mg. A stooge identifying himself as 'Dr Smith from the psychiatric department' telephoned the nurses on duty on each ward and ordered them to give a named patient 20mg of Astroten. The study found that 21 of the 22 nurses administered the drug. Superficially, this high level of obedience seems to support Milgram's findings; however, the situation was very different. Critically, the nurses did *not* believe they were going to harm the patient by obeying. Some did not notice the label and others made the judgement that the doctor simply knew better than they did.

There may be cultural variations in destructive obedience

Remember that Milgram began his investigation of obedience with the idea that there may have been something distinctive about German culture that contributed to the destructive obedience seen in the Holocaust. Since Milgram's time, a number of replications of his procedure have been carried out in different countries. Blass (1996) has reviewed these studies and found rates for complete obedience (giving the 450V shock) ranging from 28 per cent in Australia to 87.5 per cent in South Africa. These results suggest that there may be cultural differences in obedience. However, Blass also notes that replications by different researchers in the USA have found widely differing obedience rates, so we cannot be sure that these results really reflect cultural differences.

Summing it up

Asch (1955)

- The context to this study was the development of mass media in the early twentieth century and the systematic attempt to influence opinions on a large scale by the Nazis.

- A laboratory experiment was carried out with several conditions. The aim was to test whether students would conform to the obviously wrong judgements made by a group.

- Participants sat in a group of peers and each person in turn identified which of three lines matched a target line. The group was composed of stooges who regularly identified the obviously wrong line.

- In a control condition where the stooges gave the correct answer, the participants got 98 per cent of the lines correct. In the experimental condition when stooges gave the wrong answer, participants were only correct around two-thirds of the time.

- The conformity effect was sharply reduced when one of the stooges named a different line. However, when this 'truthful partner' went back to the group answer, participants began to conform again.

- Asch concluded that a person without support will conform to an obviously incorrect group opinion a significant minority of the time.

- Asch's study was carried out under controlled conditions, used a control condition and had a good sample size. On the other hand, his sample was unrepresentative and the task used to test conformity was not realistic.

- Later studies have broadly supported the idea that we conform to group judgements, although there appear to be cultural variations in this. The extent to which we internalise group opinions as opposed to just going along with them depends on the circumstances.

Milgram (1963)

- The context to this study was the high rate of destructive obedience displayed by Germans during the Holocaust.

- A laboratory procedure was carried out, designed to simulate the conditions in which destructive obedience takes place in real-life atrocities. The initial study had one condition, although later variations can be described as true experiments, comparing obedience under different conditions.

- The aim was to see to what extent people would obey orders to give potentially fatal electric shocks to a stranger.

- Volunteer participants were told they were teachers in a learning experiment. Their role was to administer a memory task to a stranger and give him electric shocks every time he got an answer wrong. There were no real shocks and the other participant was in fact an actor who simulated pain and distress.

- As the voltage of the shocks increased, most participants objected and showed signs of stress, but the experimenter gave them a series of verbal prods to encourage them to continue.

- One hundred per cent of participants gave the actor 300V or more. Sixty-five per cent gave the maximum voltage, although most showed signs of stress.

- Milgram's study had a number of features that made it quite life-like. It also made good use of quantitative and qualitative data. On the other hand, the procedure raised serious ethical issues, and some features were not effective in mirroring real life.

- Later replications and variations on Milgram's procedure, including those in real-life settings and conducted in several countries, generally support the idea that there are high levels of destructive obedience. There also appear to be some cultural variations.

Consolidate your understanding

The social studies

Use the following activities to run the information in this chapter through your mind. Each activity is designed to help you process the information in a different way, which should help you ensure you understand it and make it easier to remember.

Wordsearch

```
I  C  U  E  N  Y  C  R  D  T  T  O  D  M
E  T  V  I  V  T  I  E  R  T  S  O  A  I
E  H  M  M  L  I  B  E  E  I  U  C  T  L
Q  I  H  E  T  R  A  T  P  V  A  E  R  G
I  U  G  C  I  O  U  N  B  R  C  N  U  R
F  T  A  E  S  J  I  U  T  O  O  S  T  A
C  S  F  L  E  A  O  L  L  I  L  D  H  M
V  T  Y  I  M  R  O  F  N  O  C  F  F  F
E  O  N  N  H  T  G  V  T  D  H  N  U  N
C  O  M  P  L  I  A  N  C  E  N  I  L  C
E  G  I  P  C  E  Y  T  I  D  I  L  A  V
I  E  U  A  O  B  E  D  I  E  N  C  E  I
T  I  L  E  E  F  A  C  I  V  L  R  T  C
D  E  S  T  R  U  C  T  I  V  E  T  N  V
```

Asch	Milgram
compliance	naive
conformity	obedience
debrief	prod
destructive	qualitative
ecological	stooge
holocaust	truthful
line	validity
majority	volunteer

Crossword

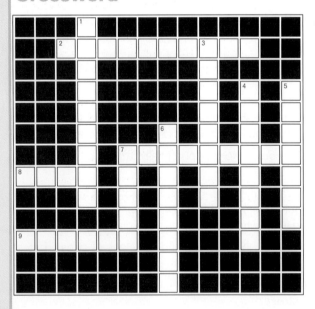

Across

2. Tested by Asch
7. The 'just obeying orders' defence
8. Posh university where Milgram study was run
9. Confederate

Down

1. Poor sampling method
3. Consent – lacking in Asch and Milgram
4. Good reliability in Asch and Milgram procedures
5. Sounds like a lightweight psychologist!
6. Non-conforming partner
7. Describes participants in both Milgram and Asch studies

Wordsearch and crossword solutions begin on page 231.

Consolidate your understanding

Cloze

Asch (1955)

The context to Asch's study was the development of mass media in the early twentieth century and the systematic attempt to influence _____ on a large scale by the Nazis. A _____ experiment was carried out with several conditions. The aim was to test whether students would conform to the obviously wrong judgements made by a group. Participants sat in a group of peers and each person in turn identified which of three lines matched a target line. The group was composed of _____ who regularly identified the obviously wrong line. In a control condition where the stooges gave the correct answer, the participants got _____ of the lines correct. In the experimental condition when stooges gave the wrong answer, participants were only correct around _____ of the time. The conformity effect was sharply _____ when one of the stooges broke ranks and named a different line. However, when this 'truthful partner' went back to the group answer, participants began to conform again. Asch concluded that a person without support will conform to an obviously incorrect group opinion a significant minority of the time. Asch's study was carried out under controlled conditions, used a control condition and had a good _____ size. On the other hand, his sample was _____ and the task used to test conformity was not realistic. Later studies have broadly supported the idea that we conform to group judgements, although there appear to be _____ variations in this. The extent to which we internalise group opinions as opposed to just going along with them depends on the circumstances.

Milgram (1963)

The context to Milgram's study was the high rate of destructive obedience displayed by Germans during the _____. A laboratory procedure was carried out, designed to simulate the conditions in which destructive _____ takes place in real-life atrocities. The initial study had one condition, although later variations can be described as _____ experiments, comparing obedience under different conditions. The aim was to see to what extent people would obey orders to give potentially fatal _____ shocks to a stranger. Volunteer participants were told they were teachers in a learning experiment. Their role was to administer a _____ task to a stranger and give him electric shocks every time he got an answer wrong. There were no real shocks and the other participant was in fact an actor who simulated pain and distress. As the voltage of the shocks increased, most participants objected and showed signs of _____, but the experimenter gave them a series of verbal _____ to encourage them to continue. One hundred per cent of participants gave the actor 300V or more. Sixty-five per cent gave the maximum voltage, although most showed signs of stress. Milgram's study had a number of features that made it quite life-like. It also made good use of quantitative and _____ data. On the other hand, the procedure raises serious _____ issues, and some features were not effective in mirroring real life. Later replications and variations on Milgram's procedure, including those in real-life settings and conducted in several countries, generally support the idea that there are high levels of destructive obedience. There also appear to be some _____ variations.

For help completing the cloze activity, see the 'Summing it up' section for this chapter.

Consolidate your understanding

Concept maps

Complete the empty boxes and you will have a visual revision plan.

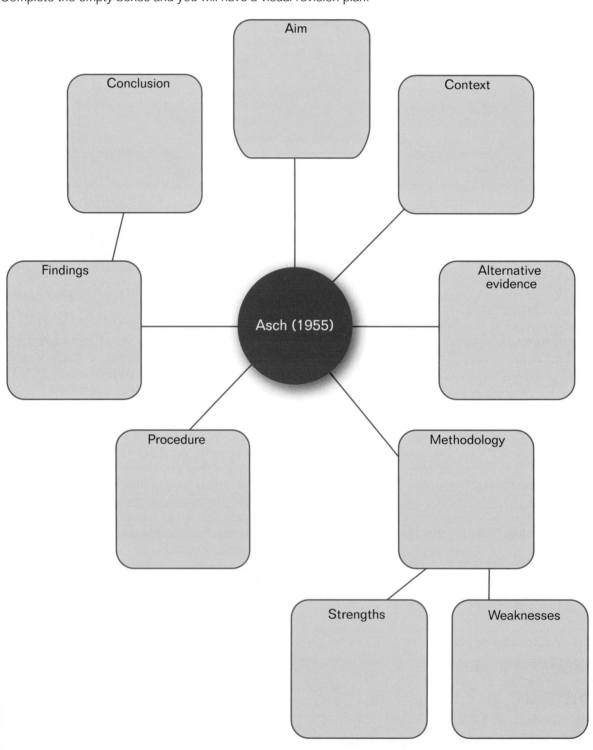

Aim

Conclusion

Context

Findings

Asch (1955)

Alternative evidence

Procedure

Methodology

Strengths

Weaknesses

Consolidate your understanding

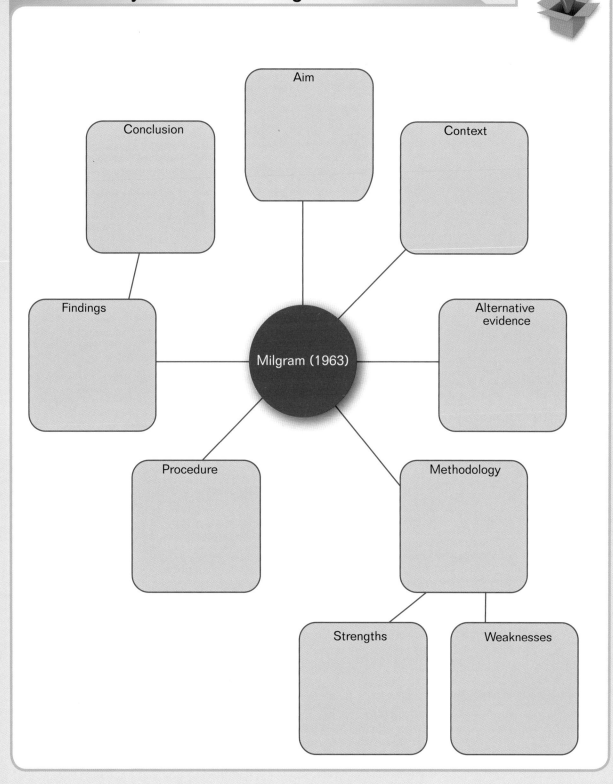

Aim

Conclusion

Context

Findings

Milgram (1963)

Alternative evidence

Procedure

Methodology

Strengths

Weaknesses

Exam focus

Trade offs – 'Rule of 4'

There is a trade-off between the amount of material you are required to know and the detail required in the answer. If there is **little material** (e.g. Gibson and Walk's procedure) then you have to be **utterly precise** in your answer. Where there is a **lot of material** (e.g. Buss's procedure) then you can **be selective** about what you learn, but you must focus your answer.

One possible technique is to use the **'Rule of 4'** for **many** questions (except Procedures) – 4 major points done in detail, each taking about 3 minutes to write. You could use capital letters to denote key ideas if it helps you structure your answer.

Asch
Context and aim

It is crucial to do at least four things in any good answer:

- Define 'conformity'
- Mention either the Jenness study or Sherif study, or both if you can
- Describe Asch's motivational background (i.e. his ancestry, Nazi Germany, conformist 1950s USA)
- State the **aim** clearly marked as such, and don't use more than a couple of sentences.

Procedure

You can mention the variations from the original procedure done at that time (**not** the later studies) but the core of the answer must be a very accurate detailed account of the procedure as detailed in the original text. This is one where every detail counts.

Findings and conclusions

Focus very clearly on the answer to the initial study – that has to be accurate and detailed. You can use a long conclusion here, using most of the text. Remember to label it clearly.

Evaluation of method

You will not be able to write something the length of the text in your **12 minute limit** answer. Pick four vital points and cover them in detail to ensure a top band mark. Use capitals to highlight how many points you have covered (e.g. 'An ETHICAL issue is…').

Critical assessment

Once again follow the **Rule of 4**. Use four studies or major points, giving you 3 minutes maximum to write about each. The text shows you how to evaluate using (rhetorical) questions such as 'Are people still as conformist as those in 1950s America?' to set up an answer. This is a great technique. What is key for the critical assessment question is what alternative evidence says about the original study. So you only need enough information about the alternative evidence to allow you to comment on how it relates to the original.

Milgram
Context and aim

Because there is little precedent for Milgram's work you need to have detail about his motivation. Look up his entry in Wikipedia or longer biographies available on the internet. The **aim** should be labelled clearly and be no more than two sentences.

Procedure

There is a huge amount of detail to summarise and you need to mention:
the sample and how it was obtained
the introduction to the stooges
the shock generator and its use
the fake procedure
the 'prods'.
Watch the **12 minute limit** here!

Findings and conclusions

You must mention both **quantitative** results (total who went to 450V, who dropped out where) and **qualitative** findings (the reactions of the participants, the groans, etc). The **conclusions** should be clearly labelled – leave time to do them!

Evaluation of method

There is a lot here and you should follow the **Rule of 4**. You must include the ethics issues but please don't just focus on these, and don't make the mistake of saying that Milgram broke all ethical rules. He didn't, and indeed he helped to develop better rules as well. He was a methodological innovator.

Critical assessment

Reference to Milgram's other studies is necessary, as is Hofling's more ecologically valid one. This is enough for a good mark, and if you have time to add some later work, you will gain a very good mark. Make sure you explain what this all means – i.e. summarise. Remember the point of this question is how alternatives reflect on the original study.

6 Core studies in physiological psychology

I should be able to:

- summarise the aims and context of Rahe, Mahan and Arthur's 1970 study of stressful life events

- outline the procedure used in Rahe *et al.*'s study

- describe Rahe *et al.*'s findings and conclusions

- evaluate the methodology of Rahe *et al.*'s study

- use alternative evidence to critically assess Rahe *et al.*'s research

- summarise the aims and context of Bennett–Levy and Marteau's 1984 study of fear of animals

- outline the procedure used in Bennett–Levy and Marteau's study

- describe Bennett–Levy and Marteau's findings and conclusions

- evaluate the methodology of Bennett–Levy and Marteau's study

- use alternative evidence to critically assess Bennett–Levy and Marteau's research.

You will recall from Chapter 1 that the physiological (or biological) approach is about the biology underlying our emotions, cognition and behaviour. It is concerned with processes and structures, including neurons, hormones and evolution, and the way that these fundamental systems affect our psychological experience – for example, when this results in stress or fear. To find out about these interactions, we must explore both the biological and the psychological aspects. As these factors cannot readily be manipulated, research in this area requires research methods that can collect information from individuals and look for patterns within that data, so in this chapter we look at two correlational studies using questionnaires.

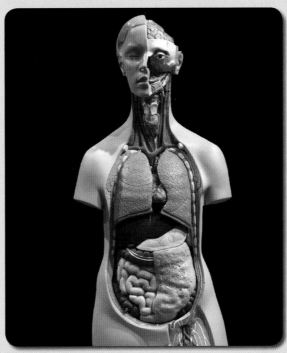

Figure 6.1 To understand psychology we must also understand physiology

Study 1: Rahe, Mahan and Arthur (1970) Stressful life events

Rahe, R.H., Mahan, J.L. and Arthur, R. (1970) 'Prediction of near-future health change from subjects' preceding life changes.' *Journal of Psychosomatic Research*, 14: 401–406.

What could I be asked?

1. **Summarise the aims and context of Rahe, Mahan and Arthur's (1970) study. [12]**

2. **Outline** the procedures of Rahe *et al.*'s (1970) study. [12]

3. **Describe** the findings **and** conclusions of Rahe *et al.*'s (1970) study. [12]

4. **Evaluate** the methodology of Rahe *et al.*'s (1970) study. [12]

5. With reference to **alternative evidence**, critically **assess** Rahe *et al.*'s (1970) study. [12]

Glossary

prospective studies – research in which participants report their recent life events and their subsequent health status is measured.
retrospective study – research which relates participants' recent life events to their current health status (e.g. present ill health).

Context

Through the 1950s, many studies explored a relationship between stress and health. One such investigation was Rosenman and Friedman (1958), who found a link between stress and coronary heart disease. Their work was based on an initial observation of patients with heart conditions in a waiting room. Unlike typical patients who relax comfortably in easy chairs, these individuals tended to leap out of their seats, apparently unable to sit still and wait. The wear on the chairs was telling – the fronts of the seats and arms had been damaged by the impatient behaviour of this particular group. Rosenman and Friedman concluded that such individuals (who they called type A personalities) experienced higher levels of stress and were more likely to suffer ill health related to heart disease. What was not clear was why they were more likely to be ill. Was it because they found life more stressful or because their personality tended to expose them to more stressful experiences? Further research has established a link between stress and ill health.

Exam tip

Make sure in a question on aims and context that you cover both. Identify what is the aim and what is the context in your answer.

Many of the early studies were conducted using participants in hospital – i.e. those whose illnesses (both physical and mental) were severe – so the findings were not necessarily relevant to the effects of more typical life stressors. Furthermore, any judgement of the stress level leading up to their illness would necessarily be retrospective and this was a problem for many studies (e.g. Greene, 1954, 1956; Rahe *et al.*, 1964). This is an issue because, if we look back on sources of stress from the perspective of being ill, we are unlikely to be fair judges.

Aim

In contrast to earlier, retrospective studies, Rahe *et al.* measured prior exposure to stress at the start of their investigation. They then followed the health of the

crew of three ships. These individuals, being isolated from other people but in one environment, were exposed to the same weather, general levels of work stress and infectious agents. They also all reported to the same medical facility, which was well used and kept detailed records. As a consequence, the situation was well controlled; any differences in health were likely to be due to differing vulnerability to illness rather than any environmental factors. As Rahe *et al.* were looking for a correlation between stressful life events and subsequent illness, this was a prospective study.

Summary of the study

Aim: To look for a correlation between stressful life events and illness.

Procedure: An estimate of life change units (LCU) from the preceding two years was obtained using the SRE questionnaire prior to six-to-eight months' deployment on board ship, during which an estimate of illness of 2,684 crew members was obtained from health records.

Findings: LCUs and illness rating were positively correlated (this relationship was stronger for older, married men and weaker for men working in more stressful situations).

Conclusion: Previous stressful life events are related to illness rates.

Procedure

The study included 2,684 naval men of varying ranks, who were asked to complete a Schedule of Recent Experiences (SRE). This questionnaire was used to assess the stressful life events each individual had experienced over four consecutive six-month periods running up to their deployment on one of three navy cruisers. Each stressful experience recorded on the SRE is assigned a life change unit (LCU), a weighting that indicates the severity of that source of stress. The allocation of weightings had been previously established using a group of American civilians and had been found to be consistent when compared to other samples. A total LCU score for each participant was calculated for each of the four six-month periods in the two years prior to disembarkation.

The sample represented between 90 and 97 per cent of each ship's crew and fell by less than 10 per cent due to transfer off the ship. The average age was 22.3 years, approximately two-thirds of the men were high-school graduates and they ranged in experience from apprentice seamen to high-ranking officers with 30 years' naval service.

Once on board, any illnesses (even minor ones) were recorded by the ship's medical facility. When the data on health were analysed, any sickness believed to be motivated by a desire to shirk work was excluded, as were any reports of pre-existing conditions. The remaining information on the number, type and severity of new health problems was used to produce an illness criterion. Neither the participants themselves, nor the ships' medical departments, were aware of the design of the study.

You can try an online version of the Holmes and Rahe Schedule of Recent Experiences at: www.mindtools.com/pages/article/newTCS_82.htm.

Table 6.1 Extract from the Schedule of Recent Experiences (SRE)

LIFE EVENTS	LIFE CHANGE UNITS
Death of spouse	100
Divorce	73
Marital separation	65
Jail term	63

(*Source*: Holmes, T.H. and Rahe, R.H. (1967) 'The social readjustment rating scale'. *Journal of Psychosomatic Research*, 11: 213–218. Copyright 1967, reprinted with permission from Elsevier.)

Findings

The relationship between stress and illness scores was investigated by testing for correlations between the individual's LCU totals for each of the four six-month periods and the illnesses reported by each man. The only significant relationship was between the LCU total for the six months immediately prior to departure and the illness score ($r = 0.118$). This indicates a positive correlation between the crew members' pre-departure life change intensity and the illnesses they reported while at sea. Only the data relating to the final six pre-departure months were used in subsequent analyses.

Overall totals were calculated by putting the participants in order of lowest to highest total LCU and dividing the list into ten bands (each a tenth of the ship's crew). The illness ratings were then compared between bands. When divided up in this way, two of the ships showed large differences, one not so great. Therefore, when the data for all three vessels were combined, the differences between the ten bands were obscured. The only big differences were at each end of the scale (see Table 6.2). To overcome this, the grouping was changed, combining some of the ten bands to make four bigger groups. These data are shown in Table 6.3. As you can see, the higher the LCU band, the higher the mean illness rating.

Table 6.2 Mean illness score for all participants (with LCU scores in each of ten different bands)

LCU BAND	MEAN ILLNESS RATE
1	1.434
2	1.377
3	1.583
4	1.543
5	1.498
6	1.685
7	1.651
8	1.693
9	2.083
10	2.049

(*Source*: adapted from Rahe *et al.* (1970))

Table **6.3** Mean illness score for all participants (with LCU scores in each of four different bands)

LCU BANDS INCLUDED IN GROUP	MEAN ILLNESS RATE
1 and 2	1.405
3, 4 and 5	1.541
6, 7 and 8	1.676
9 and 10	2.066

(*Source*: adapted from Rahe *et al.* (1970))

The results were finally analysed to look at the nature of the link between LCU and illness rates. To do this, the men's LCU scores were re-grouped into numerical ranges on LCU score (i.e. LCU 0–99, 100–199, 200–299, etc., up to 600+). These results, plotted against mean illness rates, are shown in Figure 6.2. The graph shows a linear relationship between exposure to life events and ill health.

One final piece of evidence related to the nature of each ship's mission, which differed in work level and exposure to combat stressors. For example, two ships were on military missions off the coast of Vietnam. The relationships between the LCU and mean illness rates were strongest in these two ships judged to have the easiest missions. It is possible that higher current stress levels on the other ship obscured any differences that may have been caused by preceding stressful life experiences.

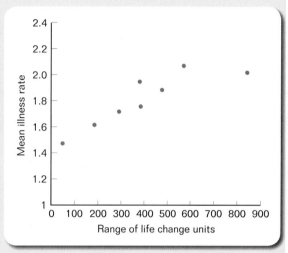

Figure **6.2** Mean illness rates are related to life changes

Conclusion

The findings suggest that higher LCUs relating to the six months prior to departure are associated with higher illness rates on board ship. There is a clear pattern. When the pre-departure life changes are low, so are on-board illness rates. However, this relationship can be masked by stressful on-board experiences because this increases the illness rate for the entire crew. Furthermore, the link was stronger for older men (over 21 years of age) and married ones than for younger, single men.

Exam tip

In a question on findings and conclusions, make sure you cover both. Clearly identify in your answer which are findings (the results) and which is the conclusion (what the findings mean or tell us in relation to the aim).

Evaluating the Rahe *et al.* study

Strengths of the methodology

This was a **prospective** study. The reporting of stress cannot, therefore, have been affected by the experience of illness, as is potentially the case in **retrospective** studies. The prospective method is thus more **valid**. Furthermore, the participants did not know that their illness rates were going to be used, so their reporting cannot have shown a **bias** based on expectations about the study.

Similarly, the medical staff were unaware of the design of the study and were accustomed to keeping full records, so would not have recorded illnesses any differently than normal.

The choice of **samples** confined on board ship was beneficial for several reasons:

- it was customary for crew members to report even minor illnesses, so the report rate would have been high
- it ensured that all incidents were recorded in the same way
- individuals would have been exposed to similar pathogens and have received similar food and general health care.

These **control** measures all improved the validity of the study as they increased the likelihood that any differences in illness were due to the individuals' previous life events rather than to any other factors. The sample itself was large and included crew members of differing ages, ranks and educational levels, representing a demographic spread. The findings were therefore likely to **generalise** beyond the sample itself.

The original version of the SRE (Hawkins *et al.*, 1957) has been revised many times to improve its validity and **reliability**. Rahe *et al.* used a military version of the SRE, based on Holmes and Rahe's (1967) updated SRE so was specific to this context. The reliability of the SRE has been tested – for example, by Mendels and Weinstein (1972), who evaluated the LCUs allocated to each event and found a high correlation between the findings of Holmes and Rahe (1967) and their own results from a sample that differed in both age and educational level. Furthermore, Mendels and Weinstein's correlation remained high when the sample was retested a year later. However, more recent studies have questioned the reliability of self-reporting of stress. Raphael *et al.* (1991) asked women to report stressful events each month over a ten-month period. When asked to recall the events again at the end of the study period, only a quarter of the originally reported categories appeared. Nevertheless, the findings in relation to Rahe *et al.* (1970) are supported by both earlier, retrospective studies (e.g. Rahe *et al.*, 1964) and subsequent prospective ones, such as Gupta and Gupta (2004), who found a significant correlation between stress and skin disorders.

You can find out more about the history of research into stress and illness:
- http://annals.highwire.org/cgi/content/full/124/7/673 – this catalogues the work of Holmes, who developed the first version of the SRE.
- Read Holmes' view on the success of the SRE: www.garfield.library. upenn.edu/classics1982/A1982PJ13900001.pdf.
- Read Rahe's explanation of the difference between SRE, SRRS (Social Readjustment Rating Scale) and LCUs: www.psychosomaticmedicine.org/ cgi/reprint/40/2/95.pdf.

Weaknesses of the methodology

The correlation coefficients found by Rahe *et al.* were quite low (e.g. $r = 0.118$). Many of these results were nevertheless significant as the sample was so large. However, a correlation only tells us that there is a relationship. Just because two factors vary together, we cannot conclude that one causes a change in the

other. Even in this prospective study, it is still possible that both the illnesses and the stressful events were caused by a third factor. Ill health is not necessarily dependent upon previous trauma. Indeed, not all studies that have looked at life events and illness have found a link (e.g. Theorell _et al._, 1975; Vidal _et al._, 2006).

The SRE is a **self-report** measure – that is, the participants fill in the question-naire themselves. In this situation, individuals may give biased responses, such as offering socially desirable answers. In a question asking about minor viola-tions of the law, participants may choose not to report events that had in fact happened. This may be especially so for this particular sample of participants; military personnel about to go into combat may feel they should answer in a particular way.

The **sample**, while large and varied in some respects, consisted only of American males and represented a somewhat narrow occupational field. Women respond to stress in rather different ways from men – for example, in the coping strategies they adopt. The findings may not, therefore, generalise from one gender to the other. Similarly, **cultural differences** in responses to stress have also been identified (e.g. Frydenberg _et al._, 2003). Occupational choice may also be an important factor in sensitivity to stress. For example, it is possible that those willing to go to war, or to spend time away from their families on board ship, are more resilient to stressors than those who choose against such a profession. This possibility is supported by the difference found by Rahe _et al._ in the strength of the link between stress and illness in older, married men compared to younger, single ones. The potential influence of such factors again limits the extent to which the findings would be **valid** if applied to the wider population. Other differences could clearly exist – for example, in the response of individuals to the death of their partner, which would depend on the nature of the preceding relationship, or to divorce, which for some may be seen positively. Furthermore, these events are assumed to be independent of each other, whereas in reality they may not be. For example, marriage and a change of jobs and residence may commonly coincide.

> ## Exam tip
>
> Evaluation questions may ask you either to evaluate the methodology or to assess using alternative evidence. Be clear what to write for each type of question.

An ethical issue was raised because, although the participants were aware that they had filled in the SRE, they were unaware that their illness records were going to be used. They had not, therefore, given **informed consent** for their health monitoring to be used in this way.

What does alternative evidence tell us?

The SRRS is still useful in understanding the link between stress and illness

The Social Readjustment Rating Scale (SRRS) continues to be a widely used tool in health research as it is important to be able to establish the role played by stress in physical disorders. Recent research has demonstrated links between specific illnesses and stress – for example, Yamada _et al._ (2003) have found that SRRS score was linked to sarcoidosis (a disease in which organs develop lumps). Higher scores were associated with a greater likelihood of sarcoidosis developing.

Similarly, Palesh *et al.* (2007) found that women who had been treated for breast cancer were more likely to relapse if they had experienced more stressful life events.

In a study conducted by Menéndez Villalva *et al.* (2002), the blood pressures and pulse rates of 236 older participants (mean age 64 years) already suffering with hypertension were measured. These patients were followed up and asked to complete an SRRS and almost half reported some life changes since the physiological test. Participants with an LCU of more than 150 showed a significant increase in blood pressure of 10.91 mmHg and heart rate (up 9.48 beats per minute), suggesting that stressful life events have a damaging effect on blood pressure in at-risk patients. Many such studies are based on samples consisting of patients who already have a health problem. In contrast, Gupta and Gupta (2004) found that life events were significantly related to skin disorders (such as scalp itching) in a sample of *healthy* people. Such information is useful so that, where a link exists, parties such as clinicians and employers, as well as the individual themselves, are better prepared to resolve the problem.

The SRRS has wider implications than just illness

Life events can also impact on other aspects of our lives. De Meuse (1985) looked at the performance of students in examinations and found that those with higher stress ratings did less well. Simantov *et al.* (2000) recorded four important life events in a group of adolescents (death of a close friend, parental divorce or separation, a parent losing their job or a parent getting in trouble with the law). Adolescents who had experienced more of these stressful life events were also more likely to smoke and to drink – behaviours that impact negatively on many aspects of life.

Figure 6.3 Bonanno *et al.* found that people in New York with fewer life events coped better with the effects of the 9/11 attacks on the World Trade Center

Stressful life events also seem to have a cumulative effect. Bonanno *et al.* (2007) investigated the effect of life events on the ability to cope with new sources of stress by studying resilience to post-traumatic stress disorder in people affected by the 9/11 attacks in New York. People who had experienced fewer recent life events coped better with the effects of the disaster: those with only one recent life event were about twice as likely to be able to resist the effects of the tragedy as those who had experienced two or three.

Not all illnesses are linked to stress

Vidal *et al.* (2006) followed up 163 patients with inflammatory bowel disease (IBD). Each participant completed a version of the SRRS in Spanish (their native language). At the time of testing, all the patients were in remission (i.e. their IBD was inactive), although all had relapsed before. For the next 11 months, the patients' health was monitored. Fifty-one patients relapsed (and eight dropped out), but there was no relationship between relapse and stressful life events, suggesting that, at least for some disorders, high levels of stressful life events are not associated with health problems. Such findings suggest that the link between stress and illness is not a simple one.

Life events are not the only factors affecting stress

Life events are the big things in life that happen to us, but little things can be a source of stress too. How often do you think 'This is driving me crazy' or 'Argh! That bugs me'? These are the habitual frustrations that Lazarus and his colleagues believed were important. The Hassles Scale (Kanner *et al.*, 1981) measures minor problems such as arguing or queuing (see Table 6.4) and people who experience more hassles suffer more symptoms of stress, such as depression and anxiety. Kanner *et al.* also devised an 'Uplifts Scale', which measures the daily positives that we experience (such as eating out or getting enough sleep). Although uplifts alone are not related to health, having uplifts can help us to cope with the hassles. DeLongis *et al.* (1988) used a revised Hassles and Uplifts scale to show that people with more stressors experienced more symptoms of stress, such as getting flu, sore throats, headaches and backache, suggesting that minor as well as major stressful experiences in life affect our health.

Table 6.4 The ten most frequent hassles and uplifts

HASSLES	UPLIFTS
1. Concerns about weight	1. Relating well with your spouse or lover
2. Health of a family member	2. Relating well with friends
3. Rising prices of common goods	3. Completing a task
4. Home maintenance	4. Feeling healthy
5. Too many things to do	5. Getting enough sleep
6. Misplacing or losing things	6. Eating out
7. Yard (garden) work or outside home maintenance	7. Meeting your responsibilities
8. Property, investment or taxes	8. Visiting, phoning or writing to someone
9. Crime	9. Spending time with family
10. Physical appearance	10. Home (inside) pleasing to you

Another factor affecting our experience of stress is our personality. The Type A personality is associated with an increased risk of stress-related illness (see page 100), whereas hardiness reduces the risk of stress-related illness (Kobasa, 1979). Hardy people have a strong sense of commitment and involvement, believe they are in control of their lives and see challenges as positive experiences. Rhodewalt and Zone (1989) found that hardy women experienced less illness and depression than non-hardy women following negative life changes, and Bartone (2000) found that soldiers with higher hardiness scores coped better with the stressors they experienced in battle zones. Such findings suggest that the life-events approach alone is insufficient to give us a full picture of the factors affecting the link between stress and illness.

Study 2: Bennett-Levy and Marteau (1984) Fear of animals

Bennett–Levy, J. and Marteau, T. (1984) 'Fear of animals: What is prepared?' *British Journal of Psychology*, **75: 37–42.**

What could I be asked?

1. **Summarise** the aims **and** context of Bennett–Levy and Marteau's (1984) study. [12]

2. **Outline** the procedures of Bennett–Levy and Marteau's (1984) study. [12]

3. **Describe** the findings **and** conclusions of Bennett–Levy and Marteau's (1984) study. [12]

4. **Evaluate** the methodology of Bennett–Levy and Marteau's (1984) study. [12]

5. With reference to **alternative evidence**, critically **assess** Bennett–Levy and Marteau's (1984) study. [12]

Context

In Chapter 2, we described the process of classical conditioning – the idea that associations can be built up between stimuli when they are repeatedly encountered together. This concept underpins one explanation of how phobias are acquired. In Chapter 1, we touched briefly on the idea that behaviours can be adaptive – that evolution has shaped our stress response to maximise our chances of survival (and evolution is considered again in Chapter 9). Many behaviours appear to have identifiable evolutionary origins and this study explores the possibility that phobic responses, like the stress response and sexual attraction, may do too.

Figure 6.4 The distribution of animal phobias is non-random: we are far more likely to fear rats than rabbits

The idea that it is beneficial – that is, adaptive – to avoid things that are potentially dangerous has very obvious selective advantages. Seligman (1971) proposed that we have evolved to become afraid of some stimuli more readily than others. This 'readiness' or predisposition to fear some stimuli but not others is called

preparedness. With regard to fear of animals, Bennett-Levy and Marteau identify four important pieces of evidence in favour of preparedness:

1   The pattern of animal phobias is non-random – not all species are equally likely to elicit phobic responses. This suggests that there is something particular about those species that are commonly the focus of a phobia, such as moving quickly or suddenly.

2   Fears are not related to actual negative experiences with a species – this suggests that characteristics of the species, such as being very different in form from humans, may be more important than its actual dangerousness.

3   Children are most likely to become afraid at about four years – this consistency would be unlikely to arise if their developing fears were related to their encounters, suggesting instead that the appearance of these fears has innate origins.

4   A phobic individual's fears persist despite their knowledge that the feared animal is harmless, such as fears of rats even when they are tame and innocuous – this suggests that there may be basic aspects of the species that elicit the response.

Since phobias are, by definition, irrational (i.e. are not based on genuine risk), any evolutionary explanation needs to be able to account for such fears. One possible explanation would be the idea of *discrepancy* (Hinde, 1974) – that is, the strangeness of an animal. This would suggest that animals with a highly unfamiliar form would be more likely to lead to phobias. The more different the animal is from a human – for example, having multiple legs or being hairy or slimy all over – the more likely it is to be a target of fear.

An alternative explanation depends on the fear-provoking properties of animals as stimuli (Schneirla, 1965). These could include having a threatening or unpleasant sound, touch or smell. Aversive stimulus properties could also relate to what an animal does, such as moving unpredictably or touching us.

Glossary

preparedness – the concept that people (and animals) have evolved a biological predisposition to become afraid of some animal species but not others.
discrepancy principle – the extent to which a species differs in form from the characteristics exhibited by humans.

Figure 6.5 Some characteristics of animals, such as moving rapidly, may make them more scary

Figure 6.6 We may be more likely to fear animals that feel or sound unpleasant

Research with primates has supported evolutionary explanations in two ways. Firstly, Hebb (1946) and Tinbergen (1951) found that monkeys are more likely

to fear model snakes than many other test objects. This provides evidence for an evolutionary origin of phobias as these primates are closely related to humans and show similar fears. Secondly, Mineka *et al.* (1980) found that laboratory-raised monkeys were more afraid of model snakes if they moved. This suggests that they had an innate fear of the kind of movement exhibited by snakes and, therefore, that particular perceptual characteristics, such as unfamiliar movement or appearance of an animal, elicit fear.

Aim

Bennett-Levy and Marteau's study aimed to explore the importance of perceptual characteristics of animal phobias. Based on the criteria for evidence for preparedness, Bennett-Levy and Marteau aimed to test several hypotheses, that:

- fear is related to an animal's perceptual characteristics
- the acceptable distance from an animal is related to its perceptual characteristics
- animals with greater discrepancy will be perceived as more ugly
- animals with greater discrepancy will be perceived as more frightening.

Summary of the study

Aim: To investigate the relationship between characteristics of animals (ugliness, sliminess, speediness, suddenness of movement) and reactions to animals (fear, nearness/ avoidance).

Procedure: Data from questionnaires and informal interviews with 54 male and 59 female health centre visitors were used to correlate opinions about animal characteristics and reactions to them.

Findings: Rats, cockroaches, jellyfish, spiders and slugs were commonly feared animals. Women feared the animals more, although the same patterns of fears were seen in both genders. Ugly and slimy animals and those moving suddenly were more feared and less likely to be approached.

Conclusion: Preparedness is specific to certain characteristics (less human, e.g. lots of legs, or threatening characteristics, e.g. unpredictability) rather than to particular animals.

Procedure

This study investigated people's responses to a range of 29 small, harmless animal species. The participants in the sample, 113 patients at a local health clinic, were randomly allocated one of two questionnaires. Sixty-four participants (34 female, 30 male; mean age 35.5 years) completed Questionnaire 1, and 49 (25 female, 24 male; mean age 35.1 years) completed Questionnaire 2. It was made clear to the participants that the animals listed were not harmful and this was written beside species for which there might be any doubt (e.g. 'grass snake' and 'jellyfish').

Questionnaire 1 asked about fear and avoidance:

- *Fear:* participants rated how afraid they were of each species on a scale of 1–3 (1 = not afraid, 2 = quite afraid, 3 = very afraid).
- *Nearness:* participants rated how they would respond to being close to each species on a scale of 1–5 (1 = enjoy picking it up, 2 = would pick it up, but unpleasant, 3 = touch it or go within 6 inches [15 cm], 4 = stand 1 to 6 feet [30 cm to 2 metres] away, 5 = move further away than 6 feet [2 metres]).

As some animals would be difficult to pick up in the wild, participants were asked to imagine that they were injured – for example, a bird with a broken wing

or a squirrel with a broken foot. Following this, there was also some informal follow-up questioning.

Questionnaire 2 asked about participants' perceptions of the characteristics of the same 29 species. They rated each one on a three-point scale (1 = not, 2 = quite, 3 = very) on four characteristics:

- UGLY
- SLIMY
- SPEEDY
- how SUDDENLY they appear to MOVE.

Findings

Table 6.5 Mean ratings of animal characteristics, fear and nearness

SPECIES	QUESTIONNAIRE 1		QUESTIONNAIRE 2			
	FEAR	NEARNESS	UGLY	SLIMY	SPEEDY	MOVES SUDDENLY
rat	2.08	3.90	2.24	1.10	2.35	2.53
cockroach	1.58	3.25	2.53	1.20	1.96	2.04
jellyfish	1.58	2.95	2.00	2.47	1.39	1.51
spider	1.81	2.88	2.43	1.06	2.25	2.52
slug	1.19	2.84	2.63	2.90	1.04	1.02
grass snake	1.55	2.78	1.80	1.78	2.12	2.42
beetle	1.33	2.50	2.10	1.18	1.55	1.57
lizard	1.25	2.45	1.88	1.54	2.53	2.78
worm	1.16	2.39	2.18	2.45	1.14	1.20
frog	1.17	2.28	1.88	2.24	1.80	2.31
moth	1.25	2.27	1.53	1.09	2.04	2.32
ant	1.14	2.22	1.86	1.04	2.04	2.14
crow	1.22	2.14	1.67	1.02	2.02	2.08
mouse	1.27	2.13	1.35	1.02	2.23	2.56
grasshopper	1.16	2.06	1.76	1.12	2.48	2.77
squirrel	1.11	2.03	1.02	1.02	2.44	2.71
caterpillar	1.05	1.84	1.65	1.24	1.14	1.12
baby seal	1.03	1.63	1.06	1.42	1.50	1.48
blackbird	1.08	1.59	1.10	1.00	2.04	2.20
hamster	1.00	1.50	1.02	1.00	1.98	2.23
baby chimpanzee	1.09	1.48	1.33	1.00	1.63	1.73
butterfly	1.00	1.33	1.06	1.02	2.08	2.36
spaniel (dog)	1.08	1.31	1.08	1.02	2.06	1.84
tortoise	1.00	1.31	1.41	1.08	1.08	1.06
robin	1.00	1.31	1.02	1.00	2.10	2.29
lamb	1.00	1.16	1.02	1.00	1.61	1.90
cat	1.03	1.14	1.02	1.00	2.17	2.31
ladybird	1.02	1.14	1.10	1.00	1.71	1.88
rabbit	1.02	1.13	1.04	1.00	2.35	2.65

(*Source:* adapted from Bennett-Levy and Marteau (1984) 'Fear of animals: What is prepared?' *British Journal of Psychology*, 75, Table 1, page 39)

Figure 6.7 Slow, predictably moving animals are less likely to be the target of phobias than quick, unpredictable ones

Participants were more fearful of rats than any other species and also rated them as speedy and likely to move suddenly. When questioned informally, participants reported perceiving rats as potentially harmful, even though the questionnaire had specified that they were not.

There were sex differences in the results for ten species (the jellyfish, cockroach, ant, moth, crow, worm, beetle, slug, mouse and spider). In each of these, females were less likely to pick up or approach the animals than males. No sex differences were found in ratings of ugliness, sliminess, speediness or suddenness of movement. So, although men were generally less fearful than women, the characteristics of animals to which they respond appear to be the same. For example, there was no significant difference between 'ugliness' ratings given by men and women. This evaluation was based on subjective characteristics, such as sliminess, hairiness, colour of the animal, perceived dirtiness, number of limbs, sticking-out antennae and the relation of the eyes to the head.

Combinations of characteristics were analysed using correlations. The key findings were that:

- *suddenness of movement* was linked to *nearness*: animals were less likely to be approached closely if they might move suddenly
- *suddenness of movement* was linked to *fear*: people were more afraid of animals if they might move suddenly
- 'ugliness' was linked to *nearness*: 'ugly' animals were less likely to be approached closely
- 'ugliness' was linked to *fear*: more 'ugly' animals elicited more fear
- 'sliminess' was linked to *nearness*: 'slimy' animals were less likely to be approached closely
- 'sliminess' was linked to *fear*: more 'slimy' animals elicited more fear.

Figure 6.8 Slimy, ugly, fast and suddenly moving animals are most likely to be feared

Table 6.6 Correlation coefficients for animal characteristics, fear and avoidance

CORRELATED VARIABLES	CORRELATION COEFFICIENT
ugly/slimy	0.75
ugly/fear	0.82
ugly/nearness	0.87
ugly/speedy	−0.20
slimy/fear	0.61
slimy/nearness	0.77
slimy/speedy	−0.29
speedy/moves suddenly	0.95
fear/nearness	0.90

(*Source:* adapted from Bennett-Levy and Marteau (1984) 'Fear of animals: What is prepared?' *British Journal of Psychology*, 75: 37–42.)

Conclusion

The findings supported the hypothesis that the perceptual characteristics of animals are related to the fear they elicit and how close a person will approach the animal. This suggests that what an animal looks like determines how a person judges it. Ugly, slimy and suddenly moving animals are more likely to be feared and more likely to be avoided than ones without these characteristics.

The concept of discrepancy is also supported. The animals at the top of Table 6.5 (after the rat) have, respectively: long antennae, tentacles, eight legs and no legs. That there are some fixed aspects to discrepancy is supported by the similarity in responses exhibited by men and women, such as the characteristics contributing to 'ugliness'. Together, the findings imply that it is not particular species that evolution has prepared us to fear, but certain perceptual aspects of animals.

The findings also support Schneirla's (1965) idea that some animals have particular fear-provoking properties. The questionnaire evidence identified the visual characteristics of speediness and suddenness of movement as important. Furthermore, the informal interviews indicated that the tactile properties ('feel') of animals and the sounds they made were also important variables in evoking fear responses. This idea of aversive stimulus properties suggests that fears are based on animals doing unpleasant things (e.g. moving unpredictably or feeling nasty if they touch us). This is supported by comments such as 'the hissing of snakes, the darting movements of their tongue…' and 'spiders can run very fast and I couldn't stand the thought of one running up my leg'.

Overall, this evidence suggests that a simple 'template' theory of specific animal fears is too simplistic. Rather than preparedness being related to a particular set of animals, the non-random pattern of animal phobias seems instead to be linked to two kinds of variables: firstly, the strangeness of an animal's physical structure in comparison to the human form, such as having antennae or many legs; and secondly, certain important threatening stimulus properties, including visual, tactile and auditory characteristics, such as moving suddenly and feeling or sounding unpleasant.

> ### Glossary
>
> **antennae** – the 'feelers' on the head of an insect.

Evaluating the Bennett-Levy and Marteau study

Strengths of the methodology

The sample used by Bennett-Levy and Marteau consisted of approximately equal numbers of males and females. This was important as previous evidence had shown that, in some respects, fears differ between the genders, so the findings are likely to be **generalisable**. The design was also a strength as different participants answered Questionnaires 1 and 2. This avoided the possibility that they were giving answers based on an understanding of the researchers' expectations as would have been likely if they had completed both, so it is unlikely that the patterns in responses were due to **demand characteristics**.

To improve **validity**, Bennett-Levy and Marteau reduced the likelihood that high fear ratings were due to the actual dangerousness of the species. The participants were explicitly told, for example, that the grass snake and jellyfish

were 'not harmful'. However, some participants said in subsequent interviews that their fear of rats was based partly on their perception of them as potentially harmful, so this precaution was not entirely successful.

By collecting both **quantitative** and **qualitative** data, Bennett-Levy and Marteau were able to obtain both a good sample size of numerical results, providing good **reliability** (demonstrated, for example, by similar responses for men and women), and in-depth explanations for the reasons behind some fears.

Weaknesses of the methodology

The questionnaire only collected data about the six key variables. In interviews, however, the participants identified other important characteristics of animals, including hairiness, perceived dirtiness, number of limbs, antennae and sensations, such as the 'feel' or sound of an animal. These might have been better indicators of fear but were not systematically recorded. This omission potentially lowers the **validity** of the study.

Another potential threat to **validity** is the use of self-report data. In both the questionnaire and interview phases of data collection, the participants were only responding to their own thoughts about the animals, not the creatures themselves. An individual may not know, or may not accurately report, how they would actually feel or behave if confronted with a live cockroach or jellyfish. Nevertheless, this method is undoubtedly more **ethical** than the more ecologically valid alternative of presenting individuals with unexpected live animals and observing their reactions directly.

The participants were an opportunity sample of attendees at a health centre – they were not specifically chosen to be **representative** of different levels or types of fear. Bennett-Levy and Marteau observed that it would be useful to know whether stronger but similar patterns of responses to animal characteristics would be found in a clinical population. In other words, would phobics, for example, perceive feared animals to be uglier and faster moving than non-phobic individuals?

What does alternative evidence tell us?

Animals have prepared fears too

The argument for the role of evolution in the development of fears is supported by evidence suggesting that animals, as well as humans, acquire specific fears. Cook and Mineka (1989) found that rhesus monkeys could learn to be afraid of fear-relevant stimuli (toy snakes and crocodiles) but not of fear-irrelevant stimuli (flowers and a toy rabbit). Since snakes and crocodiles have particular perceptual characteristics (and represent potential threats), this finding supports the idea of preparedness. Cook and Mineka (1990) also used rhesus monkeys to test whether they would learn a specific fear when exposed to the fearful reactions of other monkeys to toy snakes (which they could learn to fear) and artificial flowers (which they could not learn to fear).

We cannot learn to fear non-prepared stimuli

Support of a different kind has been provided by experimental studies of conditioning. Ŏhman and Soares (1998) found that participants could be conditioned more quickly to electric shocks paired with fear-relevant stimuli (such as pictures of snakes or spiders) than to fear-irrelevant stimuli (pictures of flowers or mushrooms). The fear-relevant stimuli chosen satisfy the requirements of both the 'discrepancy' and the 'aversive properties' criteria. This confirms that fear is more readily associated with some stimuli than with others but does not help to distinguish between the explanations.

While the findings do suggest that preparedness may relate to animal characteristics rather than individual species, this is still an incomplete explanation for the acquisition of phobias. If some animals have features that make them highly unpleasant, why do we not all fear them? Individual differences in phobias remain difficult to account for.

Regan and Howard (1995) have also demonstrated how people more readily learn fear-relevant stimuli than fear-irrelevant ones. They found that participants acquired fears to learn small animals (fear-relevant) than landscapes (fear-irrelevant). Like Ŏhman and Soares' findings, this confirms preparedness as emotional responses appear to be generated automatically to some kinds of stimuli.

Evolving a fear of disease?

If preparedness has evolved, there must be a biological imperative (i.e. some fears must have adaptive value). This could be related to risk of disease. Two studies, Matchett and Davey (1991) and Ware *et al.* (1994), investigated the link between animal fears and health risks (contamination and attack). Interestingly, when they compared predatory and 'other fear-relevant' animals, although both elicited fear only the 'other fear-relevant' animals also elicited disgust. Participants with the greatest fear response to 'disgusting' animals also had high scores on scales of fear of illness and obsessive washing.

Davey *et al.* (1998) supported the link between fear and illness with a cross-cultural study. Although cultures typically shared a fear of fierce animals, the greatest similarity was in those eliciting disgust, supporting a disease–avoidance model of animal fears. Davey *et al.* (2003) used an experiment to demonstrate the difference between fear of fierce and infection-risk animals. Although people could be classically conditioned to fear predatory animals, they learned to fear disgust-related, low-predation risk animals (i.e. ones with a disease risk) more readily than safe ones.

Survival relevance

A study by Merckelbach *et al.* (2005) provides further support for preparedness but also suggests that some research in the area may be flawed. Merckelbach *et al.* compared a range of stimuli used in tests of preparedness and asked participants to rate them for fearfulness, dangerousness and movement. They also asked expert biologists to rate them for 'survival relevance' (i.e. the real level of threat they present.) Fear correlated with survival relevance, dangerousness and unpredictability of movement in these species, supporting the concept of preparedness. However, the survival relevance ratings suggested that the current practice

of using flowers and mushrooms as 'neutral' stimuli and snakes and spiders as 'phobia–relevant' stimuli was not justified.

- www.anxietyuk.org.uk/about-anxiety/anxiety-disorders/simple-specific-phobias/ – this is one page on phobias from the website of Anxiety UK. It describes sufferers' experiences with snakes, birds, wasps, spiders, cockroaches, caterpillars and many other animals. Look to see how many have characteristics identified as important by Bennett-Levy and Marteau.
- www.biomedcentral.com/1471-244X/6/38 – this site provides free full text of an article describing an experiment comparing the brain responses of spider phobics and non-phobics.

Summing it up

Rahe, Mahan and Arthur (1970)

➡ This was a prospective correlational study, aiming to confirm the link between current stress and future illness indicated by earlier retrospective studies.

➡ More than 2,000 naval servicemen completed a Schedule of Recent Events, a questionnaire about stressful life events which had happened prior to a period at sea during which their health was closely monitored.

➡ A positive correlation was found between the number of life change units (an indicator of stressful events) experienced in the preceding six months and illness rating, showing that previous stressful life events are related to illness rates.

➡ Using a sample confined on board ensured that there were many controls; however the sample was also limited (e.g. by being exclusively male).

➡ The participants were unaware that their health monitoring would be used, which raises ethical issues, although it did ensure that their reporting of illness was unbiased by their participation in the study.

➡ The main strength of this study was that it was prospective, so the reporting of stressful life events cannot have been affected by illness, making the study more valid than retrospective investigations. The measurement of illness was also well controlled as consistent reporting of even minor illnesses was standard and all individuals were exposed to similar health risks, food and health care. As the sample was large and diverse, the findings were likely to be generalisable.

➡ The reliability of the findings can be questioned as recent studies have demonstrated that participants do not self-report accurately over time and Rahe *et al.*'s correlation coefficients were low. Also, correlations only indicate that two factors vary together, not that one causes a change in the other. The use of self-reports in general raises issues of social desirability bias, which can reduce validity, and in this study in particular, issues of informed consent as the seamen were unaware of how their illness records were being used.

➡ The SRRS is a useful tool for demonstrating links between stress and illness and recent research supports this, so it can guide practice for clinicians and employers and help stressed individuals to resolve their problems. Life events have a wider impact – for example, affecting exam performance, negative health behaviours such as smoking and drinking and our ability to resist the effects of cumulative stressors.

➡ Not all illnesses are linked to stress, suggesting that the link between stress and illness is complex. Two additional factors affecting our experience of stress are daily hassles and our personality. Minor irritations increase the risk of depression and anxiety and a type A personality increase the risk of stress-related illness, while a hardy personality reduces it.

Bennett-Levy and Marteau (1984)

➡ Preparedness is an explanation for why we become afraid of some stimuli more readily than others. This may be due to discrepancy (e.g. how different an animal is from a human), so this study tested the link between animals' characteristics and participants' reactions to them.

➡ Participants answered either a questionnaire about the characteristics of 29 animal species (how ugly, slimy, speedy or suddenly moving they were) or about fear and avoidance of the same species.

→ They found that animals such as rats, cockroaches, jellyfish, spiders and slugs were commonly feared, especially by women but also by men – the same patterns of fears were seen in both genders. Ugly and slimy animals were less likely to be approached and more likely to be feared. Animals that moved suddenly were also less likely to be approached and feared more.

→ The patterns in the results suggest that preparedness is not specific to particular animals but to ones with certain characteristics: those that are less like humans in form (e.g. have many legs or antennae) and that have potentially threatening characteristics (e.g. are unpredictable).

→ The design reduced demand characteristics because participants could not guess the aim as they only answered questions on either fear and avoidance or animal characteristics. As the sample included approximately equal numbers of males and females (whose fears differ in intensity), the findings should generalise well. Saying the species were 'not harmful' reduced the possibility that fear ratings were due to actual dangerousness, improving validity, as did the collection of both quantitative and qualitative data.

→ The limited questionnaire data omitted characteristics such as hairiness and dirtiness, which were identified as important in interviews. This threatens validity, as does the use of self-report in general as people may not accurately describe how they would actually respond. The opportunity sample is unlikely to be representative, especially not of phobics.

→ Experimental evidence with humans and animals supports the concept of learning fear-relevant stimuli more readily than non fear-relevant ones, although individual differences in fear are difficult to account for from the preparedness perspective. Alternatively, we may fear disease-causing rather than fierce animals.

Consolidate your understanding

The physiological studies

Use the following activities to run the information in this chapter through your mind. Each activity is designed to help you process the information in a different way, which should help you ensure you understand it and make it easier to remember.

Wordsearch

Y	I	D	I	E	T	T	I	E	S	S	Y	E	S	N	S	T	I
E	O	C	W	D	S	E	C	S	U	R	O	E	S	S	U	N	M
C	C	S	D	A	L	S	E	S	F	E	S	U	P	Y	I	E	D
O	E	A	U	O	L	Y	S	A	R	Y	I	H	S	C	N	S	S
L	C	I	I	N	I	P	I	V	Y	S	I	I	I	N	T	N	E
E	Y	E	U	E	L	I	I	C	L	Y	E	I	C	A	N	O	Y
V	S	I	D	G	I	R	S	U	N	E	R	O	O	P	R	C	G
J	N	N	T	R	L	S	R	A	E	I	N	N	C	E	S	D	L
E	S	S	R	E	D	I	P	S	D	L	C	H	K	R	H	E	Y
L	K	W	E	E	D	L	N	W	D	L	R	A	R	C	E	M	P
L	M	W	E	U	E	A	R	E	U	N	L	S	O	S	C	R	A
Y	T	I	L	I	B	A	R	I	S	E	D	L	A	I	C	O	S
F	O	L	L	M	E	A	C	V	G	S	C	U	C	D	S	F	A
I	G	C	S	F	S	U	I	R	N	S	E	G	H	U	O	N	G
S	N	Y	O	I	Y	S	R	E	I	H	T	R	R	U	R	I	C
H	O	E	E	A	T	R	S	T	V	A	D	C	T	I	C	L	R
A	E	P	Y	T	I	L	A	N	O	S	R	E	P	S	C	S	Y
Y	C	R	C	C	L	S	L	I	M	I	N	E	S	S	D	D	F

SRE	type A
cockroach	CHD
LCU	discrepancy
jellyfish	fear
stress	ugliness
illness	moving suddenly
social desirability	sliminess
informed consent	slug
SRRS	spiders
personality	interviews

Crossword

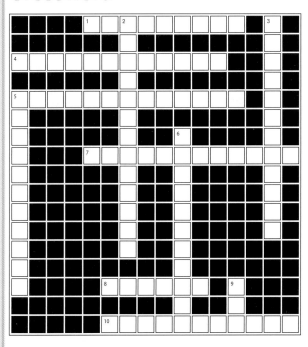

Across

1. A personality type that makes us more resistant to the effects of stress
4. Numerical data are described as this
5. A self-report method using written questions and answers
7. The idea that we have evolved the capacity to learn to fear some stimuli more easily than others
8. The least feared and most approached animal in Bennett-Levy and Marteau's study
10. A relationship between two variables that does not indicate causality

Down

2. Refers to a study which relies on participants' memory of past events
3. The short-term parallel for stressful life events – an alternative explanation of our experience of stress
5. Descriptive data are described as this
6. Refers to a study which collects data about participants' current experiences
9. The most feared and least approached animal in Bennett-Levy and Marteau's study

Wordsearch and crossword solutions begin on page 231.

Consolidate your understanding

Cloze

Rahe, Mahan and Arthur (1970)

Rahe *et al.* did a prospective _____ study looking for a link between current stress and _____ illness. They gave more than 2,000 naval servicemen the _____ before they were deployed at sea, after which _____ records were kept. A _____ correlation between the number of LCUs (indicating recent _____ events) and illness rating was found. _____ of the study is likely to be high as the reporting of life events cannot have been affected by illness, which could be the case in retrospective studies. _____ were also good as illness reporting was consistent, as was exposure to health risks. As the _____ was large and diverse, the findings were likely to be generalisable. However, the _____ of self-reports is questionable as people may not describe their life events consistently over time. Furthermore, a correlation only indicates that two factors vary together, not that one _____ the other to change. There was a risk of social desirability bias affecting participants' responses, reducing validity. The ethical issue of _____ _____ arose because the participants did not know how their health records were being used. The SRRS is a useful tool because it helps to demonstrate a link between stress and illness so can help _____ and stressed individuals. The effect of multiple life events is cumulative and extends beyond illness – for example, to poor _____ performance and _____ health behaviours such as smoking and drinking. However, not all illnesses are linked to stress and other factors such as _____ _____ and personality affect our experience of stress.

Bennett-Levy and Marteau (1984)

Preparedness explains why we become afraid of some stimuli more _____ than others, which may be due to _____ (having different features from humans, e.g. _____ of legs). The study tested the link between animals' _____ and participants' reactions to them using questionnaires about 29 animal species. These questionnaires asked participants how _____, _____, _____ or _____ moving the animals were or about _____ and _____ of the species. Animals such as rats, _____, _____, _____ and slugs were commonly feared, especially by _____ but also by _____. Ugly and slimy animals were approached _____ and feared _____. Animals that moved suddenly were also less likely to be _____ and _____ more. The results suggest that certain characteristics (e.g. being unpredictable), rather than particular _____, trigger fear as the animal is perceived to have potentially threatening characteristics. As participants were told the animals were non-harmful, _____ _____ were reduced and both _____ and _____ data were collected, so the findings had high _____. Having equal numbers of males and females would increase _____, although the _____ sample was unlikely to be representative (e.g. not including phobics). An alternative explanation is that we may preferentially learn to fear _____ -causing rather than fierce animals.

For help completing the cloze activity, see the 'Summing it up' section for this chapter.

Consolidate your understanding

Concept maps

Complete the empty boxes and you will have a visual revision plan.

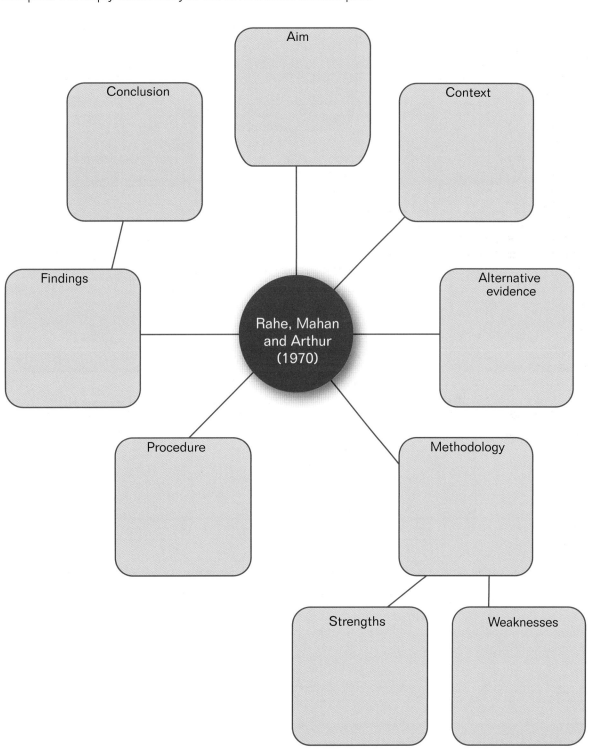

Consolidate your understanding

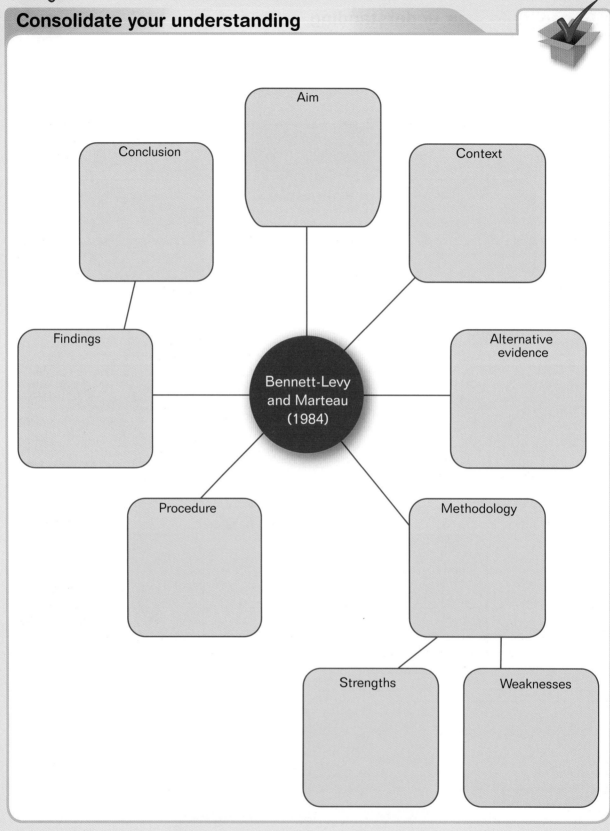

Aim

Conclusion

Context

Findings

Bennett-Levy and Marteau (1984)

Alternative evidence

Procedure

Methodology

Strengths

Weaknesses

Exam focus

Rahe, Mahan and Arthur

Context and aim

The context can be well summarised from the text but you will need to cut the **aim** down to a couple of sentences, clearly labelled. Don't forget to clearly identify this as a **prospective study**.

Procedure

Your sample details need to be **absolutely accurate**. Remember to emphasise the different stages, as well as the fact that one vessel saw action. Check this answer carefully as it is easy to over-run the **12 minute limit**.

Findings and conclusions

The first paragraph of this section in the chapter is incredibly important in your answer, as are the '**mean illness rates**' for the LCU bands. Get the figures correct.

Evaluation of method

Be very, very, careful here to prepare a **12 minute limit** answer. Stick to the **Rule of 4** very strictly here in assembling your answer.

Critical assessment

Rule of 4 alert! There is so much material you can use, but you will have to decide on **4 clear points with evidence** that you can grasp and remember. There are only punishments for writing answers that are too long! What is key for the critical assessment question is what alternative evidence says about the original study. So you only need enough information about the alternative evidence to allow you to comment on how it relates to the original.

Bennett-Levy and Marteau

Context and aim

This is a big context and you need to apply the **Rule of 4** here too – but one of the four is the **aim**. So you are looking for three detailed points – the 'preparedness' concept, the 'difference' hypothesis and some prior studies would be ideal.

Procedure

Not too long a procedure so this is a **clear trade off moment** – you must have 12 minutes of exact detail in your answer. All figures must be present and correct, plus questions.

Findings and conclusions

You have to summarise the tables of results for **half your answer (findings)** then draw **conclusions for the original hypotheses** for the rest. Mention the 'mean ratings' and then highlight key findings in the correlations (such as 'speedy/moves suddenly' = 0.95), then move onto summarising briefly (2 minutes each) 'discrepancy', 'properties' 'template' and evidence for each.

Evaluation of method

Rule of 4 time again, and pay special attention to '**validity**' as this is a key issue with this study.

Critical assessment

There are four clear points made in the text, so your work is completely done for you – except you have to cut each point down to 3 minutes writing and make it simple and memorable! Remember the point of this question is how alternatives reflect on the original study.

7 Core studies in cognitive psychology

This chapter includes:

I should be able to:

- summarise the aims and context of Loftus and Palmer's (1974) study of leading questions

- outline the procedure of Loftus and Palmer's study

- describe Loftus and Palmer's findings and conclusions

- evaluate the methodology of Loftus and Palmer's study

- use alternative evidence to critically assess Loftus and Palmer's research

- summarise the aims and context of Gardner and Gardner's (1969) study of language learning in a chimp

- outline the procedure of Gardner and Gardner's study

- describe Gardner and Gardner's findings and conclusions

- evaluate the methodology of Gardner and Gardner's study

- use alternative evidence to critically assess Gardner and Gardner's research.

The cognitive approach is concerned with how we process information, through attention, perception, thinking, reasoning, memory and language. From Chapter 4, you will recall how the cognitive approach can explain our thinking and reasoning by considering the way we process information about other people. In this section, we will consider two studies which explore the way people and animals acquire and use information in the processes of memory and language. Cognitive psychology generally lends itself to laboratory experimentation, as we will see in the first core study. However, it is not always possible to conduct lab experiments, so some cognitive research, as we will see in the second core study, uses other methods, such as case studies.

Figure 7.1 Cognitive psychology focuses on how we process information

Study 1: Loftus and Palmer (1974)
Leading questions

Loftus, E.F. and Palmer, J.C. (1974) 'Reconstruction of automobile destruction: an example of the interaction between learning and memory.' *Journal of Verbal Learning and Behavior*, 13: 585–589.

What could I be asked?

1. **Summarise** the aims **and** context of Loftus and Palmer's (1974) study. [12]
2. **Outline** the procedures of Loftus and Palmer's (1974) study. [12]
3. **Describe** the findings **and** conclusions of Loftus and Palmer's (1974) study. [12]
4. **Evaluate** the methodology of Loftus and Palmer's (1974) study. [12]
5. With reference to **alternative evidence**, critically **assess** Loftus and Palmer's (1974) study. [12]

Glossary

leading question – a question which implies a particular type of response.

Context

The accuracy of eyewitnesses is important because their testimony can be vital to the conclusions of a jury and the outcome of court cases. This particular study is about the way that the memory of an event is influenced by the form of questions that follow the formation of that memory.

Think back to the situations you have been in and people you have seen so far today. How well could you could describe any unfamiliar people or vehicles that you have seen? Or even recall seeing them at all? People are notably poor at remembering details such as faces, weapons and speed. Early research showed that verbal labels during encoding (learning) could alter memory. Carmichael *et al.* (1932) found that presenting participants with identical figures but different accompanying words influenced the way that they reproduced the images (see Figure 7.2). This suggested that information is not simply saved and regurgitated but memory is 'rebuilt' from stored elements as it is retrieved – that is, it is *reconstructed*. This reconstruction process can be affected by other sources of information, such as the verbal labels in Carmichael *et al.*'s study.

Some reproductions	Label list 1	Original stimuli	Label list 2	Some reproductions
	Curtains in a window		Diamond in a rectangle	
	Crescent moon		Letter 'C'	
	Eyeglasses		Dumbbells	
	Seven		Four	
	Ship's wheel		Sun	

Figure 7.2 Participants saw the figures in the centre and either label list 1 or label list 2. Their reproductions of the figures were affected by the words that they had seen (see figures alongside the label lists). *Source*: Carmichael *et al.* (1932) 'An experimental study of the effect of language on the reproduction of visually perceived forms.' *Journal of Experimental Psychology*, 15: 73–86. Published by APA and reproduced with permission.

Exam tip

Make sure in a question on aims and context that you cover both. Identify what is the aim and what is the context in your answer.

Accident

Leading question:
'About how fast were the
cars going when they
smashed into each other?'

Memory construction

Figure 7.3 Reconstructive memory

Aim

This study aimed to test two effects of using leading questions about a car accident. Firstly, to see whether using different verbs implying a more or less serious accident in a question influenced estimates of speed, and secondly to see whether there was a subsequent effect on the recall of damage caused in the accident.

Procedure

This study included two separate but related laboratory experiments, each with an independent measures design.

In Experiment 1, 45 students in variously sized groups watched seven film clips of traffic accidents lasting 5–30 seconds. Participants saw the film clips in different orders. Following each film clip, participants were given a questionnaire that first asked them to describe the collision and then had a series of specific questions, including one about the speed of the vehicles involved in the collision (the critical question). The critical question was '*About how fast were the cars going when they .... each other?*' Five different verbs were used (*smashed into, collided with, bumped into, hit,* and *contacted*), each being given to nine participants. These were the levels of the independent variable. The remaining questions in the questionnaire were 'filler' questions – that is, they were there simply to disguise the experimental aim. The dependent variable was the speed estimate given (in miles per hour).

In Experiment 2, 150 students in variously sized groups watched a film lasting less than one minute that contained a multiple car accident that was shown for four seconds. After seeing the film, participants were given a questionnaire that first asked them to describe the collision and then had a series of questions. For 50 participants, this included the critical question '*About how fast were the cars going when they smashed into each other?*', and for another 50, the question read '*About how fast were the cars going when they hit each other?*'. The remaining

Summary of the study

Aim: To investigate the role of leading questions about car accidents on the accuracy of recall of speed and damage caused.

Procedure: *Experiment 1*: 45 student participants saw clips of car accidents and were questioned about speed using different verbs. *Experiment 2*: a week after answering questions using 'smashed' or 'hit' as in Experiment 1, or no critical question, the 150 student participants were asked whether they had seen broken glass.

Findings: Both experiments showed that speed

estimates were higher with more severe verbs. Experiment 2 also showed that recall of non-existent broken glass was more likely when the speed question used a more severe verb.

Conclusion: Leading questions affect recall because memories include two sources of information: the original perception and post-event information. When memories are reconstructed at retrieval, these two sources become integrated and indistinguishable.

participants were not asked about the speed of the vehicles (the control group). These were the three levels of the independent variable. One week later, the participants returned and were asked another ten questions about the accident, including the critical question *'Did you see any broken glass?'* (there was no broken glass in the film). Their answer, *'yes'* or *'no'*, was the dependent variable. The position of this question was randomised.

Findings

The results of both experiments showed that questions containing verbs such as 'smashed', which suggest greater speeds and impact of the accident, produced significantly higher estimates (see Table 7.1 for the results from Experiment 1). Four of the films were staged events, in which the accidents took place at 20, 30 and 40 mph (two clips). These produced average estimates of 37.7, 36.2, 39.7 and 36.1 mph respectively, indicating that people are not very good at judging how fast a vehicle is going. The actual speed of the vehicle in the film contributed little to the overall variance in participants' estimates.

Table 7.1 Speed estimates from Experiment 1

VERB	MEAN SPEED ESTIMATE (MPH)
smashed	40.8
collided	39.3
bumped	38.1
hit	34.0
contacted	31.8

(*Source*: adapted from Loftus and Palmer (1974))

In Experiment 2, the mean estimate of speed for the group exposed to *'smashed'* (10.46 mph) was significantly higher than for those exposed to *'hit'* (8 mph). Furthermore, participants were significantly more likely to report having seen broken glass if their question about the vehicle's speed used the word *'smashed'* than if the question used *'hit'*, or if they were not questioned about speed (see Table 7.2).

Table 7.2 Answers to the question 'Did you see any broken glass?'

RESPONSE	VERB CONDITION		
	SMASHED	HIT	CONTROL
Yes	16	7	6
No	34	43	44

(*Source*: adapted from Loftus and Palmer (1974))

Participants varied considerably in their estimates of speed in both verb conditions. When classified by their speed estimates, it can be seen that participants who estimated higher speeds were more likely to report broken glass than those who estimated lower speeds (see Table 7.3). However, regardless of speed estimated, those participants exposed to *'smashed'* were consistently more likely to report seeing broken glass than those exposed to *'hit'*.

Glossary

**post-event
information** –
things arising after
the encoding of a
memory that can
affect a memory on
retrieval.
**reconstructive
memory** – the
idea that when we
retrieve information
we do not simply
have access to a
perfect copy but
instead rebuild the
scene or event,
a process which
can accidentally
incorporate extra
details.

Table 7.3 Probability of replying 'yes' to the critical question for different estimated speeds

VERB CONDITION	ESTIMATED SPEED (MPH)			
	1–5	6–10	11–15	16–20
smashed	0.09	0.27	0.41	0.62
hit	0.06	0.09	0.25	0.50

(*Source*: adapted from Loftus and Palmer (1974))

Conclusion

The findings of Experiment 1 suggest that the form of a question can system-atically affect a witness's answer. There are two possible interpretations of these results. Firstly, an individual who is uncertain about the speed (e.g. cannot decide between 20 or 30 mph) may base their decision on a response bias determined by the verb, so a more 'dangerous' sounding verb would bias them towards a higher guess. Alternatively, the form of the question may actually alter the representation of the accident in the individual's memory, thus the memory of a participant exposed to the verb '*smashed*' would be different, and more 'severe', than one whose question contained the word '*hit*'. If this change in memory were the case, participants exposed to the verb '*smashed*' would be predicted to falsely recall other details that would be expected in higher speed accidents – such as broken glass.

Experiment 2 was designed to test this and showed that it was indeed the case. This suggests that the memory of a complex event is composed of two sources of information: some from the perception of the original event (in this case from watching the films) and, subsequently, from additional external information (such as contained in the critical question in this study). Over time, these two sources of information become integrated and indistinguishable. So, in this study, the memory of the accident is reconstructed using the verb in the question. When this suggests a more severe crash, the accident is labelled as a 'smash', thus broken glass is more likely to be recalled, even though there was none.

Evaluating Loftus and Palmer's study

Strengths of the methodology

As it was a **laboratory experiment**, it was possible to exert control over the independent variable so that the verb could be systematically varied to imply greater or lesser damage (hence the five verbs). It was also possible to eliminate extraneous variables that could have affected the dependent variable, such as time allowed to encode, and delay prior to recall. Demand characteristics were also minimised by using filler questions and by the randomisation of the order of the film clips in Experiment 1 and of the position of the critical question in Experiment 2. Furthermore, in Experiment 2, it was possible to separate the effect of the verbs used from the variation in participants' speed judgement to be

Exam tip

In a question on findings and conclusions, make sure you cover both. Clearly identify in your answer which are findings and which is the conclusion.

Test your own ability as an eyewitness on this website: www.youramazingbrain.org/testyourself/eyewitness.htm. It will show you a film (which requires Real Player, Quicktime or Windows Media Player), and then ask you questions. Finally, you will be told whether you were correct.

sure that the verb was affecting memory of the accident directly, rather than only via the influence of recall of speed. Such rigorous procedures helped to improve **validity** and establish that differences in responses between groups were caused by the verbs being manipulated. The various controls, including use of standard film clips, also ensured that the findings were **reliable**. This is demonstrated by the similarity of the speed estimation results in Experiments 1 and 2.

Finally, the study attempts to simulate the experiences of an eyewitness to a car crash and, since they could be asked leading questions in court, in this sense it has mundane realism. This and the delay in asking the question about the broken glass in Experiment 2, which also reflects the real experiences of witnesses, go some way to raising the **ecological validity** of the study.

Weaknesses of the methodology

For eyewitnesses viewing a real car accident, there would be much greater motivation to observe and memorise the events than there would be for participants who know they are only watching a film for a study. Similarly, the participants would be less emotionally affected by the films than witnesses to real accidents, and emotions such as fear do have an effect on memory. The clips were also isolated events and very short, whereas real accidents occur in the context of an ongoing scene. These differences lower the **ecological validity** of Loftus and Palmer's experiments as the findings would be less likely to generalise to actual eyewitness memories.

The **sample** is also a weakness of this study as they were students, so predominantly young. This, in itself, may not be important but, as they are unlikely to have much driving experience, their ability to judge the speed of cars may not be typical of the wider population, limiting the generalisibility of the findings.

Exam tip

Evaluation questions may ask you either to evaluate the methodology or to assess using alternative evidence. Be clear what to write for each type of question.

What does alternative evidence tell us?

Many studies show that leading questions can supplement memories

The findings of Loftus and Palmer's study are supported by many other experiments into eyewitness testimony which confirm that leading questions distort memory. For example, Loftus (1975) showed that asking participants how fast a car was travelling when it passed a barn caused them to recall a non-existent barn. In a similar vein, Loftus and Zanni (1975) found that participants were more likely to answer 'yes' to questions phrased 'Did you see *the* ...' than 'Did you see *a* ...' in relation to non-existent objects.

Leading questions can cause selective forgetting

From Loftus and Palmer (1974) and many other of Loftus' studies, it has become clear that post-event information can be added to existing memories. Research has also shown that such information can be responsible for the loss of information from memory. Wright, Loftus and Hall (2001) showed participants

Elizabeth Loftus's website (www.seweb.uci. edu/faculty/loftus/) provides access to many other studies on eyewitness testimony. Look at several (the earliest ones are likely to be the easiest) and explain the findings in terms of the way memory of an event is affected by information that follows the event.

sequences of drawings of scenes in a restaurant depicting situations such as a guitar player by a table and a waitress taking an order. They then asked participants to read descriptions of the sequences from which critical scenes had sometimes been omitted, these acted as post-event information. When the descriptions omitted critical scenes, participants were *less* likely to recall these events when subsequently tested. This effect can be understood in the same context, suggesting that memories are affected by the integration of new information from leading questions. In this case, however, information is absent and the memory is reconstructed without that original content.

Sometimes leading information is ineffective

Loftus (1979) presented 100 participants with an incorrect suggestion relating to a slide they had seen of a man stealing a red purse from a woman's bag. Ninety-eight of the participants who then read an account that referred to a brown purse still recalled the colour correctly. This suggests that we are less likely to be misled about unambiguous details.

In a case study of 13 witnesses to a real theft and fatal shooting, Yullie and Cutshall (1986) also found that the participants were difficult to mislead. For example, in relation to the gunman's car, they asked some of the participants 'Did you see *the* busted headlight?' and some 'Did you see *a* busted headlight?' (there was no broken headlight). The participants were also asked about seeing '*the*' or '*a*' 'yellow quarterpanel' (there was an unmatching coloured panel but it was blue). Virtually none of the leading questions produced incorrect answers. These findings support the idea that the lack of realism in Loftus and Palmer's study may mean that their findings are lacking in ecological validity.

Study 2: Gardner and Gardner (1969) Teaching language to a chimp

Gardner, B.T. and Gardner, R.A. (1969) 'Teaching sign language to a chimpanzee.' *Science*, 165: 664–672.

What could I be asked?

1. **Summarise** the aims **and** context of Gardner and Gardner's (1969) study. [12]
2. **Outline** the procedures of Gardner and Gardner's (1969) study. [12]
3. **Describe** the findings **and** conclusions of Gardner and Gardner's (1969) study. [12]
4. **Evaluate** the methodology of Gardner and Gardner's (1969) study. [12]
5. With reference to **alternative evidence**, critically **assess** Gardner and Gardner's (1969) study. [12]

Context

The second study we will be exploring from the cognitive approach is Gardner and Gardner (1969), which records their attempt to teach language to a chimpanzee. It is a study about language acquisition that is trying to find out whether there is something special about the minds of humans that means that we can learn to use language, whereas animals cannot.

Psychologists are interested in language because it is a complex cognitive function and seems to be exclusive to humans. To find out whether this is true, and to offer insights into how language is processed, many attempts have been made to teach language to different species of non-human animals. These include chimpanzees, bonobos (pygmy chimpanzees), gorillas, dolphins and parrots. If such species cannot acquire language, this would tell us there is something special about the human mind that means we possess particular kinds of cognitive abilities that animals do not.

Early researchers such as Hayes and Hayes (1951) attempted to teach chimpanzees to use spoken English. Their chimpanzee, Vicki, was raised in the human household and was rewarded for noises that sounded like speech. However, after considerable training, she only mastered four words: 'mama', 'papa', 'cup' and 'up'. The inability of chimps such as Vicki (and others: for example, Gua, raised by Kellogg and Kellogg, 1933) to acquire spoken language can be accounted for by the difference between ape and human vocal tracts. Structural differences between the lips and larynx make it impossible for chimpanzees to make the range of speech sounds available to humans. This is compounded by the context of their spontaneous vocalisations. Chimpanzees tend only to use sound to communicate in situations of danger or excitement. Furthermore, they may be hindered by a reluctance to imitate speech sounds. Although these studies were unsuccessful in their attempts to teach chimpanzees to speak, there was some indication of a capacity for language. Gua, for example, learned to recognise approximately 100 spoken words, suggesting that her limitation was at least in part one of language production.

Figure 7.4 Gardner and Gardner (1969) attempted to teach language to a chimpanzee

Following the lack of success in earlier studies, Gardner and Gardner used American Sign Language (ASL) rather than speech. This is more suitable as chimps have a considerable capacity for manual dexterity and for physical imitation. This is a complete language, using a large vocabulary of gestural signs, which can be combined to express complex ideas. Thus any limitation in the development of language could be isolated to the chimpanzee's cognitive ability (i.e. its capacity to understand), rather any physical restraints upon reproduction of the elements (i.e. speech sounds or signs).

Aim

The aim of this study was to raise a very young chimp in a manner similar to that of a human child, giving it the opportunity to learn language and to chart the chimp's progress. This would allow the exploration of the processes of language acquisition and indicate the extent to which language could be learned by a young chimp, so exposing any innate limitations to that learning process. Specifically, to look for evidence of the acquisition of a *vocabulary* (using signs consistently and without prompting), *differentiation* (the use of different signs in different contexts, thus indicating an understanding of specific meanings), *transfer* (the generalisation of usage of a sign from the original context to new ones) and *combinations* (the consistent and meaningful use of two or more words with new or specific meanings).

Summary of the study

Aim: To find out whether language is unique to humans by attempting to teach language to a chimp.

Procedure: A case study of a chimp learning ASL through social learning and operant conditioning. Production of new signs was recorded to track language acquisition.

Findings: Washoe acquired a large vocabulary of signs and used them consistently. She differentiated between signs with similar meanings, transferred signs to new contexts and combined signs to make new meanings.

Conclusion: Washoe learned to communicate effectively using ASL and showed some, though not all, of the criteria required for language.

Procedure

Washoe, a female chimpanzee aged 8–14 months at the start of the study, was the study's only participant. Her exact age was unknown as she was wild-caught. This was essential as laboratory-reared chimps could not be obtained so young. For the study to expose any genetic limitations on language learning, intervention needed to begin as soon as possible after birth. Washoe was taught American Sign Language (ASL), a gestural language for the deaf. This is not simply finger-spelling of letters in English words but a language in which words and concepts correspond to precise manual patterns.

A social environment was created for Washoe in which all humans communicated exclusively in ASL, whether interacting with her or each other. This ensured that signing could not be perceived to have a lower social status than talking. Three techniques were used to train Washoe to use gestures:

1 *Imitation* – a researcher would show Washoe a gesture and if she imitated it she was rewarded (e.g. with being tickled). Once Washoe had learned some signs, imitation could be initiated by making the sign for 'sign' or asking 'What is this?' in ASL.

2 *Babbling* – human babies engage in vocal babbling (the production of random speech sounds) and it was anticipated that Washoe would produce similar manual 'babbling' which could be reinforced with positive feedback, such as clapping and imitating, much as adults smile at babbling infants and go 'goo goo' back to them.

3 *Operant conditioning* – it was possible to shape arbitrary movements in Washoe's behaviour, by reinforcing closer and closer approximations to an actual sign, until Washoe reliably produced a correct sign when appropriate.

Situations such as games and outings were devised to maximise opportunities for signing and introducing new signs. Initially, a complete record of Washoe's signing was kept, but as her vocabulary expanded, only new signs were recorded (from the sixteenth month). These were systematically recorded when new signs were acquired only if the sign:

- was spontaneous (i.e. arose without prompting)
- occurred in an appropriate context
- was recorded by three researchers independently
- was used at least once a day on 15 consecutive days.

As contexts appropriate for demonstrating signs do not always arise, some additional, consistent signs were recorded even though they did not fulfil the frequency criterion at 22 months.

Findings

Washoe had learned 34 signs within the first 22 months. These are listed in Table 7.4. They were the product of three language experiences: Washoe's spontaneous manual babbling, operant conditioning and imitation.

Washoe did babble manually, although later than had been expected. As with human infants, she would sometimes make a gesture that resembled a sign, which was responded to as if it were correct and reproduced in an accurate form in an appropriate context. For example, in an imitation game, Washoe made a gesture like the sign for 'funny'. The sign for 'funny' was repeated by the researchers, accompanied by laughing and smiling. This sign was then used whenever something funny happened and Washoe eventually came to use it in appropriate circumstances. Other signs used by Washoe, such as 'hurry', may have arisen out of her own babbling rather than being imitative.

Imitation was used successfully with Washoe. For example, her teeth were brushed after every meal and, although she initially resisted this, she did submit. The sign for toothbrush was regularly used but Washoe had not imitated it. On seeing a mug of toothbrushes in a bathroom (at ten months), she signed 'toothbrush' spontaneously, suggesting that she had learned the sign and was using it purely to communicate (as it was unlikely that she was requesting to have her teeth cleaned). This is an example of 'delayed imitation'.

Operant conditioning (as described in Chapter 2) involves reinforcing desired behaviours. This was used to train Washoe to perform signs and to use them in the correct context. The sign for 'open' starts with the hands side-by-side, palms down, then they are 'opened' like a book, to palms up. Washoe's response to a closed door she wanted to get through – pounding with both palms on the door – provided a starting point for shaping this sign. When she placed her hands on the door spontaneously, they were lifted to complete the sign, and it was demonstrated for her to imitate. By prompting in this way, Washoe produced a version of the sign for open and was reinforced by having the door opened. After training with three doors, this sign generalised to all doors and then to other objects that could be opened, such as cupboards, drawers, boxes and jars. Washoe also employed this sign to ask for taps to be turned on. This process, although using a combination of imitation and operant conditioning, also used guidance – training by placing the hands into the desired positions.

Figure 7.5 Washoe

In respect of the four language criteria, Gardner and Gardner found the following:

- *Vocabulary:* 34 signs met the criteria for acquisition by 22 months (see Table 7.4).

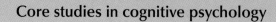

Table 7.4 Within 22 months, Washoe's vocabulary included 34 signs, which she used reliably. They are listed here in order of appearance. They include nouns (e.g. flower), verbs (e.g. open) and emphasisers (e.g. more)

SIGNS	DESCRIPTION	CONTEXT
Come-gimme	Beckoning motion, with wrists or knuckles as pivot.	Sign made to persons or animals, also for objects out of reach. Often combined: "come tickle", "gimme sweet", etc.
More	Fingertips are brought together, usually overhead. (Correct ASL form: tips of the tapered hand touch repeatedly.)	When asking for continuation or repetition of activities such as swinging or tickling, for second helpings of food, etc. Also used to ask for repetition of some performance, such as a somersault.
Up	Arm extends upward, and index finger may also point up.	Wants a lift to reach objects such as grapes on vine, or leaves; or wants to be placed on someone's shoulders; or wants to leave potty-chair.
Sweet	Index or index and second fingers touch tip of wagging tongue. (Correct ASL form: index and second fingers extended side by side.)	For dessert; used spontaneously at end of meal. Also, when asking for candy.
Open	Flat hands are placed side by side, palms down, then drawn apart while rotated to palms up.	At door of house, room, car, refrigerator, or cupboard; on containers such as jars; on faucets (taps).
Tickle	The index finger of one hand is drawn across the back of the other hand. (Related to ASL "touch".)	For tickling or for chasing games.
Go	Opposite of "come-gimme".	While walking hand-in-hand or riding on someone's shoulders. Washoe usually indicates the direction desired.
Out	Curved hand grasps tapered hand; then tapered hand is withdrawn upward.	When passing through doorways; until recently, used for both "in" and "out". Also, when asking to be taken outdoors.
Hurry	Open hand is shaken at the wrist. (Correct ASL form: index and second fingers extended side by side.)	Often follows signs such as "come-gimme", "out", "open" and "go", particularly if there is a delay before Washoe is obeyed. Also, used while watching her meal being prepared.
Hear-listen	Index finger touches ear.	For loud or strange sounds: bells, car horns, sonic booms, etc. Also, for asking someone to hold a watch to her ear.
Toothbrush	Index finger is used as a brush, to rub front teeth.	When Washoe has finished her meal, or at other times when shown a toothbrush.
Drink	Thumb is extended from fisted hand and touches mouth.	For water, formula, soda, pop, etc. For soda pop, often combined with "sweet".
Hurt	Extended index fingers are jabbed toward each other. Can be used to indicate location of pain.	To indicate cuts and bruises on herself or others. Can be elicited by red stains on a person's skin or by tears in clothing.

SIGNS	DESCRIPTION	CONTEXT
Sorry	Fisted hand clasps and unclasps at shoulder. (Correct ASL form: fisted hand is rubbed over heart with circular motion.)	After biting someone, or when someone has been hurt in another way (not necessarily by Washoe). When told to apologise for mischief.
Funny	Tip of index finger presses nose, and Washoe snorts. (Correct ASL form: index and second fingers used; no snort.)	When soliciting interaction play, and during games. Occasionally, when being pursued after mischief.
Please	Open hand is drawn across chest. (Correct ASL form: fingertips used and circular motion.)	When asking for objects and activities. Frequently combined: 'Please go', 'Out, please', 'Please drink'.
Food-eat	Several fingers of one hand are placed in mouth. (Correct ASL form: fingertips of tapered hand touch mouth repeatedly.)	During meals and preparation of meals.
Flower	Tip of index finger touches one or both nostrils. (Correct ASL form: tips of tapered hand touch first one nostril, then the other.)	For flowers.
Cover-blanket	Draws one hand toward self over the back of the other.	At bedtime or naptime, and, on cold days, when Washoe wants to be taken out.
Dog	Repeated slapping on thigh.	For dogs and for barking.
You	Index finger points at a person's chest.	Indicates successive turns in games. Also used in response to questions such as "Who tickle?", "Who brush?".
Napkin-bib	Fingertips wipe the mouth region.	For bib, for washcloth, and for Kleenex.
In	Opposite of "out".	Wants to go indoors, or wants someone to join her indoors.
Brush	The fisted hand brushes the back of the open hand several times. (Adapted from ASL "polish".)	For hairbrush, and when asking for brushing.
Hat	Palm pats top of head.	For hats and caps.
I-me	Index finger points at, or touches, chest.	Indicates Washoe's turn, when she and a companion share food, drink, etc. Also used in phrases, such as "I drink", and in reply to question such as "Who tickle?" (Washoe: "you"); "Who I tickle?" (Washoe: "me").
Shoes	The fisted hands are held side by side and strike down on shoes or floor. (Correct ASL form: the sides of the fisted hands strike against each other.)	For shoes and boots.
Smell	Palm is held before nose and moved slightly upward several times.	For scented objects: tobacco, perfume, sage, etc.

SIGNS	DESCRIPTION	CONTEXT
Pants	Palms of the flat hands are drawn up against the body toward waist.	For diapers, rubber pants, trousers.
Clothes	Fingertips brush down the chest.	For Washoe's jacket, nightgown, and shirts; also for our clothing.
Cat	Thumb and index finger grasp cheek hair near side of mouth and are drawn outward (representing cat's whiskers).	For cats.
Key	Palm of one hand is repeatedly touched with the index finger of the other. (Correct ASL form: crooked index finger is rotated against palm.)	Used for keys and locks and to ask us to unlock a door.
Baby	One forearm is placed in the crook of the other, as if cradling a baby.	For dolls, including animal dolls such as a toy horse and duck.
Clean	The open palm of one hand is passed over the open palm of the other.	Used when Washoe is washing, or being washed, or when a companion is washing hands or some other object. Also used for "soap".

(*Source:* adapted from Gardner and Gardner (1969), Table 1)

<table>
<tr><td>

Explore the website of the Chimpanzee and Human Communication Institute: www.cwu.edu/~cwuchci/index.html.
This includes three 'chimpcams' and a link to the 'Friends of Washoe' site, which provides a history of her life and that of other chimps in language projects, with video clips of each chimp. Look at the biography of Loulis. In what key way has Loulis acquired language differently from Washoe?

</td></tr>
</table>

- *Differentiation:* Some signs became differentiated. For example, Washoe used 'more' largely to mean 'do it again' (e.g. for an action she could not name), and 'flower' to mean 'smell' (e.g. in response to the smell of tobacco). For this latter context, Washoe acquired a new sign for smell, although 'flower' was sometimes still used with this meaning.
- *Transfer:* Signs such as 'more' and 'open' generalised readily from their original contexts to new ones. 'Flower' was applied not only to different flowers and contexts (e.g. indoors and outdoors) but also to pictures of flowers, the same sign being used in each instance.
- *Combinations:* Although the researchers signed in strings, no effort was initially made to train Washoe to do so; when she did, it was spontaneous (although this may have been inadvertently reinforced by the researchers responding more readily). However, as Washoe's vocabulary expanded, she combined signs more often. Some of these could not have been imitative (e.g. 'gimme tickle' before Washoe had ever been asked to tickle anyone else). Several signs were commonly used in combinations (*please, come-gimme, hurry, more, go, out, open and hear-listen*), often as emphasisers (e.g. in *please open hurry*) but this was not always the case (e.g. *open key* to a locked door or *eat listen* to the sound of a meal bell).

Conclusion

The findings suggest that sign language was a good choice for achieving two-way communication between humans and a chimpanzee. Washoe's expanding vocabulary, including nouns and verbs, her spontaneous transfer of meanings and rudimentary combinations of signs all suggest that she was intellectually capable of acquiring signs and using them to communicate.

Evaluating Gardner and Gardner's study

Strengths of the methodology

A chimpanzee was an appropriate choice of study animal as the species is both sociable and intelligent; sociability was essential as it is a key factor in human language learning. A language based on movements rather than sounds was chosen for several reasons:

- chimpanzee vocal communication is used for different purposes than that of humans
- previous studies had demonstrated that chimps could not acquire spoken language (e.g. Hayes and Hayes, 1951)
- chimps are very dexterous, using their hands to manipulate objects in the wild. Even caged, laboratory animals spontaneously develop gestures such as 'begging' and those with extensive human contact develop a variety of such communicative movements.

As human and chimp hands are so similar, it would be possible for Washoe to replicate the signs easily. Washoe was also provided with an appropriate language learning environment, a context in which she was immersed in a shared language as a child would be, and that language environment (of signing) was a genuine human one (for deaf children). This ensured that any important social cues and sources of motivation were present. This meant that Washoe was likely to exhibit any language she had learned as it was both familiar and would result in valued social rewards (such as tickling), as well as primary reinforcers such as food. Together these factors make the study practical and therefore more **valid** than earlier studies, since it provides a more effective measure of language acquisition.

ASL signs are arbitrary, although some are more obvious than others. The sign for 'flower', for example, is made by extending the fingers of the signing hand, touching the fingertips together and holding them under each nostril as if sniffing a flower. This meant that it was unlikely that Washoe could randomly generate the correct sign in a given context. Observers working 'blind' (i.e. unaware of the object Washoe was looking at when she signed) were used to record her vocabulary. These precautions helped to avoid the risk of **observer bias**, which would have reduced the validity of the findings.

For a sign to be recorded as learned, strict criteria were adhered to (see page 132). These helped to improve the **reliability** of the data about Washoe's vocabulary. For example, a sign had to be seen independently by three researchers and used at least once a day on 15 consecutive days.

Weaknesses of the methodology

Washoe developed a large vocabulary but this does not necessarily indicate that she acquired language, which is more than just the understanding of symbols; it also relies on syntax – that is, a system of rules that determine the meaning of strings of symbols (e.g. by use of word order or word endings). This ability to combine words meaningfully is called structure-dependence. Although Washoe did use word combinations, these did not appear to contain 'more' meaning than that of the individual words themselves. For example, would Washoe have

Glossary

structure-dependence – a characteristic of language. It requires the understanding that meaning can be dependent on the construction of an utterance – for example, that saying 'Washoe tickle me' is different from 'me tickle Washoe'.

understood the difference between 'Washoe tickle' and 'tickle Washoe'? For this to be a **valid** test of language acquisition, there needed to be systematic testing of Washoe's understanding of structure-dependence (i.e. by testing word combinations and word order).

The study raises **ethical issues** as Washoe was caught from the wild and, at least during Gardner and Gardner's study, was deprived of social contact with other chimps. As chimps form strong social bonds, these conditions were likely to have caused her some distress.

As this was a **case study** of a single chimp, the findings may not be typical of all chimps. Indeed, other studies have drawn different conclusions (see below).

What does alternative evidence tell us?

Other studies have replicated the ability of apes to learn sign language

Terrace (1979) taught ASL to a chimp called Nim Chimpsky, named after the famous linguist Noam Chomsky, who proposed that humans have a 'language acquisition device', which determines our linguistic ability – for example, our capacity to understand structure-dependence. Like Washoe, Nim learned to use sign language proficiently but Terrace doubted that Nim's (or Washoe's) two-word combinations represented an understanding of syntax.

More recent studies suggest that chimps can demonstrate structure-dependence

Further work on language has been conducted on many animals, including Kanzi, a bonobo. Kanzi uses a lexigram, a board with visual symbols representing words and concepts. He uses this extensively to communicate with humans and can ask and answer questions using it. For example, he can correctly respond to instructions, such as:

- put the pine needles on the ball
- put the ball on the pine needles
- get the ball that is in the group room (when there was a ball next to him)
- take the television outside.

These findings begin to overcome the criticism of the Washoe project that chimps' use of word combinations is too simplistic to be called language. Tasks such as those given to Kanzi demand an understanding of the importance of structure-dependence. This is an important criterion in differentiating between mere replication of utterances combined with trial and error learning and a level of genuine linguistic competence.

Other species may have language capacities too

In the wild, whales and dolphins communicate using complex sounds. Herman *et al.* (1984) explored the language ability of two captive bottlenosed dolphins. Akeakamai was taught a language based on visual signs and Phoenix was taught an acoustic language. Phoenix could respond to five-word sentences, with instructions involving a verb relating two objects, each of which had a modifier, such as 'surface hoop fetch bottom basket' (go to the hoop at the surface and take it to the basket at the bottom). This indicates a more sophisticated comprehension than Washoe's – although Phoenix could only respond with actions to indicate understanding, not with *production* of language. Akeakamai could respond to novel, four–word sentences, the meaning of which was dependent on word order. This indicated a comprehension of structure–dependence.

Figure 7.6 Herman *et al.* (1984) found a comprehension of structure-dependence in dolphins

You can find out more about Kanzi at:

- www.greatapetrust.org/about-the-trust/meet-our-apes/kanzi – part of the website of the Great Ape Trust, Iowa (with several video clips of Kanzi)
- www.npr.org/templates/story/story.php?storyId=5503685 – a radio station with an accompanying funny video of Kanzi at a cook-out (under 'interactive' *social connection*)
- http://pubpages.unh.edu/~jel/SGMonKanzi.html – a Kanzi article.

Summing it up

Loftus and Palmer (1974)

➡ This study is set in the context of the need for accurate eyewitness testimonies and the demonstration that additional information, such as is present in leading questions, could alter memories, so the study aimed to test how leading questions affect recall of speed and damage in a car accident.

➡ There were two laboratory experiments. The first used five different verbs in a question about the speed of cars in filmed accidents. The second was similar, using questions with two of the same verbs and a control condition. The participants were asked about (non-existent) broken glass a week later.

➡ Both experiments found higher speed estimates with more severe verbs. Non-existent broken glass was more likely to be recalled when a more severe verb was used.

➡ Loftus and Palmer concluded that recall is affected by leading questions because they provide 'post-event information' which is integrated with information from the original perception.

➡ The controls, hiding of the critical questions and use of the second experiment raise both the validity and reliability of the study. However, eyewitnesses to real accidents would have greater motivation and emotional involvement, which would affect memory, lowering ecological validity.

➡ Although many other lab studies show that leading questions reduce the accuracy of recall (by causing additions to memory or omissions), this is not always the case. We are less likely to be misled about unambiguous details or in real, high-emotion situations, such as shootings.

Gardner and Gardner (1969)

➡ Early studies tried to teach chimps verbal language and failed as they do not have the vocal ability, so this study aimed to teach Washoe sign language to find out whether language was a unique human ability.

➡ Gardner and Gardner used a case study to teach Washoe ASL through imitation and operant conditioning. Production of new signs was recorded to track language acquisition.

➡ Washoe acquired a large vocabulary of signs (34 words in 22 months, including nouns, verbs and emphasisers) and used them consistently. She differentiated between signs with similar meanings, transferred signs to new contexts and combined signs to make new meanings.

➡ Gardner and Gardner concluded that Washoe had learned to communicate effectively using ASL and that she showed some of the criteria required for language, although further research would be needed to confirm some aspects, such as the combination of symbols.

➡ One strength of Gardner and Gardner's research was their effort to make language accessible to Washoe – by choosing ASL rather than spoken language and providing a motivating social context. They achieved this while maintaining objectivity; as ASL signs are arbitrary, strict definitions were used to decide on acquisition of new signs and blind judges were used.

➡ A weakness was that Washoe was not rigorously tested for her understanding of structure-dependence. In addition, ethical issues are raised as Washoe was wild-caught and lacked social contact with other chimps.

➡ Another chimp, Nim Chimpsky, also learned to use sign language proficiently, but Kanzi, a bonobo, uses a lexigram board in a more linguistically sophisticated way than either chimp and shows structure-dependence, as do some trained dolphins, although they can only comprehend, not produce, language.

Consolidate your understanding

The cognitive studies

Use the following activities to run the information in this chapter through your mind. Each activity is designed to help you process the information in a different way, which should help you ensure you understand it and make it easier to remember.

Wordsearch

U	B	I	I	A	D	I	H	S	D	B
D	E	D	M	A	C	B	I	I	E	U
C	O	L	L	I	D	E	D	G	T	M
D	H	L	M	M	T	G	L	N	C	P
I	S	D	E	H	S	A	M	S	A	E
G	A	H	L	H	B	U	T	C	T	D
A	W	O	B	A	B	B	L	I	N	G
S	Y	R	A	L	U	B	A	C	O	V
S	S	L	C	I	C	E	S	E	C	N
S	O	U	C	H	A	P	S	V	B	B
D	T	L	V	T	N	S	O	C	C	D

Washoe
imitation
vocabulary
signs
babbling

smashed
collided
bumped
hit
contacted

Crossword

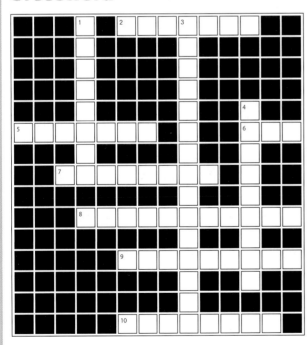

Across

2. A type of question which tends to produce inaccurate answers
5. A kind of conditioning based on rewards used to teach Washoe
6. A sign language used by deaf people and learned by some chimps
7. Differences between these in lab experiments and real-world settings make lab studies of eyewitness testimony less ecologically valid
8. Animal Noam Chomsky

9. Information that eyewitnesses receive after perceiving a crime scene, which may combine with their existing memory and alter it
10. The ability to use a word correctly in different contexts

Down

1. A board of symbols used to teach chimps language
3. The ability to distinguish between the meanings of similar words
4. One of Washoe's sign combinations used to refer to the meal bell

Wordsearch and crossword solutions begin on page 231.

Consolidate your understanding

Cloze

Loftus and Palmer (1974)

This study responded to the issue of the inaccuracy of eyewitness testimonies when _____ questions are used as these could alter memories. Loftus and Palmer's _____ experiments aimed to test how such questions affected the recall of the _____ of vehicles and the damage caused using car _____ scenes. Experiment 1 used _____ different verbs in a question about the speed of cars in filmed accidents. Experiment 2 also used film clips of accidents and used questions with two of the same verbs, plus a _____ group who were not asked about speed. All the participants in the second experiment were asked a week later whether they had seen (non-existent) _____ _____. Both experiments found higher speed estimates with more severe verbs (e.g. smashed). Non-existent broken glass was _____ likely to be recalled when a severe verb was used. Loftus and Palmer concluded that recall is affected by leading questions because they provide '_____-_____ information' which is integrated with information from the original perception. The controls, hiding of the critical questions and Experiment 2 raise both the _____ and reliability of the study. However, eyewitnesses to _____ accidents would have greater motivation and _____ involvement, which would affect memory, so the _____ _____ of this study is low. Although many other lab studies show that leading questions _____ the accuracy of recall (by causing additions to memory or omissions), we are not always misled. We are affected _____ by leading questions about unambiguous details or in real, high-emotion situations, such as shootings.

Gardner and Gardner (1969)

Early studies tried to teach chimps _____ language and failed as they do not have the vocal ability, so this study aimed to teach Washoe _____ language to find out whether language was a unique _____ ability. Gardner and Gardner used the _____ _____ research method to study Washoe, learning ASL through _____ and operant conditioning. Production of new signs was recorded to track language acquisition. Washoe acquired a large _____ of signs (34 words in 22 months, including nouns, verbs and emphasisers) and used them consistently. She _____ between signs with similar meanings, _____ signs to new contexts and _____ signs to make new meanings. Gardner and Gardner concluded that Washoe had learned to communicate effectively using ASL and showed some of the criteria required for language, although further research would be needed to confirm some aspects, such as the combination of symbols. The main strength of Gardner and Gardner's research was their effort to make language accessible to Washoe – by choosing ASL rather than spoken language and providing a motivating social context. They also maintained objectivity – as ASL signs are _____, strict definitions were used to decide on acquisition of new signs and _____ judges were used. A weakness was that Washoe was not rigorously tested for her understanding of _____-_____. In addition, _____ issues are raised as Washoe was wild-caught and lacked social contact with other chimps. Another chimp, Nim Chimpsky, also learned to use sign language proficiently but Kanzi, a bonobo, uses a _____ board in a more linguistically sophisticated way than either chimp and shows structure-dependence, as do some trained dolphins, although they can only comprehend, not _____, language.

For help completing the cloze activity, see the 'Summing it up' section for this chapter.

Consolidate your understanding

Concept maps

Complete the empty boxes and you will have a visual revision plan.

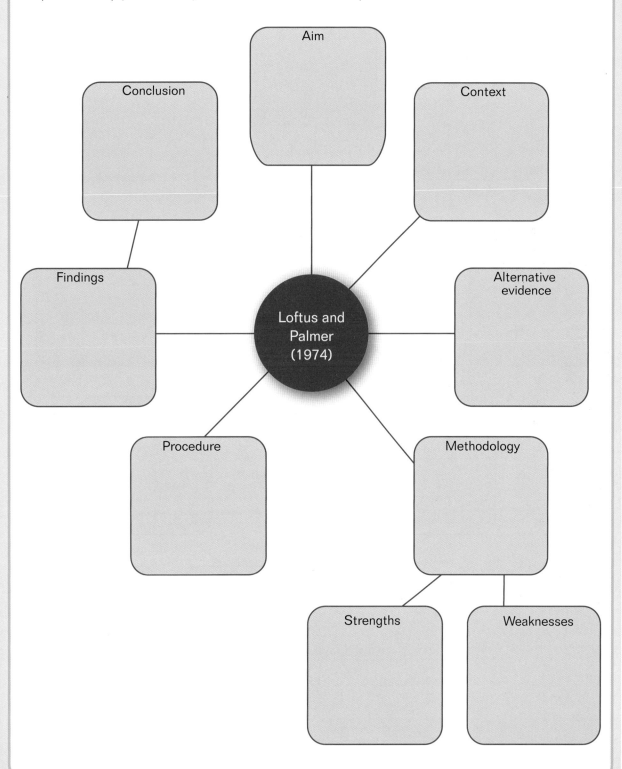

Consolidate your understanding

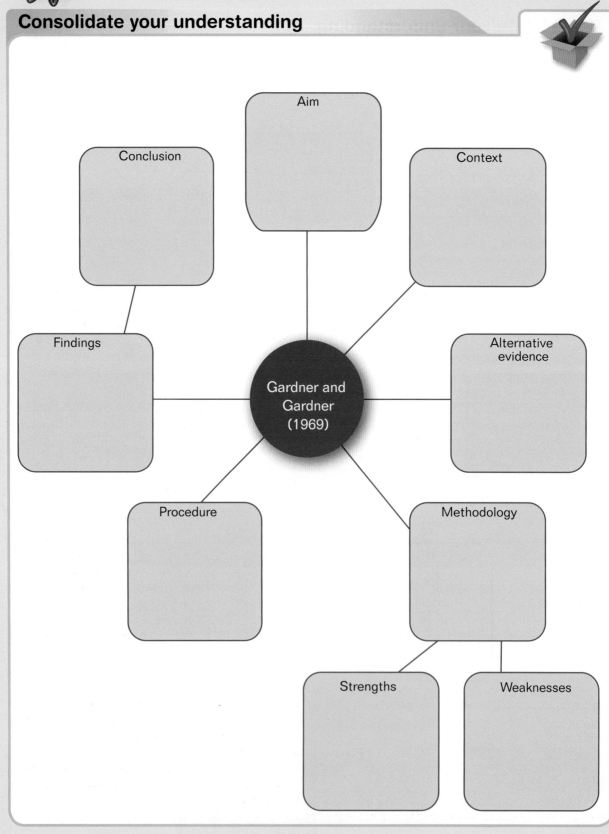

Aim

Conclusion

Context

Findings

Alternative evidence

Gardner and Gardner (1969)

Procedure

Methodology

Strengths

Weaknesses

Exam focus

Loftus and Palmer

Context and aim

The usual **Rule of 4** observed here means that there should be a minimum of three major points made plus the aims. **Reconstructive memory** is crucial here, plus **prior research evidence** and the importance of **eyewitness testimony in real life** are the prime candidates.

Procedure

Remember there are **two experiments** to describe. You need precise sample numbers in both. The verbs need to be correct in both experiments, and the control group noted in Experiment 2.

Findings and conclusions

This is where **absolute precision** is necessary. You must have the **exact** speed estimate in Experiment 1 and the **exact** 'broken glass' numbers likewise in Experiment 2. In Experiment 2 remember that most participants did not notice any broken glass. **You must have conclusions from both studies too.**

Evaluation of method

Be very careful with classic lab experiments, not to have totally generic evaluation (i.e. without any actual reference to the studies). Be positive, not just critical.
'This is a classic lab experiment, with tight control of variables. One example is the **verb IV** manipulated in otherwise identical circumstances for all Ps.' Obviously the big issue here is **ecological validity**!

Critical assessment

The main focus must be the discrepancy between real-life studies and lab work. You should also note Loftus's later work which adjusts her position somewhat. The text gives you the material but you need to cut it down. What is key for the critical assessment question is what alternative evidence says about the original study. So you only need enough information about the alternative evidence to allow you to comment on how it relates to the original.

Gardner and Gardner

Context and aim

This can be a big section! **Rule of 4** here, with three major points plus **aim**. Previous work needs a mention; the evolutionary part-link between humans and chimps and the language use controversy should be the other two. Make sure you show why the question of animals using language was so important.

Procedure

Big and complicated! You need to section this up into training details (especially the reinforcements) and recording details; the **set of criteria for counting a new sign as established** is vital for your answer. Important: Washoe was female! Write 'she' not 'he' as many students do, alas.

Findings and conclusions

Again, long and complicated. Progression in sign acquisition needs noting as well as some examples of spontaneous utterances.

Evaluation of method

Do not criticise the Gardners – as so many students do for most of their answer – for taking little Washoe away from Mum and out of the jungle. They didn't. And don't criticise them for dumping Washoe when their research money was cut off. Their assistant, Roger Fouts, made huge efforts to get a colony home for Washoe, eventually successfully. You **can** criticise them for bringing up Washoe unnaturally, away from other chimps. Stress the positives of the very rigorous method.

Critical assessment

You have to answer the question 'What did the study show' and marshal your evidence to do that. **Rule of 4** again! Be careful with Terrace's Project Nim – look it up on the internet as there are many severe criticisms of it and pointing out its lack of validity is an extra mark boost. Remember the point of this question is how alternatives reflect on the original study.

8 Core studies in developmental psychology

I should be able to:

- summarise the aims and context of Langer and Rodin's 1955 study of the effect of choice and responsibility in older people

- outline the procedure used in Langer and Rodin's study

- describe Langer and Rodin's findings and conclusions

- evaluate the methodology of Langer and Rodin's study

- use alternative evidence to critically assess Langer and Rodin's research

- summarise the aims and context of Gibson and Walk's study of babies' depth perception

- outline the procedure used in Gibson and Walk's study

- describe Gibson and Walk's findings and conclusions

- evaluate the methodology of Gibson and Walk's study

- use alternative evidence to critically assess Gibson and Walk's research.

Developmental psychology is concerned with how we develop as we grow and age. Clearly, childhood is a period of intense growth and development, so much of the work of developmental psychologists has focused on childhood. A minority of developmental psychologists study adult development and older age. Psychologists study human development using a range of research methods. One approach is to use laboratory experiments. These involve testing children's abilities and behaviours under controlled conditions. Another approach is to carry experiments outside the laboratory into the real world. In this chapter, we look at a field experiment into the effect of personal choice and responsibility in older people and a laboratory experiment into infant depth perception.

Figure 8.1 Developmental psychology looks at how we grow

Study 1: Langer and Rodin (1976) Choice and personal responsibility in older people

Langer, E.J. and Rodin, J. (1976) 'The effects of choice and enhanced personal responsibility for the aged: a field experiment in an institutional setting.' *Journal of Personality and Social Psychology*, 134: 191–198.

What could I be asked?

1. **Summarise** the aims **and** context of Langer and Rodin's (1976) study. [12]
2. **Outline** the procedures of Langer and Rodin's (1976) study. [12]
3. **Describe** the findings **and** conclusions of Langer and Rodin's (1976) study. [12]
4. **Evaluate** the methodology of Langer and Rodin's (1976) study. [12]
5. With reference to **alternative evidence**, critically **assess** Langer and Rodin's (1976) study. [12]

Context

Langer and Rodin were concerned with the relationships between choice, self-determination and health. Both researchers had already conducted experiments into the importance of choice, finding, for example, that people would take greater risks when they perceived that they had more choice. Ellen Langer, in particular, was concerned with choice in health settings, looking, for example, at how choice could be used to reduce stress for surgical patients.

The theoretical background to this study is a debate about the extent to which the decline in physical and psychological abilities often observed in older people is the result of physical ageing and the extent to which it results from the typical environment and lifestyle of older people. It had already been established in other settings that beliefs in personal choice had significant health benefits. The aim of this study was to test the principle in a real-world setting – whether giving residents in a home for older people greater choice would affect their alertness and activity.

> ### Exam tip
> Make sure in a question on aims and context that you cover both. Identify what is the aim and what is the context in your answer.

Aim

The aim of the study was to investigate whether being given greater choice and personal responsibility had a positive impact on older people living in a residential home. Specifically, residents were given the choice of a plant, films and how to arrange their furniture, and they were given responsibility for managing a complaints procedure.

Figure 8.2 Older people may not be given enough choice or responsibility

Summary of the study

Aim: To test the effect of choice and personal responsibility on well-being in older people.

Procedure: Ninety-one residents on two floors of a nursing home took part. In one condition, they were given choice and responsibility in planning their environment. In the control condition, they were not.

Findings: Those with choice and responsibility improved on several measures, while those in the control condition declined.

Conclusion: Choice and responsibility are good for well-being in older people.

Procedure

The study was a field experiment carried out in a large, modern nursing home in Connecticut, USA. The home was built on four floors. Two floors were used for the two conditions of the experiment. Residents were already living on these floors and were not assigned there for the purposes of the study. Although staff believed that the two groups were similar, there was no procedure to match them. Technically, then, this was a quasi-experimental, rather than a true experimental, design. Because there was very little contact between residents living on different floors, participants in the two conditions were unlikely to become aware that anything was different for them.

Participants were the residents on the fourth and second floors. The 39 women and eight men living on the fourth floor took part in the experimental condition. The 35 women and nine men of the second floor made up the control group. Participants ranged in age from 65 to 90 years.

In each condition, the hospital director called a meeting of residents in the lounge on each floor. In both conditions, he gave a friendly talk in which he gave residents a plant, offered a new complaints procedure and told them there would be films screened regularly. In the experimental procedure, designed to enhance choice and responsibility, he told fourth-floor residents that they could choose their plant and take care of it as they wished. He also said that they could rearrange furniture as they liked and choose the films to be shown. With regards to complaints, the director told residents that it was their responsibility to make the home the way they wanted it. In the control condition, second-floor residents were given a plant (they could not choose) and told a nurse would water it for them. They were also told that their rooms had been arranged for maximum comfort and that they would be told what films would be shown. No mention was made of responsibility when the complaints procedure was introduced. Three days later, he visited each group and repeated the message.

Patients rated themselves for happiness, activity and perceived control over their lives on a scale of 0–8 (where 0 = none and 8 = total) one week prior to the director's talk and three weeks later. The nurse giving the questionnaire rated each resident for alertness, also using an eight-point scale. Nurses also recorded measures of resident behaviour – for example, how much time they spent visiting each other and other people.

Findings

On several measures, patients in the enhanced choice and responsibility condition came out as better off than those in the control condition. A summary of results is shown in Table 8.1.

Typically, patients in the experimental condition of enhanced choice and responsibility were happier, more active and more alert following the director's talk. However, most of those in the control group were less happy, active and alert. An odd result is that residents in the control condition reported feeling that they had more control over their lives than those in the experimental condition. However, as many participants said they did not understand the question relating to control, the researchers decided to disregard it. Nurses also rated all patients for overall functioning. Of the experimental group, 93 per cent were judged to have improved, as opposed to only 21 per cent of the control group.

Figure 8.3 Nurses rated patients on a number of measures

Table 8.1 Outcomes of the Langer and Rodin procedure

MEASURE	EXPERIMENTAL GROUP BEFORE TALK	EXPERIMENTAL GROUP AFTER TALK	CHANGE	CONTROL GROUP BEFORE TALK	CONTROL GROUP AFTER TALK	CHANGE
Happiness (0–8)	5.15	5.44	+0.28	4.9	4.78	−0.12
Activity (0–8)	4.07	4.27	+0.2	3.9	2.62	−1.28
Control (have it) (0–8)	3.26	3.42	+1.6	3.62	4.03	+0.41
Alertness (0–8)	5.02	5.31	+0.29	5.75	5.38	−0.37
Time visiting other residents (hours per week)	13.03	19.81	+6.78	7.94	4.65	−3.3

(*Source*: adapted from Langer and Rodin (1976) 'The effects of choice and enhanced personal responsibility for the aged: a field experiment in an institutional setting.' *Journal of Personality and Social Psychology*, 134: 191–198. Published by APA and reproduced with permission.)

Exam tip

In a question on findings and conclusions, make sure you cover both. Clearly identify in your answer which are findings and which is the conclusion.

Glossary

double-blind – a procedure to avoid participant and experimenter bias. Participants and the experimenters dealing directly with them are unaware of the purpose of the study or which condition they are in.

Conclusion

Langer and Rodin concluded that the welfare of the elderly residents of the nursing home was profoundly affected by the extent to which they had choice and responsibility. Importantly, a standard intervention, in which people were treated sympathetically but not given choice and responsibility, actually made people less happy, alert and active. By contrast, the experimental condition, in which people received a similar message but one that emphasised their responsibility and choice, led to significant improvements on all these measures. As the only thing that varied between the two conditions was the element of choice and responsibility in the experimental condition, it seems that this was what had the effect.

Evaluating the Langer and Rodin study

Strengths of the methodology

Figure 8.4 The study has good ecological validity as it was carried out in a real nursing home

The design of the study had important strengths. It was conducted in a real nursing home with real residents. The things that were said to residents in each condition were realistic. Both the setting and the intervention were natural and so the **ecological validity** of the study can be said to be good. This is particularly important in a study like this one because it was aiming to test whether ideas that seemed to work in the laboratory would actually work in a real-life setting.

Often when experiments are carried out in natural settings and ecological validity is high, there is a trade-off with experimental control. In this study, however, there was good experimental control because of the similarity of the two floors on which the study was conducted. Care was taken to see that the only variables differing between the two conditions were choice and responsibility. This is why both groups were given a similar talk by the same person. The procedure could easily be replicated elsewhere; therefore, both **internal** and **external reliability** are good.

Glossary

single-blind – a procedure to avoid participant bias. Participants are unaware of the purpose of the experiment or which condition they are in.

A range of measures of outcome was used, including questionnaires and ratings by nurses. A problem in some studies involving rating by observers is **bias**. This takes place because the observers know what the study is testing and what they expect to find. Importantly in this study, the nurses who rated patients for alertness and time spent visiting were not aware of the purpose of the study. This is called a **double-blind** procedure. They were thus not biased by their own opinions about what was likely to happen.

Weaknesses of the methodology

The major limitation of the study was the fact that two pre-existing groups of patients took part in the two conditions. Technically, this makes the study a *quasi-experiment* (although the authors describe it as a field experiment). In a true experiment, the patients would have been randomly allocated to the two conditions, but this could not be done in this study because it would have

meant separating friends. This would have been ethically unacceptable. Because two existing groups were used, we cannot be sure that they were well matched. Looking at Table 8.1, you can see that, before the experimental procedure, the enhanced choice and responsibility group had slightly higher levels of happiness and activity and slightly lower levels of alertness. Crucially, they spent almost twice as long as the control group visiting other residents. This apparent greater sociability in the experimental group as opposed to the control group might be a serious **extraneous variable**.

There are also problems with the **generalisability** of Langer and Rodin's findings. The sample size is reasonable and neither a strength nor a weakness of the methodology. However, the representativeness of the sample is less good. The small number of men in the study means that results might be hard to generalise to a setting with a more equal gender balance (or a single-sex environment, for that matter). Also, the study was conducted in a single nursing home. Without knowing how typical the home was, it is hard to say how well results would generalise to other residential care settings.

Another problem with the design of the study was the poor wording of the question concerning how in control patients felt. Many patients simply did not understand the question and so the results had to be abandoned. This measure had poor **validity**. Actually, this was an important measure and it would have been useful to know whether patients actually felt more in control as a result of the experimental condition.

> ### Exam tip
>
> Evaluation questions may ask you either to evaluate the methodology or to assess using alternative evidence. Be clear what to write for each type of question.

What does alternative evidence tell us?

The role of choice in motivation has been studied extensively since the work of Langer and Rodin. Stefanou *et al.* (2004) found that giving children choice in their classroom seating arrangement, choice of learning materials and the chance to work independently and take responsibility for generating solutions to problems led directly to better motivation to learn. Patall, Cooper and Robinson (2008) reviewed 41 studies looking at the effects of giving people choices. These studies included both laboratory experiments and trials set in real-life settings. They concluded that choice generally led to increased motivation, improved performance and perception of greater ability. These findings provide support for Langer and Rodin's conclusion that choice is beneficial for people.

Figure 8.5 Choice improves motivation in the classroom

Research into the role of choice in the care of older people has continued since Langer and Rodin's study. However, most modern research takes a quality assurance approach, looking for indicators of good quality care. The problem with a quality assurance model is that, by definition, it places responsibility on staff to meet the needs of service users and so shifts attention away from personal responsibility. Saliba and Schnelle (2002) identified 19 indicators of good quality care. However, only two of these refer to choice (and those refer to documenting rather than providing it) and none

Glossary

autonomy – sense of personal independence.

refer to responsibility. Some actually suggest taking choice and responsibility away from residents. Langer and Rodin's research would suggest that this move towards quality assurance is a bad thing because it undermines the motivation and independence of residents.

Langer and Rodin's findings fit in neatly with a modern theory of motivation: Deci's self-determination theory. Ryan and Deci (2000) suggest that people enjoy and are motivated to take part in activities when they have a sense of autonomy (independence). By increasing people's sense of autonomy, we increase their enjoyment and participation in tasks. This would neatly explain Langer and Rodin's findings – once the residents at the nursing home were given choices and responsibility, they would have felt they had more autonomy and so enjoyed events more.

Study 2: Gibson and Walk (1960) The visual cliff

Gibson, E.J. and Walk, R. (1960) 'The visual cliff.' *Scientific American*, **202: 67–71.**

What could I be asked?

1. **Summarise** the aims **and** context of Gibson and Walk's (1960) study. [12]
2. **Outline** the procedures of Gibson and Walk's (1960) study. [12]
3. **Describe** the findings **and** conclusions of Gibson and Walk's (1960) study. [12]
4. **Evaluate** the methodology of Gibson and Walk's (1960) study. [12]
5. With reference to **alternative evidence**, critically **assess** Gibson and Walk's (1960) study. [12]

Context

Psychologists have long been interested in the extent to which we acquire our visual ability through experience and the extent to which we are born able to perceive the world. The latter is called the nativist view (not to be confused with naturist, which involves not wearing clothes!). Eleanor Gibson and Richard Walk were particularly interested in whether depth and distance perception had to be learned. Early studies had involved rearing animals in the dark and seeing whether their lack of visual experience affected their ability to perceive distance normally. Lashley and Russell (1934) had reared rats in the dark and found that they could still jump the correct distance on to a platform. However, Gibson and Walk were unimpressed by this sort of test. Because the rats had to be trained to jump, they could simply have learnt to judge the distance correctly in the course of this training. Instead Gibson and Walk (1960) developed a visual cliff technique. This is pictured in Figure 8.6.

Figure 8.6 The visual cliff

The visual cliff has a glass top under which a real drop can be set up, clearly signalled by a pattern such as a check (as in Figure 8.6). There is thus apparently a deep and a shallow side to the cliff. The glass top not only keeps the participant safe but also means that any clues to depth are visual and not available via the other senses. The visual cliff can be used to test depth perception in human infants as well as animals. The study reported here used both.

Aim

The aim of the study was to investigate whether depth perception was innate or learned. Specifically, it aimed to test whether mobile infants of various species (including humans) would avoid a visible drop.

> **Summary of the study**
>
> **Aim**: To test whether depth perception is innate or learned.
>
> **Procedure**: Thirty-six babies, plus neonates from a range of other species, were placed on a visual cliff, which simulated the appearance of a dangerous drop.
>
> **Findings**: In virtually every case, across all species tested, infants avoided the simulated drop.
>
> **Conclusion**: Depth perception is innate in a range of species, including humans.

Procedure

The study involved 36 human infants aged between 6 and 14 months and their mothers. All the babies were able to crawl. Each child was placed in the centre of the visual cliff on a centreboard (see Figure 8.6). Their mothers then called to them from the cliff side and the shallow side. The idea was to see whether they would be less inclined to crawl across the 'cliff' than the shallow side. If they would not cross the 'cliff', this would suggest that their depth perception was intact as soon as they could crawl. This would in turn suggest that human depth perception is innate, supporting the nativist position.

It takes a few months before humans learn to crawl. It was possible, therefore, that if the babies tested in this study would not cross the visual cliff, it was because they had had time to learn depth perception. To test this possibility, the researchers ran a similar procedure on a range of animal species, including rats, chicks, lambs, kids, puppies and kittens. The procedure with the animals simply involved placing the neonate on the centreboard and seeing which way they would move. Of particular interest were the chicks, kids and lambs because they could stand and so be tested within 24 hours of birth. They would thus have had no opportunity to learn to perceive depth.

A further test was carried out on the kids and lambs. An adjustable cliff was set up so that the apparently shallow surface could be lowered once the animal was on it. The idea was to test how the animal would respond to the visual cues suggesting that the depth of its surroundings was suddenly descending.

An additional condition was set up in which the pattern that displayed the depth cues was replaced by a uniform grey surface. This was to test whether it was the pattern that allowed the participants to perceive distance. If it were indeed the pattern that allowed the depth perception, it would be expected that the participants would no longer show a preference for the shallow side.

Glossary

neonate – newborn human or animal.

Findings

Figure 8.7 This kitten placed on the 'deep' surface freezes

Twenty-seven of the 36 human babies crawled off the centreboard. Of these, all 27 crawled on to the 'shallow' side at least once. By contrast, only three crawled on to the 'deep' side. In addition, many of them crawled away from the mother when she called to them from the deep side. Of the lambs, kids and chicks, none at all ventured on to the 'deep' side; all moved to the shallow side of the centreboard. When placed on the deep side, they 'froze.' This is shown in Figure 8.7.

In the condition with the lowered surface, all the animals similarly adopted an immobile defensive posture when the visual surface dropped more than 12 inches from the top glass. The animals did not adapt when this procedure was repeated a number of times, but continued to freeze. Turtles, the species tested with the poorest eyesight, showed the poorest depth perception as measured by the visual cliff. Seventy-six per cent of them crawled to the shallow side, but a number did crawl on to the 'deep' side. When the pattern was replaced by uniform grey, the animals showed no preference for the deep or shallow side.

Conclusion

All the species tested, including humans, showed intact depth perception by the time they could move independently. In some species, this was within a few hours after birth. This suggests that their ability to perceive depth was present at birth. The nativist position was thus supported. The fact that in the 'grey' condition, no species showed any preference for the shallow side allowed the researchers to conclude as well that the innate mechanism for depth perception involved interpreting changes in patterns indicating depth.

Evaluating the Gibson and Walk study

Strengths of the methodology

The major strength of the study was the ingenious design of the visual cliff. This was arguably the first successful procedure to be used for measuring depth perception in infants. The infants' movement was an easily identifiable measure of their perception. As well as allowing depth perception to be tested in relative safety, the design of the visual cliff allowed researchers to eliminate the role of other senses, such as touch. This ensured that what was assessed was *visual* perception. This gave the study **validity** because it helped ensure that the study measured what it set out to measure.

Previous research into depth perception in animals could be criticised on the basis that it was unclear how well the findings could be applied to humans. A strength of the Gibson and Walk study was that they were thorough in testing their procedure on a range of species, including humans. The consistency of findings across a range of species gives their conclusions particular credibility.

The procedure is straightforward. This is a strength because it means that participants had very much the same experience – that is, there was good internal reliability. The procedure could easily be replicated, meaning that it also has good external reliability.

Weaknesses of the methodology

The **sample** size of 36 human infants was relatively small. Also the age range was quite large (6–14 months), considering this was meant to be a sample of humans only just capable of crawling. It could even be argued that there was little point in including human babies in the study as humans have ample time to learn depth perception by the time they can crawl. However, the authors are clear that it is the combined findings from humans and other species that justify their conclusions.

The **validity** of the measure of depth perception – the preferred direction participants moved from the centreboard – is open to question. It is hard to surmise from this sort of visible behaviour what is happening in the mind of the participant. Clearly, neither babies nor animals could tell the researchers whether they were motivated to avoid a drop. We should always be a little cautious about making judgements like this.

There are **ethical** issues with Gibson and Walk's procedure. The sight of the visual cliff may have distressed the babies, even though they were in no danger of falling. They were not capable of giving real consent to risking distress, although their mothers did give consent for them. They did not have a right of withdrawal if they suffered distress. It is even conceivable that the babies might have been particularly distressed by their mothers appearing to persuade them to fall off a cliff! Fortunately, there is no evidence of this.

What does alternative evidence tell us?

Studies have continued to investigate the question of whether basic perception processes like depth perception are innate or acquired through experience. Tondel and Candy (2007) presented two-to-five-month-old babies with the image of a fast-moving clown. Most of the babies were able to track the clown, even when it moved at speeds of 50 cm/second. This suggests that the ability to track moving objects is innate, in line with the nativist position, and in support of Gibson and Walk's conclusions.

However, Pei, Pettet and Norcia (2007) have shown, using a range of different textures and patterns, that although human infants can make use of crude patterns like the squares in the visual cliff, they cannot detect more subtle differences in texture like adults can. It thus appears that, while some basic perceptual processes are intact at birth, more advanced visual perception does require experience. This contradicts Gibson and Walk's conclusions.

Research continues to show the importance of texture patterning as a source of information about depth. Sinai, Ooi and He (1998) tested adults on their ability to judge distance up to seven metres. They found that, when the ground was even, participants could use texture as a cue and judge distance very accurately. However, when other stimuli were put in the way – for example, a ditch – the accuracy of their distance estimates declined. This supports Gibson and Walk's emphasis on texture patterns as a distance cue.

Summing it up

Langer and Rodin (1976)

➔ The context of the study was prior research into the effects of choice on health and a debate over the extent to which health decline in older people reflects inevitable biological decline or decline in activity.

➔ A field experiment was designed to test the effect of choice and responsibility on the well-being of older people in residential care. This was carried out in a nursing home for older people.

➔ Patients on two floors of the nursing home took part in the two conditions, one floor per condition. In the experimental condition, the director gave a talk emphasising choice and responsibility.

➔ In the control condition, a similar talk was given but it emphasised instead the responsibility of staff to look after residents.

➔ Residents in each condition were rated on a number of measures of well-being before and after the talk, using questionnaires and observations.

➔ Residents in the experimental condition improved significantly in happiness, activity and alertness. Those in the control condition declined on all these measures.

➔ It was concluded that choice and personal responsibility had beneficial effects.

➔ This study has good ecological validity because it was carried out in a natural environment. It also used a good range of well-being measures and a double-blind procedure in which observers were not aware of the aims of the study.

➔ The major weakness of the study is the matching of the two groups in the experimental and control conditions. They were not matched precisely before the interventions so the outcome may have been partly a result of individual differences between the participants.

➔ Modern research has supported the idea that choice has positive effects on motivation. Results can now be understood using Deci's self-determination theory.

Gibson and Walk (1960)

➔ The context to the study was the debate about whether visual perception is present at birth and the extent it is learnt. This forms part of the nature–nurture debate.

➔ The study aimed to test whether neonates from a range of species would respond to texture-gradient depth cues.

➔ A visual cliff was set up. This involved a glass surface covering a surface, the pattern on which displayed depth cues. One half of the surface appeared to have a drop, while the other half appeared to be the height of the glass.

➔ Thirty-six human babies aged 6–14 months took part in the study. They were placed on a board in the centre of the visual cliff. Their mothers called them over from the deep and shallow sides.

➔ Twenty-seven crawled on to the 'shallow' side at least once. Only three crawled on to the 'deep' side.

➔ The procedure was repeated using a range of animal species. In most species, all moved to the 'shallow' side and none to the 'deep' side.

- When the patterned surface was replaced with uniform grey, the animals displayed no preference for either side.

- The major advantages of the study were the clever design of the visual cliff and the consistency of findings across species.

- The major limitation with any research of this sort is inferring from babies' behaviour what they are thinking or perceiving. The study also raises ethical issues.

- Modern research continues to show that some aspects of visual perception appear to be innate, as suggested by Gibson and Walk. However, results are not consistent and it is still unclear whether this is true of depth perception.

Consolidate your understanding

The developmental studies

Use the following activities to run the information in this chapter through your mind. Each activity is designed to help you process the information in a different way, which should help you ensure you understand it and make it easier to remember.

Wordsearch

O	E	I	C	C	H	O	I	C	E	U	H	A	I	O
N	I	T	M	W	I	I	E	N	T	Y	N	T	O	E
D	I	E	A	S	A	P	H	S	T	Y	S	N	E	T
F	N	L	I	N	D	A	I	I	L	D	A	E	T	A
O	K	B	N	B	N	V	D	I	A	V	M	M	H	N
A	B	I	C	C	I	I	N	E	N	L	P	P	I	O
H	I	L	E	T	L	A	C	I	G	O	L	O	C	E
S	I	D	A	A	B	N	S	I	E	E	E	L	S	N
A	D	N	V	S	E	X	P	E	R	I	M	E	N	T
H	I	F	F	I	L	C	L	A	U	S	I	V	H	O
Y	T	I	L	I	B	I	S	N	O	P	S	E	R	V
S	I	D	I	I	U	T	F	L	T	F	N	D	I	I
E	G	I	B	S	O	N	I	O	B	L	O	N	E	I
N	P	S	A	A	D	E	N	X	C	C	I	N	C	E
N	V	T	D	E	E	O	I	M	P	M	N	T	N	U

development
experiment
Langer
choice
responsibility
enhanced
ecological
double blind
bias

Gibson
Walk
visual cliff
nativist
sample
validity
ethics
neonate
innate

Crossword

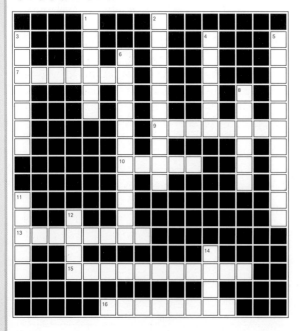

Across
7. Newborn
9. Type of reliability in which all participants have a similar experience
10. Used to create high or low control
13. This was rated by nurses
15. An extraneous variable in Langer and Rodin's study
16. Believes in innate abilities – and wears clothes!

Down
1. Present at birth
2. A type of validity
3. In Langer and Rodin, a condition with low choice and responsibility

4. Species with poor eyesight
5. Ageing pop singer's video or a device creating the illusion of depth
6. Age-related change
8. Studied choice in health settings
11. French almost-hero carried out almost-experiment
12. Participated in the Gibson and Walk study, in both the human and goat sense
14. Occurs when experimenters or participants understand the whole study

Wordsearch and crossword solutions begin on page 231.

Consolidate your understanding

Cloze

Langer and Rodin (1976)

The context of Langer and Rodin's study was prior research into the effects of _____ on health and a debate over the extent to which health decline in older people reflects inevitable biological decline or decline in activity. A field _____ was designed to test the effect of choice and responsibility on the well-being of older people in residential care. This was carried out in a nursing home for older people. Patients on _____ floors of the nursing home took part in the two conditions, one floor per condition. In the experimental condition, the director gave a talk emphasising _____ and _____. In the control condition, a similar talk was given but it emphasised instead the responsibility of _____ to look after residents. Residents in each condition were rated on a number of measures of well-being before and after the talk, using questionnaires and _____. Residents in the experimental condition improved significantly in happiness, activity and alertness. Those in the control condition declined on all these measures. It was concluded that choice and personal responsibility had _____ effects.

This study has good _____ validity because it was carried out in a natural environment. It also used a good range of well-being measures and a double-_____ procedure in which observers were not aware of the aims of the study. The major weakness of the study is the matching of the two groups in the experimental and control conditions. They were not matched precisely before the interventions so the outcome may have been partly a result of individual differences between the participants. Modern research has supported the idea that choice has positive effects on motivation. Results can now be understood using Deci's self-_____ theory.

Gibson and Walk (1960)

The context to Gibson and Walk's study was the debate about whether visual perception is present at birth and the extent it is learnt. This forms part of the nature–_____ debate. The study aimed to test whether neonates from a range of species would respond to texture-gradient depth cues. A visual _____ was set up. This involved a glass surface covering a surface, the pattern on which displayed depth cues. One half of the surface appeared to have a drop, while the other half appeared to be the height of the glass. Thirty-six human _____ aged 6–14 months took part in the study. They were placed on a board in the centre of the visual cliff. Their mothers called them over from the deep and shallow sides. Twenty-seven crawled on to the 'shallow' side at least once. Only three crawled on to the 'deep' side. The procedure was repeated using a range of animal species. In most species, all moved to the 'shallow' side and none to the 'deep' side. When the patterned surface was replaced with uniform grey, the animals displayed no _____ for either side.

The major advantages of the study were the clever design of the visual cliff and the consistency of findings across species. The major limitation with any research of this sort is inferring from babies' behaviour what they are thinking or perceiving. The study also raises _____ issues. Modern research continues to show that some aspects of visual perception appear to be _____, as suggested by Gibson and Walk. However, results are not consistent and it is still unclear whether this is true of depth perception.

For help completing the cloze activity, see the 'Summing it up' section for this chapter.

Consolidate your understanding

Concept maps

Complete the empty boxes and you will have a visual revision plan.

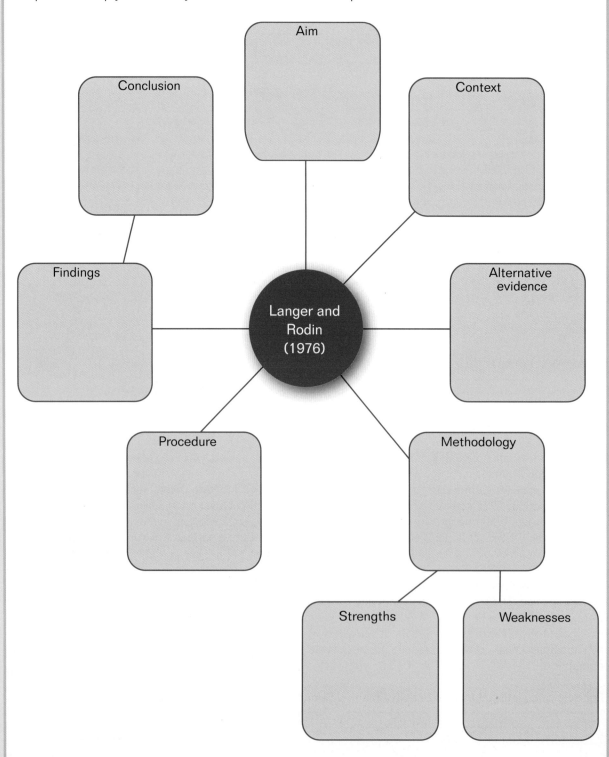

Consolidate your understanding

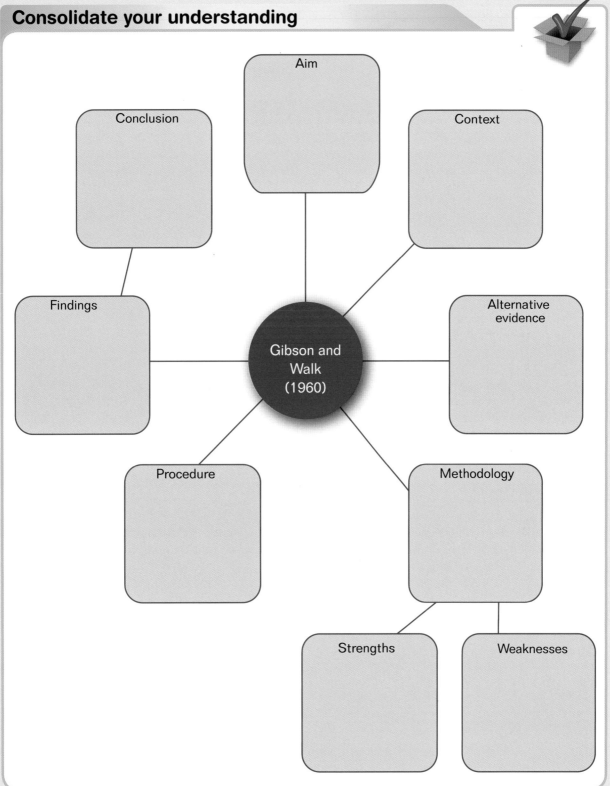

- Aim
- Conclusion
- Context
- Findings
- Gibson and Walk (1960)
- Alternative evidence
- Procedure
- Methodology
- Strengths
- Weaknesses

Exam focus

Langer and Rodin

Context and aim

The important issue here is choice and health, Langer did a lot of work on self-determination so the focus is on her work. An internet search could be useful here – there's lots of really interesting stuff on Langer and you may want to add your own material here about ageing and the mind. Whatever you do, don't forget the **Rule of 4** including the **aim.**

Procedure

The text is quite clear here and you can do no better than make your own version from it.

Findings and conclusions

Table 8.1 is vital. You need to use some examples along with the general results in the text – the '**time visiting other residents**' and '**happiness**' self report scale results are probably the best to give as exact examples. Finish off with the '**overall functioning**' estimates.

Evaluation of method

Stress the positives of the extremely valid methodology! There are four good points to be had in the text. A valid discussion point is how **ethically fair** was treating the control group in the way they did if the researchers thought (correctly) that the experimental group would have their lives and health enhanced.

Critical assessment

The **Rule of 4** and the text coincide here – use it! You'll just need to cut a little of the text out. What is key for the critical assessment question is what alternative evidence says about the original study. So you only need enough information about the alternative evidence to allow you to comment on how it relates to the original.

Gibson and Walk

Context and aim

You can make a bit more of the nature/nurture argument in the context, to produce a good three points to go with the **aim**. In the 1950s and 1960s there was an interminable clash between proponents of **nurture** (e.g. the behaviourist approach) and those leaning towards the **nature/ nativist** view (e.g. the biological approach) – at least in English-speaking psychology. There was little in the way of evidence then, and many techniques you are familiar with (e.g. genetic techniques) did not exist. (Neither did computers, mobile phones or the internet, and colour TV was just catching on.) Looking this controversy up in your library or Wikipedia could be useful.

Procedure

There is so little in the way of procedure, **every little detail has to be spot on** (e.g. age range of children, ages of animals).

Findings and conclusions

Exactly the same as the procedure, **every detail has to be exactly right** if you want top band marks!

Evaluation of method

The main part of the answer must concern the age of the children and whether the method – which requires mobile children – can tell us anything about the onset of depth perception. You can also ask just how relevant animal studies are – a theme that occurs elsewhere with Gardner and Gardner.

Critical assessment

There is a lot of subsequent work on depth perception in infants, and if you use the **Rule of 4** you have three examples from the text to compare and contrast with the study. Do some further research in your library or on the internet to pick up another point if you want, otherwise you will need to be very accurate in your answer. Remember the point of this question is how alternatives reflect on the original study.

9 Core studies in the psychology of individual differences

This chapter includes:

I should be able to:

- summarise the aims and context of Buss's 1989 study of mate preference
- outline the procedure used in Buss's study
- describe Buss's findings and conclusions
- evaluate the methodology of Buss's study
- use alternative evidence to critically assess Buss's research
- summarise the aims and context of Rosenhan's 1973 study of the psychiatric system
- outline the procedure used in Rosenhan's study
- describe Rosenhan's findings and conclusions
- evaluate the methodology of Rosenhan's study
- use alternative evidence to critically assess Rosenhan's research.

As the name suggests, the psychology of individual differences is about the ways humans differ from one another. The bulk of psychological research is more concerned with what we have in common than how we vary. Research into our physiology, cognition, social behaviour and development has mainly been concerned with establishing broad rules about human psychology – that is, how we *all* function. The field of individual differences takes a different approach and looks at how people differ from one another. We differ from one another in numerous ways, as a function of our age, sex, and our cultural, genetic and family background. Some of the most studied aspects of individual differences include intelligence, personality and mental health. The two studies in this chapter are concerned with sex differences and mental health.

Figure 9.1 The psychology of individual differences looks at what makes us unique

Study 1: Buss (1989) Sex differences in human mate preferences

Buss, D. (1989) 'Sex differences in human mate preferences.' *Behavioural & Brain Sciences*, **12: 1–49.**

What could I be asked?

1. **Summarise** the aims **and** context of Buss's (1989) study. [12]
2. **Outline the procedures of Buss's (1989) study.** [12]
3. **Describe the findings and conclusions of Buss's (1989) study.** [12]
4. **Evaluate** the methodology of Buss's (1989) study. [12]
5. With reference to **alternative evidence**, critically **assess** Buss's (1989) study. [12]

Context

In the 1870s, Charles Darwin suggested that mate selection (choosing a sexual partner) was a matter of evolution because it determined which members of a species got to reproduce and pass on their characteristics to future generations. More recently, psychologists have developed a whole field of evolutionary psychology. Evolutionary psychologists are interested in how behaviours like mate selection might be affected by instincts designed to maximise the chances of reproducing and passing on our genes. There are now a number of theories in this area. Buss was particularly interested in three ideas: parental investment, reproductive value and paternal probability.

Parental investment

Trivers (1972) proposed that one factor affecting mate selection is *parental investment*. In humans, females invest more time and energy in reproduction than men. Men *can* invest as little as a few minutes of casual sex impregnating a woman, who will then carry the child through pregnancy and typically take the bulk of responsibility for raising that child to adulthood. The fact that women invest so much more in reproduction means that they will tend to be fussier in their mate choice. It also means that selection of men should be influenced by their likelihood and ability to contribute to child rearing. Put bluntly, this theory predicts that women will favour ambitious, hardworking and rich men, who are most likely to be able to look after them and their children.

Reproductive value

Evolutionary psychologists have proposed other factors affecting mate choice. Fertility and reproductive value are two related factors. These primarily affect males' choice of females because, for men, access to fertile females is the major factor affecting their chances of reproducing. *Fertility* is the probability of reproduction now. *Reproductive value* is the probability of reproduction in the future. Fertility in women peaks in their late teens or early twenties and obviously the younger the woman, the longer she is likely to remain fertile. This whole approach therefore predicts that men will favour younger women. Because facial

Glossary

chastity – lack of current sexual activity.
fertility – the short-term probability of reproduction.
reproductive value – the long-term probability of reproducing.

appearance gives clues to age and therefore to fertility and reproductive value, this approach also predicts that facial attractiveness
in women will be very important to men.

Paternal probability

A third line of research is based on the idea that we want to be
sure that any investment we make in reproduction ensures that we
pass on *our* genes to future generations. For women, this is easy
– unless there is an unfortunate mix-up in the maternity ward,
there is little doubt that your child is biologically your own. For
men, on the other hand, it is much harder to know that a child is
theirs. This line of thinking predicts that men, to a much greater
extent than women, will value chastity (lack of sexual activity) in
their partner (Dickemann, 1981).

Figure 9.2 Stereotypically attractive
women appear fertile

Aim

Evolutionary psychologists are often interested in how behaviour varies across
cultures. In general, the more something holds true across a range of cultures,
the more likely it is to be a result of evolution. Using a cross-cultural design,
Buss (1989) tested a range of predictions from evolutionary theory about sex
differences in mate selection. It was predicted that, regardless of culture, women
would tend to prefer men who were ambitious, industrious (hardworking) and
financially well off. It was also predicted that men would prefer young, attractive
and chaste women.

Summary of the study

Aim: To investigate whether men and women in
a range of cultures consistently rated the same
characteristics as important for mate preference.

Procedure: Ten thousand people from 33
countries were surveyed about what characteristics
they thought were important in a mate.

Findings: Across a range of cultures, men
preferred younger women, whereas women
preferred older men. Men rated looks and
chastity as more important than women
did. Women placed more emphasis on
industriousness and ambition.

Conclusion: Men and women prefer mates
to have characteristics associated with fertility,
paternal probability and parental investment.

Procedure

Thirty-seven samples were obtained from 33 countries covering six continents.

Countries with separate populations, such as Israel, Canada and South Africa,
had separate samples taken from each group. For example, separate samples
of English- and French-speaking Canadians were taken. The total number of
participants was 10,047. Of these, 4,601 were male and 5,446 were female.
Their average age was 23.05 years. Sample sizes for each country are shown in
Table 9.1.

Table 9.1　Sample size from each country

COUNTRY	SAMPLE SIZE
Nigeria	172
South Africa	228
Zambia	119
China	500
Indonesia	143
Iran	55
Israel	582
Japan	259
Taiwan	566
Bulgaria	269
Estonia	303
Poland	240
Yugoslavia	140
Belgium	145
France	191
Finland	204
Germany	1,083
Great Britain	130
Greece	132
Ireland	122
Italy	101
Netherlands	417
Norway	134
Spain	124
Sweden	172
Canada	206
USA	1,670
Australia	280
New Zealand	151
Brazil	630
Colombia	139
Venezuela	193
India	247

(*Source*: adapted from Buss (1989) 'Sex differences in human mate preferences.' *Behavioural and Brain Sciences*, 12: 1–49)

Sampling methods varied from one country to another, but were generally either opportunity or self-selecting in nature. The New Zealand sample consisted of secondary-age schoolchildren. The Estonian participants were those applying for marriage licences in particular districts. A number of countries used university students. The German participants responded to newspaper adverts.

Two questionnaires were administered to all participants in their native language. The first measured the importance of factors affecting mate choice. Eighteen characteristics were assessed for importance. Some were irrelevant to the study – for example, sociability. Others were the target variables of age, good looks, good financial prospects, chastity, ambition, industriousness and no previous sexual experience. Participants rated the importance of each factor on a 0–3 scale, where 0 was irrelevant and 3 was indispensable. The second questionnaire asked participants to rank 13 factors affecting mate choice in order of importance. Within the 13 factors were 'good earning capacity' and 'physical attractiveness'.

Remember that evolutionary theory predicts that women will tend to prefer men who are ambitious, industrious and financially well off. It also predicts that men will tend to prefer young, attractive and chaste women.

Figure 9.3 Women prefer men to have good earning capacity

Findings

Broadly, the results were in line with evolutionary theory, although there were some cultural differences in mate selection priorities. In 36 out of 37 cultures, women placed significantly more importance on good financial prospects in a mate than men. The exception was Spain, where women placed only fractionally more importance than men on finance. In 34 of the 37 cultures, women placed more emphasis on ambition and industriousness than men, although the difference was only great enough to be statistically significant in 29 cultures. In three samples, Spanish, Colombian and Zulu South African, the position was reversed. Men rated ambition and industriousness in women as more important than women did in men. In all 37 cultures, the average age of men's ideal woman was significantly younger than themselves and that of women's ideal man. Similarly, in all 37 samples, women's ideal man was older than themselves. The average age difference between the ideal man and the ideal woman was four years. This is shown in Table 9.2.

Figure 9.4 Against the trend, Colombian men rated ambition and industry higher than women

Table 9.2 Ideal mate age

| Men's ideal woman | 24.83 |
| Women's ideal man | 28.81 |

In all 37 cultures, men rated good looks as more important than did women. In 34 cultures, this difference was great enough to be statistically significant. Chastity and lack of previous sexual experience was the factor that varied most

across cultures. Out of the Western European countries, only Ireland placed much emphasis on chastity. In only 23 of the 37 cultures was there a gender difference in the importance placed on chastity in a potential mate. However, the findings were still broadly in the direction predicted by evolutionary theory; overall, men placed more importance than women on chastity. In no culture did women place significantly more emphasis on chastity in a partner than men.

Conclusion

Buss concluded that there was support for all the predictions from evolutionary theory tested in the study. Across the 37 cultures tested, a strong trend emerged for men to choose mates based on age and attractiveness – and, to a lesser extent, chastity. Women, on the other hand, placed more emphasis on ambition, industriousness and earning capacity. These findings suggest that parental investment, reproductive value and paternal probability all play a role in mate selection in humans.

Evaluating the Buss study

Strengths of the methodology

Sample size was large. This is important as it makes it more likely that the sample will fairly **represent** the populations it is taken from. The scale of Buss's study is very impressive, with over 10,000 participants taking part and 33 countries being represented. Buss was very thorough in representing every inhabited continent and a wide range of differing cultures. This thoroughness increases the **generalisability** of the findings.

The **validity** of measures is a strength of the study for two main reasons. Firstly, two separate measures were used to assess mate preference. Whenever we use a single questionnaire, it is hard to know what extraneous variables might creep in and affect people's answers. Using two different questionnaires reduced the chances of this. Secondly, using a questionnaire method is a valid way of finding out about mate *preferences*. Other studies, which use measures such as marriage records, have been criticised on the basis that they really measure mate *selection*. Local cultural factors, such as arranged marriage, affect mate selection as well as mate preference. Answers to questions are probably a more valid measure of mate preference.

Weaknesses of the methodology

Glossary

opportunity sample – a sample made up of the most easily available participants.
self-selecting sample – a sample of volunteers.

Although the scale of Buss's study is impressive, his sampling procedures were much less so, and he admits himself that the samples were not **representative** of the populations looked at in the study. Opportunity and self-selecting sampling are by definition not methods for obtaining a representative sample of people. The sample size in some countries was also quite small; for example, only 28 men and 27 women represented Iran. In addition, the majority of participants (77 per cent) were from industrialised nations. Although the results were remarkably consistent across countries, we cannot be entirely sure that they would have been so if more representative samples had been tested.

There are always limitations to research that relies on people answering question-naires. When asked, most people say no to completing it. This means that no sample, however well thought-out, is ever really **representative**. Questionnaires also only work for those who can read and write. This becomes a problem if we are trying to access the views of people representing the whole world; some cultures do not place particular value on literacy or think of it as having unequal value for men and women. **Participant bias** can also become a problem in questionnaires, especially when we ask people to place options in rank order; participants can see the options and make guesses about what the researcher expects or wants to find.

Studies of this type are **socially sensitive** for a number of reasons. Evolutionary ideas are sensitive when applied to psychology in general because they are deter-ministic, suggesting that we have little free will and are in fact governed by our biology. Most people dislike thinking of themselves in this way. Evolutionary psychology is also offensive to some feminists, who suggest that it justifies discrimination in which women are valued on the basis of their age and looks, and are pressured into chastity.

What does alternative evidence tell us?

Research confirms that mate preference is influenced by fertility

Mate preference and selection remain important areas of current evolutionary psychology. Evidence has continued to mount from a range of sources that mate choice is influenced by instincts to maximise successful reproduction and child rearing. In a fascinating recent study, Pillsworth, Hasleton and Buss (2004) tested whether sexual desire in general, and for long-term partners in particular, increases when women are ovulating. The study questioned 202 female university students about how sexy they felt that day, both in relation to their partner and to other attractive men, and where they were in their menstrual cycle. It emerged that sexual desire peaked around ovulation in women with partners, but not others. In addition, among the women with partners, women expressed more desire towards their partner relative to other men when ovulating.

There is evidence that men rate women as more attractive when they are ovulating (Roberts *et al.*, 2004). Another study by Little *et al.* (2007) showed that people from Britain and the Hazda, an African hunter-gatherer culture, both found facial symmetry attractive. Studies like these support Buss's most basic idea: that mate preference is affected by evolution. Thus indicators of 'good genes' and fertility affect mate preference.

Cross-cultural research still shows universal sex differences in mate preference

There is also evidence to support the idea that there are universal sex differences in mating preferences. One of the important hypotheses has been that men, with their low parental investment, seek sex with a range of women, while women are choosier, seeking sex with fewer men. In a major cross-cultural study by Schmitt (2003), this was tested in 16,288 people from 53 countries. In every culture, there was a significant difference on each of several measures between women's and men's preferences for variety in mates. In every case, men desired

You can read the Buss paper online at: http://homepage. psy.utexas.edu/ HomePage/ Group/BussLAB/ publications.htm.

a larger number of mates. Studies like this support Buss's conclusion that there are cross-cultural universals in sex differences in mating behaviour.

Debates about evolutionary psychology continue

There have been serious challenges to the whole idea of evolutionary psychology. In direct opposition to the notion of instinctive sexual behaviour, social constructionists place their emphasis on the role of culture in affecting our social behaviour. The debate over culture versus evolution has been particularly bitter over the issue of rape.

Evolutionary psychologists believe that one of the instincts guiding our behaviour is to reproduce and pass on our genes. Thornhill and Palmer (2000) suggest that rape has evolved as a mechanism for sexually unsuccessful men to pass on their genes. For support, evolutionary psychologists can draw on examples of similar behaviours in other species. A number of species – for example, mallards – use forced sex as a reproductive strategy. Rose and Rose (2000) have challenged this perspective, proposing instead that rape is actually a cultural phenomenon. They go on to suggest that the evolutionary perspective contributes to the social acceptability of rape by suggesting that it is inevitable and, in some ways, beneficial to the species. Instead of instinct, social constructionists emphasise how cultural practices benefit those with social power at the expense of those with less power. As most rape is carried out by men (who generally hold more social power than women) against women, a social constructionist view is that rape is a way for men to uphold their dominant social position over women.

Study 2: Rosenhan (1973) On being sane in insane places

Rosenhan, D.L. (1973) 'On being sane in insane places.' _Science_, 179: 250–258.

What could I be asked?

1. **Summarise** the aims **and** context of Rosenhan's (1973) study. [12]
2. **Outline** the procedures of Rosenhan's (1973) study. [12]
3. **Describe** the findings **and** conclusions of Rosenhan's (1973) study. [12]
4. **Evaluate** the methodology of Rosenhan's (1973) study. [12]
5. With reference to **alternative evidence**, critically **assess** Rosenhan's (1973) study. [12]

Context

Rosenhan begins his paper with the question 'If sanity and insanity exist how shall we know them?' (1973: p250). People have wrestled with the notion of mental illness since long before the birth of psychology. Rosenhan is clear that he is not questioning the existence of mental disorder. As he puts it, 'Anxiety and depression exist. Psychological suffering exists. But normality and abnormality, sanity and insanity and the diagnoses that flow from them may be less substantive than many believe them to be.' (1973: p250) In other words,

Rosenhan is suggesting that, although mental disorder exists, we are not particularly good at recognising it.

Since the early twentieth century, psychological abnormality had been dealt with by means of medical diagnoses. It has been customary to diagnose mental illness from a patient's symptoms, in the same way that physical illness is diagnosed. In 1952, the American Psychiatric Association published its own system, the DSM (Diagnostic and Statistical Manual of Mental Disorder). This is now in its fourth edition. Although it is standard practice to make a diagnosis using one of these systems, there have always been concerns about their reliability and validity. Rosenhan points out that the assumption behind all such systems is that it is possible to tell the 'sane' (not mentally disordered) from the 'insane' (mentally disordered). However, this is questionable, and other people writing in the late 1960s and early 1970s suggested that diagnosis is 'in the minds of the observers' (1973: p250) rather than the patients. Rosenhan set out to investigate this.

Rosenhan suggested that one test of the validity of psychiatric diagnosis was whether doctors and other health professionals could recognise that in fact some of their patients had no symptoms at all. This could be tested by using pseudopatients – mentally healthy people who could gain entry to the psychiatric system by faking a symptom, and then who acted normally. Rosenhan believed that if the mental health system was capable of valid diagnosis, professionals would soon spot pseudopatients.

> ## Glossary
>
> **pseudopatient** – a participant who fakes one or more symptoms in order to become a patient so as to gather data on the health system.
> **sane** – technically a legal term meaning mentally competent to make decisions. Often used as a non-technical term to mean mentally healthy.

> ## Exam tip
>
> Make sure in a question on aims and context that you cover both. Identify what is the aim and what is the context in your answer.

Aim

This was a pseudopatient study looking at the success of the mental health system to spot pseudopatients at the point of diagnosis and during hospitalisation. The first specific aim was to see whether they would be identified as 'sane' when they presented themselves for diagnosis. The second specific aim was to record their experiences as psychiatric in-patients.

> ## Summary of the study
>
> **Aim**: To investigate the ability of mental health professionals to identify pseudopatients.
>
> **Procedure**: Eight volunteers faked a single symptom at 12 hospitals. They then acted normally and recorded staff behaviour. In a follow-up study, staff at a hospital were challenged to spot a pseudopatient over a three-month period.
>
> **Findings**: In all cases, pseudopatients were admitted to hospital. Once there, staff made little effort to interact and labelled ordinary behaviour as symptoms. All were released with a diagnosis of schizophrenia (11) or manic depression (1) in remission. In the follow-up, 41 of 193 real patients were wrongly judged to be pseudopatients.
>
> **Conclusion**: The validity of diagnosis is poor, and workers in the system tend to misinterpret behaviour as symptoms of mental disorder once a patient has been labelled.

Figure 9.5 All the pseudopatients were admitted to hospitals after reporting a single symptom

Procedure

Eight pseudopatients took part in the study. Five were men and three women. Three were psychologists, one a psychology student and one a psychiatrist. The others were not mental health experts: one was a paediatrician (a medical doctor specialising in treating children), another a housewife and the other a painter and decorator. All used false names so that they would not have a diagnosis on their own medical records after the study. The mental health professionals also gave false information about their occupation so that they would not receive any special treatment.

Twelve hospitals were targeted for the study. In one case where Rosenhan himself was the pseudopatient, his identity and the purpose of the study were known to the hospital authorities. In all other cases, the hospitals were entirely unaware of the study. A wide range of hospitals was deliberately chosen: one was private and one attached to a university. The others were all publicly funded. Some were new, others old. Some had much better staff–patient ratios than others.

Each pseudopatient called a hospital and then attended an appointment where they reported hearing voices. In each case, the voice was the same sex as the pseudopatient and unfamiliar to them. The voices were sometimes unclear but the words 'empty', 'hollow' and 'thud' could be made out. Apart from the voices, they gave accurate descriptions of their mental state. Once admitted to the hospital's psychiatric wards, they acted normally with staff and patients. They accepted (but did not take) medication from staff. When asked, they reported no further symptoms. In three hospitals, the pseudopatients recorded the number of patients who expressed doubts that they were genuine. In four hospitals, they attempted to ask doctors and nurses questions and recorded their responses.

A follow-up to the main study took place at another hospital whose staff had expressed doubt that they would be fooled by pseudopatients. They were informed that one or more pseudopatients would present themselves over the next three months. Staff rated all new patients on a 1–10 scale for how likely each new admission was to be a pseudopatient. In fact, no pseudopatients approached them in this time; the idea was to record how many real patients were falsely judged to be pseudopatients.

Findings

Quantitative and qualitative data were gathered. In 100 per cent of cases, the pseudopatient was immediately admitted to hospital. The length of stay ranged from 7 to 52 days (average 19 days). Eleven patients were diagnosed with schizophrenia and one with manic depression. While in hospital, no doctors or nurses questioned the genuineness of the pseudopatients. However, of the 118 patients in the three hospitals where patient responses were recorded, 35 (30 per cent) challenged the pseudopatients. In the four hospitals where staff responses to questions were recorded, in no case did they make an effort to answer the questions. Their responses are shown in Table 9.3.

Table 9.3 Staff responses to pseudopatient questions

	PSYCHIATRISTS	NURSES AND ATTENDANTS
Responses (per cent):		
Moves on; head averted	71	88
Makes eye contact	23	10
Pauses and chats	2	2
Stops and talks	4	0.5

(*Source*: adapted from Rosenhan (1973))

Qualitative data was available in the form of notes taken by the pseudopatients and hospital staff. These illustrate how staff interpreted the behaviour of the pseudopatients in line with their beliefs that they were mentally disordered. One nurse recorded daily that her pseudopatient 'engaged in writing behaviour', seeing this as a compulsive behaviour (in fact, the pseudopatient was keeping notes). Another interpreted the bored pacing of a pseudopatient as nervousness. One patient mentioned how in childhood he was closer to his mother but more recently had got on better with his father. In his notes, this was presented as follows: '... manifests a long history of considerable ambivalence in close relationships, which begins in early childhood. A warm relationship with his mother cools in adolescence. A distant relationship with his father is described as becoming very intense.' This makes the normal ups and downs of family life sound dysfunctional.

Figure 9.6 Ordinary behaviour like note taking was interpreted as a symptom

Further data came from the follow-up study. Over the three months of the study, 193 genuine patients and no pseudopatients were admitted. Forty-one were judged with a high level of confidence to be a pseudopatient by at least one member of staff. In 23 cases, at least one psychiatrist and, in 19 cases, a psychiatrist and another staff member believed they were dealing with a pseudopatient.

Exam tip

In a question on findings and conclusions, make sure you cover both. Clearly identify in your answer which are findings and which is the conclusion.

Conclusion

The major conclusion of the study was that even experienced mental health professionals could not reliably distinguish between real and false patients. Faking a single symptom on a single occasion was sufficient to receive a psychiatric diagnosis. Furthermore, once in the mental health system, patients' normal behaviour was interpreted as symptoms of their disorder. This indicates that the validity of psychiatric diagnosis was poor. It is important to remember that Rosenhan did not use his data to criticise the competence or conduct of doctors or nurses. Instead he blamed the poor results on the 'system' of diagnosis.

You can read Rosenhan's paper in full at the following: www.walnet.org/llf/ROSENHAN-BEINGSANE.PDF.

Evaluating the Rosenhan study

Strengths of the methodology

This was a field study, carried out in 12 real hospitals. Real doctors and nurses were involved and they were not aware that they were taking part in a study (at least until the follow-up stage). These factors are important because they ensured that all doctors, nurses and patients behaved naturally. In addition, the doctors and nurses in the study believed they were carrying out their normal duties. The study can thus be said to have good **ecological validity**.

Although the study involved only eight pseudopatients and 12 hospitals, care was taken to ensure that the hospitals chosen were representative of the range available to the public. We can thus say that the study had a small sample but quite a **representative sample**.

The procedure can be said to have good **internal reliability**. This is because the pseudopatients and the professionals they came into contact with had consistent experiences. Moreover, the conclusions of the main procedure are highly consistent with those of the follow-up. Findings are also consistent with those of replications, meaning that the study also has good external reliability.

A good range of data was gathered, both quantitative and qualitative. From the quantitative data, we get the headline figures – how many patients were admitted, how many pseudopatients were falsely identified, etc. From the qualitative data, we get further useful information about the kind of things doctors and nurses said to and about the pseudopatients. This study thus made good use of both **qualitative** and **quantitative** data.

Weaknesses of the methodology

The study raises serious **ethical issues** centred around consent and deception. The doctors, nurses and patients in the hospitals did not give consent to take part in a psychological study. In addition, the pseudopatients set out to deliberately deceive them. There was a risk of stress to everyone involved, including the pseudopatients. A further problem is the effect the study had on public confidence in the mental health system. The publicity generated by the study may have done more harm than good if it discouraged people concerned with their mental health from seeking help. This is particularly true now when diagnostic procedures have improved out of all recognition, but the study is still taught to thousands of psychology and sociology students every year. There is a risk of continuing to bring mental health services into disrepute without just cause.

There are also important methodological questions about this study. Clearly, the study showed that it is possible to fool the system (at least as it was nearly 40 years ago). However, does this really mean that the system does not work under normal circumstances? The study can be said to lack **mundane realism** (see page 200 for a discussion) because the task of identifying fake patients is entirely different to the task of assessing real patients.

There is also something of a gap between the data gathered, which actually paints quite a mixed picture of diagnosis, and the entirely negative conclusions reached by Rosenhan. For example, Ruscio (2004) points out the fact that it is a

positive finding that, in 11 of the 12 cases, the same diagnosis was reached. It at least shows very good *reliability* (i.e. consistency) in psychiatric diagnosis. In addition, it was noticed in every case (admittedly after varying time lags) that the patient no longer had symptoms and they were thus released from hospital. The diagnoses of a psychosis in remission is entirely consistent with the behaviour of the pseudopatients.

> ## Exam tip
>
> Evaluation questions may ask you either to evaluate the methodology or to assess using alternative evidence. Be clear what to write for each type of question.

What does alternative evidence tell us?

Procedures have changed since Rosenhan's time

There have been important changes to systems of psychiatric diagnosis since Rosenhan's study. At that time, the standard system was the second edition of the DSM (DSM-II). We are now on the fourth edition with revisions (DSMIV-TR). One of the major reasons for continuing to work on newer versions of systems like this is to improve the validity of diagnosis. One way that newer versions have tightened up on diagnosis is in specifying that symptoms must occur with particular frequency or over a particular period. For example, in the DSM-IV system, hearing voices must now take place for over a month before this can be used as a basis for diagnosing schizophrenia. This suggests that Rosenhan's conclusions are now dated and cannot be applied to the current systems of diagnosis.

The system may still be fooled

Because of the ethical issues involved, mental health professionals and academics do not normally carry out pseudopatient designs any more. However, journalists and others still attempt to catch the system out. Rosenhan suggested that one test of the validity of diagnosis was whether doctors and other health professionals could recognise that in fact some of their patients had no symptoms at all. Slater (2004) claims to have presented herself to nine hospital emergency rooms with the same symptom as Rosenhan's pseudopatients. In most cases, she reports receiving a diagnosis of psychotic depression. Slater's reported findings are very consistent with Rosenhan's. However, according to Moran (2006), a number of experts have challenged the truthfulness of Slater's claims, so the credibility of her evidence is unclear.

In 2008, the BBC asked a panel of three mental health experts to assess ten volunteers and distinguish the five real patients from five pseudopatients and to identify their condition. The experts achieved a 50 per cent success rate. Two patients and their conditions were successfully identified, and a third patient was correctly identified but wrongly diagnosed. In the other two cases, the experts wrongly identified two pseudopatients. These results support Rosenhan's conclusion that mental health professionals cannot reliably identify people with genuine mental health problems.

In another recent attempt to fool the system, in 1999, novelist Ian McEwan submitted a false case study based on one of his novels to the *British Journal of Psychiatry*. This described a case of the fictitious De Clerambault's Syndrome, which involves sexual stalking and is named after the French psychiatrist who

There are still concerns over the process of psychiatric diagnosis. Visit the following website: www.critpsynet.freeuk.com/antipsychiatry.htm. This is the centre of the critical psychiatry network. Have a read of some of the perspectives put forward here. How strong is the case for critical psychiatry?

first identified it. The case report was never published, suggesting that the psychiatric establishment has become wiser since Rosenhan's day!

Other sources of evidence show moderately good validity

An alternative way to assess the validity of psychiatric diagnosis is to assess patients using different systems, like DSM and ICD (the World Health Organization's system of diagnosis), and see whether the two systems lead to the same diagnosis. This is an example of concurrent validity, which is discussed in detail on page 201. In a study of concurrent validity of diagnosis, Andrews *et al.* (1999) assessed 1,500 people using DSM-IV and ICD-10. Overall, the agreement between the systems was 68 per cent. Very good agreement between the systems was found for the diagnosis of depression, substance dependence and generalised anxiety. However, there was agreement only 35 per cent of the time on post-traumatic stress, with ICD-10 identifying twice as many cases as DSM-IV. Generally, people were more likely to receive a diagnosis according to ICD-10 than according to DSM-IV. Unlike Rosenhan's study, this shows moderately good validity for psychiatric diagnosis.

Summing it up

Buss (1989)

➔ Evolutionary theory suggests that men will choose mates with particular characteristics, while women will choose mates according to different criteria.

➔ The study was a cross-cultural comparison of the factors affecting mate preferences in men and women.

➔ The aim was to test the predictions of evolutionary psychology that men would prefer young attractive and chaste women, while women would favour industrious, ambitious and high-earning men.

➔ A survey method was used with two separate measures of preferred mate characteristics.

➔ The study surveyed 10,047 participants from 33 countries and 37 cultural groups.

➔ In 36 of 37 samples, women placed more emphasis than men on financial prospects and, in 34 samples, they placed more emphasis on industriousness and ambition.

➔ In all 37 samples, men placed more emphasis on attractiveness than women.

➔ In all 37 samples, the ideal age men gave for women was significantly younger than that women specified for men. Attitudes to chastity varied widely between cultures.

➔ The greatest strength of the study was its scale. More than 10,000 people were surveyed.

➔ A major limitation was the sampling method, which varied from one country to another and was generally unrepresentative. The study also suffers from the limitations of all questionnaire studies.

➔ Later studies have supported cross-cultural similarities in mate preference and the idea that mate preferences are influenced by evolutionary factors.

Rosenhan (1973)

➔ The context to the study was concern over the validity of psychiatric diagnosis.

➔ A field study was carried out in order to test how mental health professionals would respond to pseudopatients faking a single symptom on a single occasion and then acting normally once in the role of psychiatric patient.

➔ Rosenhan himself and a set of volunteers made hospital appointments. At the appointments, they told doctors they heard voices.

➔ All were admitted to psychiatric wards where they stayed for between 7 and 52 days.

➔ In 11 of 12 cases, they were released with a diagnosis of schizophrenia in remission. In the other case, the diagnosis was manic depression in remission.

➔ Thirty per cent of fellow patients challenged the genuineness of pseudopatients, but no doctors or nurses noticed there was nothing wrong with them. In fact, doctors and nurses made very little effort to interact with patients.

➔ Normal behaviour in the pseudopatients was interpreted as symptoms of mental disorder.

➔ In a follow-up procedure, staff in another hospital rated all new patients for likelihood of being Rosenhan's pseudopatients.

- Forty-one of 193 new patients over the next three months were judged to be pseudopatients. In fact, all were genuine patients.

- The major strengths of the study were its real-life setting and importance to the mental health system.

- The major limitation is that the task of spotting fake patients lacks realism. This is not part of the day-to-day work of mental health professionals.

- Studies like this also raise ethical issues of deceit, consent and potential harm to others suffering symptoms who might be put off the mental health system.

- Although for ethical reasons mental health professionals do not normally carry out pseudopatient studies, journalists have done so and found that it is still possible to fool the system.

Consolidate your understanding

The individual differences studies

Use the following activities to run the information in this chapter through your mind. Each activity is designed to help you process the information in a different way, which should help you ensure you understand it and make it easier to remember.

Wordsearch

```
A  S  S  E  U  L  I  E  R  U  T  L  U  C  E
Y  I  L  T  I  M  O  C  T  S  T  B  D  D  V
T  S  A  Y  A  E  V  O  I  A  S  T  T  R  I
I  O  B  T  O  Y  V  L  I  P  M  P  C  E  M
T  N  E  I  T  A  P  O  D  U  E  S  P  O  O
S  G  L  L  R  A  I  G  L  T  S  Y  E  P  A
A  A  T  I  O  I  O  I  R  U  V  C  A  M  P
H  I  N  T  I  U  V  C  B  E  T  H  B  I  I
C  D  D  R  E  L  I  A  B  I  L  I  T  Y  L
P  A  R  E  N  T  A  L  L  S  T  A  O  A  P
P  I  N  F  C  S  R  E  V  I  R  T  I  N  A
E  U  T  T  I  E  C  E  O  A  D  R  S  S  I
M  Y  C  T  L  T  I  N  S  A  N  I  T  Y  M
T  L  C  I  I  S  P  T  R  T  B  S  T  T  V
Y  L  T  I  S  O  T  C  E  E  B  T  I  Y  U
```

Buss	ecological
mate	culture
evolution	insanity
Trivers	pseudopatient
parental	diagnosis
fertility	psychiatrist
chastity	reliability
ambition	deceit
validity	

Crossword

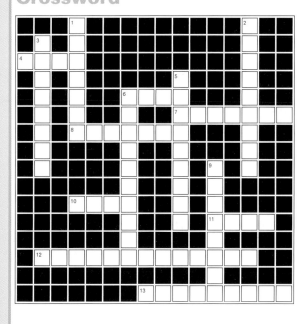

Across

4. What the pseudopatients' voices said
6. Mentally healthy enough to manage one's own affairs
7. A problem with Rosenhan's procedure
8. Confirmed that women are choosier over sexual partners
10. A problem with all questionnaire studies
11. Example of a study with a very small sample
12. Dodgy sampling procedure used by Buss
13. Process of identifying a disorder in a patient

Down

1. Showed reasonable validity for modern diagnosis
2. Object to the implications of evolutionary psychology for women
3. Not currently having sex
5. The probability of immediately reproducing
6. Strength of Buss's study
9. Rated as important by women in men

Wordsearch and crossword solutions begin on page 231.

Consolidate your understanding

Cloze

Buss (1989)

Evolutionary theory suggests that men will choose mates with particular characteristics, while women will choose mates according to different criteria. The study was a cross-_____ comparison of the factors affecting mate preferences in men and women. The aim was to test the predictions of _____ psychology that men would prefer young, attractive and chaste women, while women would favour industrious, ambitious and high-earning men. A _____ method was used with two separate measures of preferred mate characteristics. The study surveyed 10,047 participants from 33 countries and 37 cultural groups. In 36 of 37 samples, women placed more emphasis than men on financial prospects and, in 34 samples, they placed more emphasis on industriousness and _____. In all 37 samples, men placed more emphasis on attractiveness than women. In all 37 samples, the ideal age men gave for women was significantly _____ than that women specified for men. Attitudes to chastity varied widely between cultures. The greatest strength of the study was its scale. More than 10,000 people were surveyed. A major limitation was the _____ method, which varied from one country to another and was generally unrepresentative. The study also suffers from the limitations of all _____ studies. Later studies have supported cross-cultural similarities in mate preference and the idea that mate preferences are influenced by evolutionary factors.

Rosenhan (1973)

The context to the Rosenhan study was concern over the validity of psychiatric _____. A field study was carried out in order to test how mental health professionals would respond to pseudopatients faking a single symptom on a single occasion and then acting normally once in the role of psychiatric _____. Rosenhan himself and a set of volunteers made hospital appointments. At the appointments, they told doctors they heard voices. All were admitted to psychiatric wards where they stayed for between 7 and 52 days. In 11 of 12 cases, they were released with a diagnosis of schizophrenia in remission. In the other case, the diagnosis was manic depression in _____. Thirty per cent of fellow patients challenged the genuineness of pseudopatients, but no doctors or nurses noticed there was nothing wrong with them. In fact, doctors and nurses made very little effort to interact with patients. Normal behaviour in the pseudopatients was interpreted as symptoms of mental disorder. In a _____-up procedure, staff in another hospital rated all new patients for likelihood of being Rosenhan's _____. Forty-one of 193 new patients over the next three months were judged to be pseudopatients. In fact, all were genuine patients. The major strengths of the study were its real-life setting and importance to the mental health system. The major limitation is that the task of spotting fake patients lacks _____. This is not part of the day-to-day work of mental health professionals. Studies like this also raise _____ issues of deceit, consent and potential harm to others suffering symptoms who might be put off the mental health system. Although for ethical reasons mental health professionals do not normally carry out pseudopatient studies, journalists have done so and found that it is still possible to fool the system.

For help completing the cloze activity, see the 'Summing it up' section for this chapter.

Consolidate your understanding

Concept maps

Complete the empty boxes and you will have a visual revision plan.

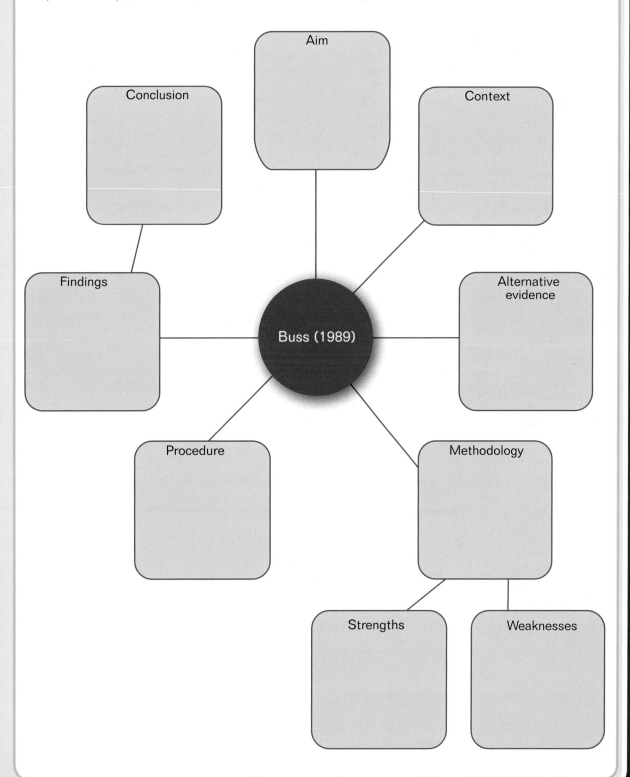

Consolidate your understanding

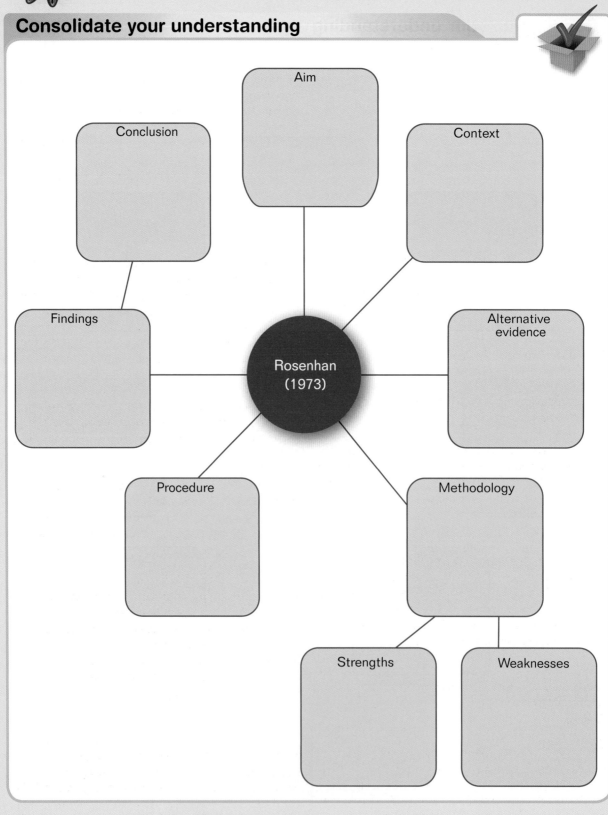

Aim

Conclusion

Context

Findings

Rosenhan
(1973)

Alternative
evidence

Procedure

Methodology

Strengths

Weaknesses

Exam focus

Buss
Context and aim

Evolutionary theory is the key here. You need to be clear about the pressures on a population that may have driven humans to display consistent mating choices and behaviours. And there are three clear points here in the text. You don't have to introduce evolution, just get on with the points! Oh, and don't forget the **aim**!

Procedure

It's enormous! The overall numbers in the sample should be exact. You have to **pick specific details** of the sampling to emphasise, with examples (e.g. small samples in some countries, differences in sampling details, exceptions). Plan this from the start: select and make notes no bigger than you could write out in **12 minutes**.

Findings and conclusions

It's enormous too. You must cover the major conclusions but you will have **less than 3 minutes** for each so you will need a sentence or two with an example in each case. This one will need planning! The Table 9.2 results must be memorised! Write your version out again and again until your teacher and your watch say you have a **good 12 minute answer.**

Evaluation of method

You must **stress both positives and negatives** here. It is a reasonable attempt to get a cross-cultural sample but it falls well short of ideal (e.g. some tiny samples). There is also the issue of whether the method of questioning would in some cases evoke social norm-type responses.

Critical assessment

There are two strands to the argument. One is obviously 'compare and contrast' with other studies. This will be enough for very good marks but pay attention to the **Rule of 4** and the **12 minute limit**. The other strand is the 'leap of faith' backwards from results to hypothesising about evolutionary history. Steven Rose (*Psychology Review*,16.3, Feb 2011) makes the case for doubting that leap. **We have no actual behavioural evidence from the past.** Buss is speculating based on current, often disputed, evidence. Studies of remote groups are still 'polluted' by global values and not historical throwbacks.

Unfortunately Buss is a very bullish proponent of his brand of evolutionary study and attracts considerable and well-founded criticism from biologists in particular. What is key for the critical assessment question is what alternative evidence says about the original study. So you only need enough information about the alternative evidence to allow you to comment on how it relates to the original.

Rosenhan
Context and aim

You will need to tease out three good points from the text to go with the **aim**. You must emphasise that this investigation sprang from a clash between the medical approach and those who believed there was a social component to all behaviour – so diagnosis had a social dimension and was less clear-cut than the medical approach suggested.

Procedure

There were two studies, so you do need details from each. The details need to be **exact**. Be clear about what the pseudopatients did in the first study.

Findings and conclusions

Divide the findings of the first study up under **headings** of '**Quantitative**' (timing of discharges) and '**Qualitative**' (comments by staff and patients, staff logs of patient behaviour). Keep the findings of the second study short and exact.

Evaluation of method

Please remember that **the participants were the medical staff**, not the pseudopatients, so any ethical criticism relates to them (e.g. the staff were deceived, their self-esteem may have been damaged when the deception was revealed, etc). Criticism in the second study relates to the deception of the staff by Rosenhan.

Critical assessment

The study itself can be criticised, and the grounds for doubting whether there was misdiagnosis – or just appropriate 'playing safe' – **must** be aired. Rosenhan's conclusions may not be fully justified. Be careful about the validity of some follow-up studies – flag up any doubts about Slater for instance. You will have to cut this one down to size and follow the **12 minute limit**! Remember the point of this question is how alternatives reflect on the original study.

10 Research methods

This chapter includes:

I should be able to:

Define and give advantages and disadvantages of qualitative and quantitative research methods, including:

- laboratory experiments
- field experiments
- natural experiments
- correlations
- observations
- questionnaires
- interviews
- case studies.

What could I be asked?

There is no guarantee that future exams will keep precisely to this wording or mark allocation. However, it is likely that any questions you are asked about research methods will be much like the following:

1. Outline **one advantage** and **one disadvantage** of using a natural experiment in this research [3]

2. Outline **one advantage** and **one disadvantage** of using a correlation in this research [3]

Throughout the chapters on the approaches and studies, you have encountered different research methods and considered some of their strengths and weaknesses. This chapter will help you to consolidate and extend your understanding.

Figure 10.1

Qualitative and quantitative data

Some investigations produce numerical data; this is called **quantitative data** as it indicates the *quantity* of a psychological measure. For example, the speed of a reaction time or the rating of a personality factor. These kinds of measures are most often associated with particular research methods, such as experiments and correlations. It is, however, possible to produce quantitative data from observations, questionnaires or interviews – for example, by recording the number of times a behaviour is observed or by counting responses to closed questions. In Chapter 12, we look in more detail at the kinds of quantitative data that can be obtained and how they are described.

Qualitative data indicates the *quality* of a psychological characteristic and comes from research that generates in-depth, descriptive findings. This is typical of observations in which particular behaviours are the focus of an observer's detailed account or questionnaires, interviews and case studies in which responses to open questions elicit elaborate reporting of feelings, beliefs or opinions. For example, rather than counting the number of times a behaviour occurs, behaviours may be described in detail.

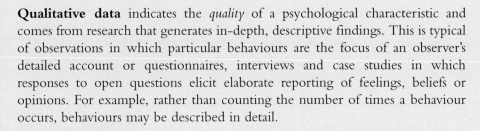

Box 10.1

Qualitative and quantitative approaches to research

Quantitative approaches aim for objectivity in data collection. The researcher should be independent and unbiased in their observations. Qualitative research, in contrast, is concerned with deriving a fuller understanding of the meaning of the data, especially within its social context. A characteristic of such research is thus that the researcher aims to gain an internal perspective on the data. The researcher, rather than some inanimate tool such as a questionnaire, becomes the primary instrument for data collection. They therefore try to understand the participants' perspective. To this end, participants in qualitative research may sometimes be included within the research team. In quantitative research, on the other hand, efforts are made to reduce the participants' knowledge of the aims of a study and they may even be deceived in order to achieve this.

In the study conducted by Rosenhan (see page 170), the pseudopatients recorded qualitative data about the way that they were responded to by nurses, doctors and other patients – for example, writing down what was said to them. They also collected quantitative data – for example, recording the total number of times they were spoken to or ignored by staff.

Experiments

An experiment is a way to carry out an investigation in which one variable is manipulated by the experimenter and the effect of this change on another variable is observed or measured. In this way, the experimenter can see whether the variable they are manipulating *causes* the other variable to change too. If it does, there is said to be a cause-and-effect relationship between the two variables. The variable causing the change, the one being manipulated by the researcher, is called the **independent variable** (or IV). The variable being measured, which varies as a consequence of the changes in the IV, is called the **dependent variable** (or DV). The measure of the DV provides quantitative

Glossary

dependent variable – the factor in an experiment that is measured by the researcher. Changes in this factor are predicted to be caused by (i.e. dependent upon) changes in the independent variable.

independent variable – the factor in an experiment that is manipulated, changed or compared by the researcher. It is expected to have an influence upon the dependent variable.

control condition – a condition in an experiment characterised by the absence of the IV. It is used as a baseline to compare with an experimental condition.

experimental design – the way in which participants are allocated to levels of the IV.

counterbalancing – a way to ensure that participants do not all carry out the different conditions in an experiment in the same order. This overcomes order effects by making sure that the levels of the IV are completed in different orders by different participants in a repeated measures design.

data. An experimenter can be sure that it is only the IV that is causing a change in the DV as all other variables are closely controlled.

The independent variable of a study will exist in two or more forms, called **levels** or **conditions**. A simple example would be the measurement of performance under high and low-stress conditions. The IV here is the stressor and two levels might be achieved by having a large or small audience present. The DV, of performance, could be measured as speed to perform a task, such as assembling a simple jigsaw puzzle. Two more complex examples are from your core studies. In the first experiment, in Loftus and Palmer's study (see page 125), there were five levels of the IV – five different verbs used in a leading question. The DV in this case was the participant's estimate of speed. Sometimes an experimental condition is compared to one in which the IV is absent – this is called the **control condition**. In Asch's study (see page 81), accuracy of the participants' judgements was recorded both in the presence of an opposing majority and when the participants were not under pressure from the majority. As the influence of conformity is absent in the latter situation, it is described as a control condition. In this study, the DV was indicated by whether or not the participant denied his senses and raised his hand to agree with the majority judgement about line length or not.

If an investigation uses the experimental method, it will also have a *design*. This relates to the way that participants are allocated to different levels of the IV.

Two common experimental designs are as follows:

- **Independent groups** – a separate set of participants is used for each level of the IV (i.e. each condition is 'independent'). For example, Loftus and Palmer (see page 125) used different participants for each verb (smashed, hit, etc.) and Langer and Rodin (see page 147) used different elderly residents in the groups with high and low control over their home environment. One problem with this design is that any difference between conditions might be due to individual differences between the participants rather than the effect of the IV.
- **Repeated measures** – the same group of participants is used in every level of the IV (i.e. they 'repeat' the test but under different conditions). Gibson and Walk's comparison between the reaction of a participant to the deep or shallow side of the visual cliff was a repeated measures design (see page 152). The main problem with this design arises because participants experience the experimental task more than once. As a result, their performance may improve (a practice effect) or worsen (a fatigue effect).

Laboratory experiments

A laboratory experiment is conducted in an artificial setting (i.e. the participants are in a situation that has been created for the purpose of the study). They will therefore be aware that they are participating in a study (although they may be unaware of its aims). The experimenter can then readily manipulate the independent variable to create two or more conditions and can measure the dependent variable accurately.

The contrived set-up in a laboratory experiment is important as it means that the researcher can control any extraneous variables that are thought to be likely to influence the DV. As a consequence, they can be sure that any changes in the

DV can only have been caused by the IV. This certainty is important because it means that the validity of the study is high. The degree of precision that can be exercised also means that the measurement of the DV is very accurate, increasing both validity and reliability. The high reliability is also due to having a stand-ardised procedure, which, in addition, means that replication is possible.

Think about two ways to measure attention in class. You could do it either by timing how long is spent making eye contact with the teacher or by counting the number of times students daydream. Time spent making eye contact will be very reliable as it can be measured exactly. A count of the number of times each student daydreams, however, depends on the observer's judgement of 'daydreaming' and it could not take into account the length of time they were not paying attention. Eye contact would also be a more valid measure if students daydreamed for reasons other than a lack of attention.

One problem with laboratory experiments is that, in general, the measure of the DV tends to be quite artificial; in other words, the participants' responses are being measured in a way that does not reflect day-to-day life. This is described as a lack of mundane realism. For example, Loftus and Palmer asked participants to estimate the speed of a filmed car – we are not usually asked to respond to film clips in this way.

Field experiments

Field experiments are conducted in the participants' normal environment for the situation or activity being explored. For example, field experiments might be conducted in the home for babies, in the park for dog walkers or in court for eyewitnesses. As in a laboratory experiment, the researcher creates or manipulates the levels of the independent variable. In Langer and Rodin's field experiment, the researchers set up the levels of the independent variable by creating the situations of high and low control of the environment (by allowing residents to decide where to put their plant or not, for example).

Figure 10.2 Langer and Rodin conducted a field experiment

Participants in a field experiment are in a less artificial setting than those in a laboratory setting so may be more likely to behave in true-to-life ways. If this is the case, the study would be said to have higher ecological validity. The effect of demand characteristics would also be lower as the aims of the study would be

Glossary

demand characteristics – features of an experimental setting that indicate to participants the aims of the study and so can influence their behaviour.

fatigue effect – a decline in participants' performance that arises because they have experienced an experimental task more than once. They may be bored or tired.

order effects – either practice or fatigue effects. In a repeated measures design, they can produce changes in performance between conditions that are not due to the IV so can obscure the effect of the DV.

practice effect – an improvement in participants' performance that arises because they have experienced an experimental task more than once. They may become more familiar with the task or recall their previous answers.

Glossary

reliability – whether a study produces findings that are consistent. This applies to both items within a set of data (e.g. questions in an interview) and over different occasions or with different researchers.

validity – whether a study is a true measure of the intended effect. If so, the findings should apply to situations other than that of the research setting itself.

mundane realism – the extent to which an experimental task represents a real-world situation.

less apparent. Furthermore, as participants may be unaware that the experiment is taking place, this is also likely to make their behaviour more realistic. However, not telling the participants about the experiment in advance has advantages and disadvantages in terms of ethics. On the one hand, it means that they have not been given the opportunity to give their informed consent to participate (see Chapter 11), but on the other, there is no need to deceive them about the aims.

Natural experiments

It is not always possible for the researcher to actually manipulate the IV – it may not be possible or ethical to do so. This would be the case in a study assessing people's stress levels before and after the building of a noisy road or one comparing levels of aggression in children who have violent or non-violent parental models. In cases such as these, it may still be possible to use an experimental design by finding contrasting situations that already exist and taking measures of the DV in each instance. This is called a natural or 'quasi' experiment.

Of course, it is much more difficult to impose controls in a natural experiment than in either field or laboratory experiments. There is therefore less certainty that any observed changes in the DV have necessarily arisen as a consequence of the IV. However, if the contrasting situations are chosen carefully, there may be very few extraneous variables. For example, in Chapter 2, we described natural experiments conducted by Joy *et al.* (1977) and Charlton *et al.* (2000), who compared the levels of aggression before and after the introduction of transmitted TV. It is highly unlikely that there were other, coincidental changes that could have obscured or exaggerated the effect of the IV in these instances (see page 32).

Figure 10.3 Natural experiments have investigated the effects of the introduction of transmitted television on levels of aggression in remote communities

As with field experiments, there are advantages in comparison to contrived situations. Since the difference is naturally occurring, it is less likely that demand characteristics will be apparent (although this will also depend on how obviously the measure of the DV is taken). In addition, the ecological validity of the situation is necessarily high, since the change or difference is a real one. It is likely, therefore, that the test will be a valid one and the findings will be highly representative. However, it is likely to be difficult or impossible to replicate a natural experiment.

Correlations

A correlation is a link between two variables. In a study with a correlational design, a measure is taken of two variables, each of which varies on a scale (i.e. the data collected is quantitative). The relationship between the two factors can be a:

- *positive correlation* – in which both variables increase together, for example, hours spent watching TV and frequency of aggressive behaviour
- *negative correlation* – in which one variable increases as the other decreases, for example, increasing stress and decreasing health.

Of course it is also possible for there to be *no* correlation between two factors.

Rahe *et al.* (1976) used a correlational analysis. They found a positive correlation between stressful life events and health.

The findings of a correlational study can be represented graphically, using a scattergram. This is a graph with one variable along each of the axes, with each data point (each participant's two scores) representing a single point (see also page 221).

A correlational design is useful in situations where variables can only be measured, rather than manipulated or compared, so an experimental design is not possible. This may be the case if changing the variables would not be practical, such as amount of pre-school exposure to TV, or would be unethical, such as increasing real-life exposure to violence. However, if a correlation is found between two variables, this only tells us that the two factors are related; it does not mean that one factor necessarily causes a change in the other. A correlation does not allow us to make judgements about cause and effect. Unlike in an experimental design, we cannot be sure that the changes in one variable are dependent upon the changes in another; either might be causing the effect or they may both be affected by another, different variable. This is illustrated by the example in Box 10.2.

Box 10.2

Can we tell if this pattern is causal?

Siân and Angharad have been selling friendship bracelets in the local market for over a year and are looking at the way their takings have varied. Siân looks at the pattern and it reminds her of an article in the local newspaper about thieving from shops in the town centre. When they look at the incidence of thefts and of their bracelet sales, there is a clear positive correlation. The more bracelets they sell, the higher the number of thefts. Angharad wonders whether they have made the bracelets wrong; the effect is not one of friendship at all – they seem to be making people more selfish instead!

What is the most likely explanation for this apparent relationship?

Figure 10.4 Correlations cannot tell us about causal relationships

Observations

In **observations**, data is collected by watching participants' behaviour. This is useful when direct methods, such as asking questions, are impossible (e.g. with animals) or not preferable (e.g. if this would produce demand characteristics). The findings can be analysed and interpreted in different ways depending on the nature of the data collected. Initially, recordings tend to be non-focused – that is, the observer looks at the range of possible behaviours to investigate. Subsequently, in focused observations, a set of behaviours which have been clearly defined are used. Observations of these specific actions can be made using techniques such as:

- *time sampling* – the action being performed at preset intervals is recorded (e.g. watching one child in the playground and recording every ten seconds whether he or she is behaving aggressively, non-aggressively or is not interacting with others)
- *event sampling* – a checklist of behaviours is drawn up and a tally is kept of an individual's performance of each of the items on the list.

Observations can therefore generate either qualitative or quantitative data. When detailed descriptions of events are gathered, qualitative data are produced. This could be done in non-focused observations or when long time intervals allow for in-depth recording. Alternatively, checklists or short-interval time sampling can generate quantitative data. This can readily be analysed using statistical methods and findings can be illustrated graphically.

In relation to the social setting, the observer may be either:

- a *participant* observer – so are part of the social setting, such as a researcher investigating stress at work who is employed alongside the participants
- a *non-participant* observer – they are not involved in the situation being observed, such as a researcher who comes into a workplace once a week to record employee behaviour.

In addition, an observer may be:

- *overt* – their role as observer is obvious to the participants (e.g. when the researcher is holding a clipboard)
- *covert* – the nature of the observer's role is hidden from the participants; for example, if they are disguised as a member of the social group (such as the colleague described in the first example above) or if they are physically hidden (e.g. using CCTV).

The environment in which observations take place can be natural, such as in a familiar work environment, or contrived, such as in a university laboratory. In Gardner and Gardner's observations of sign language in a chimp (see page 130), they observed Washoe both in what had become her normal environment and in test settings. In their interactions with her using ASL, they were participant observers. However, there were also non-participant observers who watched Washoe's replies but were not interacting with her.

One advantage of the observational method is that, in some situations, it is possible to ensure that participants are unaware that they are being observed. This reduces demand characteristics as participants cannot be affected by their expectations about the research. This is possible when the observer is covert, either as a participant or as a non-participant observer. For participant observers, there is the added advantage that they become involved in the social experience, so can gain insights into the emotions or motivation felt by participants. As a consequence, their findings may be more detailed and more valid. In self-reports (e.g. interviews or questionnaires), people may not describe their behaviour accurately. Observations may therefore be more valid than these methods.

There are also disadvantages to the observational method. Especially if they are participant, observers may become too involved in the situation, and will thus produce subjective, biased records. A strict scientific approach would see this as problematic, although a more qualitative approach may not (see page 185). If an observer is covert but participant, it may be difficult for them to record their findings immediately, thus errors may arise as they have to remember events. If researchers attempt to overcome these issues or to increase the volume of data generated by having multiple observers, another problem may arise: each observer does not necessarily arrive at the same record of behaviours having viewed the same scene. This is described as having low inter–observer reliability – that is, the consistency between observers is poor. Finally, there are issues of privacy and consent as participants may be unaware that they are involved in a study. This is particularly so in instances of covert observation in which the observer's role is disguised.

Questionnaires

A questionnaire is called a 'self-report' measure as participants provide information directly about themselves. They consist of a set of written questions that can use a range of different questioning techniques. These include:

- *closed questions* – these have a small number of fixed choices for answers, such as 'yes' or 'no'; for example, 'Did you have a holiday this year?'
- *open questions* – these can elicit longer, fuller answers; for example, 'Describe a stressful aspect of your holiday' or 'How did your feelings change during the time you were taking medication?'
- *semantic differentials* – opposing pairs of words are placed at each end of a line along which the participant places a mark (see Box 10.3); they can be used to measure emotions
- *Likert scales* – a statement is presented and a range of simple responses is offered; the participant selects one from several choices (see Box 10.3); they can be used to measure attitudes.

Glossary

inter-observer reliability – the extent to which two observers will produce the same records when they watch the same event.

self-report measures – data collection techniques, such as interviews and questionnaires, in which the participant is required to provide information about their own experiences (e.g. their beliefs or feelings).

Box 10.3

Examples of question types in questionnaires

Likert scale:

• I am an easy-going person	strongly agree	agree	don't know	disagree	strongly disagree
• There is not much that really bothers me at work	strongly agree	agree	don't know	disagree	strongly disagree
• People generally think I get wound up too easily	strongly agree	agree	don't know	disagree	strongly disagree
• I feel sorry for people who are stressed	strongly agree	agree	don't know	disagree	strongly disagree
• I work best under pressure	strongly agree	agree	don't know	disagree	strongly disagree

Semantic differential:

How did you feel during the robbery?

calm	|...|	tense
afraid	|...|	bold
confused	|...|	clear-headed
interested	|...|	fed up

Questionnaires are important tools as they can be used to investigate people's feelings and thoughts – for instance, their attitudes, beliefs or intentions. This is useful as these things cannot be investigated by observations alone. The method itself is very flexible as the different questionnaire techniques provide a range of ways to obtain different styles of data. Closed questions produce numerical (i.e. quantitative) results, which are easy to collate, score and compare, and can be analysed statistically. Furthermore, because such questions are readily understood and answered, they tend to produce relatively reliable and replicable findings. Open questions, in contrast, produce detailed qualitative data and can give greater insight into the reasons behind people's responses, such as their attitudes or beliefs. Bennett-Levy and Marteau (see page 108) used a questionnaire with closed questions about feelings towards different kinds of animals. This meant that particpants' responses to different species could readily be analysed and compared.

In comparison to interviews, questionnaires have the advantage of being less threatening as the participant is not face-to-face with the researcher. People are therefore more likely to respond honestly to questions about socially sensitive issues, such as stress, sexuality or drug use. Questionnaires are also cheaper and quicker than interviews because they do not require a specialist to administer them.

However, questionnaire techniques have disadvantages too. Closed questions offer a small number of possible answers so may not allow participants to say exactly what they mean. If this is the case, results may not reflect the individual's true opinions or feelings, thus lowering the validity of the findings. Validity may also be affected by participants' response biases. People tend to answer questions in rather set ways, preferring to make consistent responses, such as always answering 'yes'. Participants also tend to give the answers that they think people ought to; this is called a **social desirability bias**. Validity and reliability may be reduced because people may simply be unable to self-report accurately. They may not, for example, be able to recall how they felt about an event or know why they behaved in a particular way. Their responses may therefore not accurately reflect their emotions or behaviours. Further distortion of the results can arise if there is a sample bias. If a questionnaire has to be returned by post, for example, certain sorts of people may be more likely to put a stamp on the envelope and so contribute to the sample.

Interviews

Unlike a questionnaire, the questions in an interview are direct – that is, asked face-to-face (or sometimes over the telephone). In other ways, however, the methods are similar – for example, employing open and closed questioning techniques. A good interview uses questions that are non-leading and clearly understandable. The language used should also be jargon-free and questions should avoid double negatives. The responses given by participants are organised by the interviewer and may be interpreted. Depending on the style of interview used, the sequence of questions may or may not be predetermined. In *structured interviews*, the wording of questions and their order are fixed. In *unstructured interviews*, the topics to be covered may be pre-decided, but the order and nature of questions tend to follow the participant's lead.

Glossary

sample – the members of the target population who become participants in a study.

The structured interview technique enables researchers to elicit information about the same issues from many participants. As questions are consistent, the reliability is likely to be higher than in unstructured interviews. As the data produced is simpler (i.e. quantitative), structured interviews are also easier to analyse than unstructured ones. However, unstructured interviews allow researchers to gather more detailed, qualitative data and provide access to information that may not be obtained in inflexible structured interviews. For example, while it is easy to count up how many times an individual says 'yes' to closed questions about sources of stress to which they are exposed, a researcher is more likely to understand how the individual is feeling from answers to open questions. Clinical interviews, as used in the psychodynamic approach (see page 53), are unstructured, allowing the researcher to explore avenues of interest.

Figure 10.5 Interviews are flexible as the researcher can respond to the participant's comments

Unlike when responding to a questionnaire, participants being interviewed may be more likely to respond in socially desirable ways because they are face-to-face with another person. The interviewers themselves may also be affected by the social situation. They may have preconceived beliefs about what they expect to find, or about the individual, and this may bias the questions they ask or the interpretation they place on the answers. These are issues of subjectivity and are especially problematic in unstructured interviews where the questions can vary. The potential for differences between interviewers also lowers inter-interviewer reliability. Different researchers investigating the same topic with the same participants are less likely to gain the same results if they are using an unstructured technique than a structured one. This inconsistency in unstructured interviews also means that analysis, comparison and generalisation of the findings are more difficult than for structured interviews.

Case studies

There are several key differences between case studies and other research methods. A case study focuses on a single instance – usually one person (or animal), although it could be a family or an institution. This individual is explored in detail, using other methods such as interviews, observations and tests. Another difference is that the reasons for conducting case studies may be different from other research. Experimental studies and other methods aim to discover new evidence, whereas case studies are often conducted as a consequence of an event or situation that has already happened. This was not so in Gardner and Gardner's investigation of Washoe, but is in many case studies in psychodynamic psychology, such as in Freud's study of Little Hans (see page 46). This case study aimed to help relieve Little Hans's distress, which illustrates a further difference – that, in case studies, we can investigate situations that would be unethical to generate, so they offer an invaluable source of information about unusual events.

One advantage of case studies is the detail of the data collected. Although quantitative data can be collected – as Gardner and Gardner did with Washoe

– more typically, qualitative data are obtained. Using several different techniques, a researcher can gather much varied information and can then explore the findings that seem most interesting or useful in depth. The use of several techniques also enables the researcher to be more certain about their findings if each method suggests the same conclusion (i.e. it increases validity). This is called triangulation. However, case studies are impossible to replicate as no two cases are the same. As a consequence, they cannot be replicated to improve reliability or to verify findings. The uniqueness of case studies also means that the findings cannot be generalised to other people. Finally, the researcher may lack objectivity. This may be a consequence of their theoretical perspective or the intensity of their relationship with the participant, which causes them to ask questions or interpret responses in biased ways.

Qualitative and quantitative methods compared

In general, quantitative data is relatively reliable. For example, the use of closed questions in an interview or a checklist in an observation is more likely to generate consistent findings than are open questions or non-focused observations. Numerical data is also easier to analyse. Numbers can readily be used in a mean, median or mode to indicate the 'average' score in a group. Such data can also be illustrated graphically so sets of data can be easily compared. This would also help to show any trends or patterns in the results. Finally, only quantitative data can be used in statistical testing. This is important when a decision needs to be made about whether a particular pattern that can be seen in a data set could simply have arisen by chance (rather than being due to the IV, for example).

Qualitative data, by contrast, is more informative in terms of detail. It can provide both a depth and a breadth of coverage of a topic that is likely to be absent in quantitative data. As a consequence, it is possible that quantitative data may fail to identify the key issues in an investigation if that particular variable was not the focus of the study. For example, in an experiment, there is likely to be only one (or a small number) of measures or manipulated variables – if the particular factors chosen for attention are not, in reality, the most important, the investigation may misrepresent the situation. The findings may attach greater significance to the particular factors that were tested than they really deserve. A similar distortion may occur in an interview or questionnaire using closed questions. In the absence of the opportunity to say what really matters, respondents would be forced to misrepresent their views or feelings. In these cases, qualitative data would be more likely to provide an accurate representation of the real world.

Summing it up

- Qualitative data are detailed and descriptive and can be obtained from questionnaires, interviews and case studies using open questions and from observations.

- Quantitative data are numerical and are obtained using methods that score variables, such as experiments, correlational studies, observations using checklists and self-report methods using closed questions.

- In an experiment, an IV is manipulated and the effect on a DV is measured. Participants are allocated to levels of the IV and other possible variables are controlled.

- Experiments may be conducted in laboratory or field settings; the former giving greater control. The researcher can therefore be more certain that changes in the DV are the result of changes in the IV. Natural experiments utilise situations in which an existing change provides the different levels of the IV. Such situations are likely to be highly representative of the real world.

- A correlational study measures two variables. These may correlate positively (both increase together) or negatively (one goes up as the other goes down). Alternatively, no correlation may be found. In correlations, variables that cannot be manipulated can be studied, which is useful. However, if a link is found, this does not imply a causal relationship.

- Observational studies record behaviour by watching participants. The role of the observer in relation to the observed situation can vary – for example, in the extent of their involvement and visibility. Records may be highly structured (e.g. using checklists) or less focused. Observations are useful when participants cannot be asked questions, especially when they are unaware that they are being watched. However, observers may be biased, reducing validity.

- Self-report methods include questionnaires and interviews and can investigate feelings or attitudes. Each method can ask open or closed questions. Both allow the collection of data that cannot be observed but in either case there may be response biases such as social desirability.

- Interviews are conducted face-to-face and can be relatively fixed in nature (structured) or unstructured.

- Questionnaires are in written form and can use additional questioning techniques, such as Likert scales and semantic differentials.

- Compared to interviews, questionnaires are less threatening and need less specialist training to use, but interviews are more flexible.

- A case study collects in-depth data about one individual using a range of methods. Although they provide information about unusual instances that it would be unethical to create, they cannot be replicated, the findings may not generalise to other people and the researcher may become biased.

Consolidate your understanding

Research methods

Use the following activities to run the information in this chapter through your mind. Each activity is designed to help you process the information in a different way, which should help you ensure you understand it and make it easier to remember.

Crossword

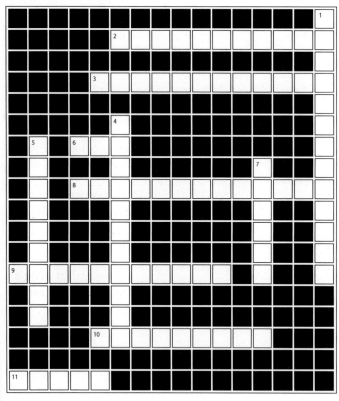

Across

2. A research method looking for a relationship between two variables
3. Data which is in numerical form
6. A type of experiment based in a controlled environment
8. A research method asking participants for information using written questions
9. Data which is detailed and descriptive
10. A research method asking participants for information face-to-face
11. A type of experiment based in the normal environment for the activity being studied

Down

1. A type of reliability that says two observers will produce the same records from the same event
4. A research method in which the researcher watches and records behaviour
5. A research method which looks at a single individual in detail
7. A type of experiment using existing differences for the IV

Crossword solutions begin on page 231.

Consolidate your understanding

Cloze

Qualitative data – for example, from interviews, _____ and case studies – are _____ and descriptive. Quantitative or _____ data come from research methods such as correlational studies, _____, questionnaires and interviews using closed questions and observations using checklists. An experiment has an _____ _____, which is manipulated, and a _____ _____, which is measured. Participants are allocated to levels of the IV and other possible variables are _____. Laboratory experiments offer more control than _____ experiments, so the researcher can be more sure of the _____ effect of the IV on the DV. _____ experiments use existing situations to provide the different levels of the IV, so they are likely to be highly representative of the real world. A correlational study measures two variables that may correlate _____ (increase together) or _____ (one goes up as the other goes down), or there may be no correlation. A correlation enables researchers to study variables that cannot be manipulated. However, if a link is found, this does _____ imply a causal relationship. In observations, the researcher watches participants. The observer's role varies in the extent of their involvement (_____ or not) and visibility (_____ or covert). Records may be highly structured (e.g. using checklists) or less focused. Observations are useful when participants cannot be asked questions and, although _____ is increased if participants are unaware they are being watched, it is reduced by observer bias. Questionnaires and _____ can investigate feelings or attitudes using _____ or closed questions to collect data that could not be obtained by observation, but response biases (e.g. social desirability) may reduce validity. Interviews are face-to-face and can be either structured or more flexible (i.e. _____). Questionnaires are in written form and can use Likert scales in questions. Questionnaires are less threatening than interviews and need less specialist training but are _____ flexible. A _____ _____ collects in-depth data about a _____ individual using a range of methods. This uniqueness is an advantage as it provides access to unusual situations it would be unethical to create, but means they cannot be replicated and the findings may not _____. The researcher may also become biased.

For help completing the cloze activity, see the 'Summing it up' section for this chapter.

11 Practical and ethical issues in research

I should be able to:

- explain what is meant by reliability and identify issues of reliability in studies
- suggest ways to ensure reliability, including split-half, test-retest and inter-rater
- explain what is meant by experimental and ecological validity
- identify issues of validity in studies and suggest ways to ensure validity, including content, concurrent and construct
- discuss ethical issues in research, including informed consent, deception, right to withdraw and risk of harm
- outline and evaluate alternative sampling methods, including opportunity, quota, random, self-selected, systematic and stratified.

What could I be asked?

There is no guarantee that future exams will keep precisely to this wording or mark allocation. However, it is likely that any questions you are asked about practical and ethical issues will be much like the following:

1. Identify **one** issue of reliability in this research, and **describe** how you would deal with this issue of reliability. [3]
2. Identify **one** issue of validity in this research, and **describe** how you would deal with this issue of validity. [3]
3. **Discuss** one ethical issue raised by this research. [3]
4. Give **one advantage** and **one disadvantage** of the sampling method used in this research. [3]

These questions will be accompanied by a summary of a study. Questions will refer to that study.

Figure 11.1 Protecting participants from physical and emotional harm is an ethical issue in psychological research

Reliability and validity

In psychological research and practice, we often have to measure things. In everyday life, we use the term 'accuracy' when we are concerned with how well something is measured. We would be worried, for example, if our electricity meter did not accurately measure how much electricity we used because we might end up paying too much in our electricity bill. When we are dealing with something like electricity consumption, defining accuracy is quite straightforward. Does the meter record correctly how much electricity we got through? There is a precise amount of electricity; we just need an accurate way of measuring it. However, the things we are trying to measure in psychological research are rarely this clear-cut. There is never a precise 'amount of intelligence' or 'amount of personality' to measure. All we can do is *estimate* how accurate our procedures and measures are. There are two estimates of accuracy: reliability and validity.

Reliability

Reliability means consistency. This is slightly different from how we use the word in everyday speech. If a student is consistently late or consistently fails to do their homework, then to a psychologist their behaviour is reliable. 'Reliable' is probably not, however, the first word that their teacher would think of to describe them! A psychological procedure or measure is reliable if it consistently measures something. Say, for example, we test a person's IQ on two occasions. If the test is reliable, we would expect them to achieve the same or very nearly the same score each time. We can ensure reliability in a number of ways:

- **Test–retest reliability**: this is the simplest way to assess reliability. As in the IQ example above, we can simply administer our test or procedure to the same people on two occasions. If there is a strong relationship between the results on the two occasions, this indicates good reliability.
- **Split-half reliability**: a slightly more complicated way to assess reliability is to split a test or procedure into two smaller tests. If the two halves of the test indicate the same thing, this is also an indicator of good reliability.
- **Inter-rater reliability**: sometimes a psychological test involves observing people and recording their actions. Alternatively, we might ask people questions. The information we obtain from observations and interviews can be used to classify people. If two or more observers or interviewers using a standard observation or interview schedule classify people the same way, then this indicates good reliability. See page 191 for further discussion.

Box 11.1

Reliability in experiments

In the core studies we looked at earlier in this unit, some of the methodological strengths and weaknesses we identified were concerned with reliability.

- Internal reliability refers to the consistency of the procedures within the experiment. If all participants had much the same experience, then the procedure has good internal reliability.
- External reliability refers to the consistency between the procedures and findings of the study and later replications. If other studies have followed the same procedures and found similar results, then the study has good external reliability.

Glossary

counterbalancing – ensuring that participants do not all carry out the different conditions in the same order.
double-blind – a procedure in which the experimenters who deal with participants are not aware of the point of the study.
experimenter bias – the phenomenon in which researchers unconsciously influence their findings because they know what they wish to find.

Validity

The other major estimate of accuracy of a psychological procedure or measure is validity. Put simply, a test or procedure is valid if it measures what it sets out to measure. In an experiment, validity means the extent to which an experimental study or method investigates what it intends to and generates results that can be generalised to other people who did not participate. The validity of an experiment can be assessed in various ways, including internal and ecological validity.

Experimental (internal) validity

Experimental validity is the extent to which we can be sure that the results of a study are a product of what we think they are. In other words, is the dependent variable (the thing we measure and makes up our results) a product of the independent variable (the thing that differs between the experimental conditions)? One factor that can affect internal validity is the reliability of our measures. Another is experimenter bias – if we know what we expect or wish to happen in an experiment, we may communicate this to participants and influence their results.

The design of a study is also important in affecting internal validity. If we use independent groups (an independent measures design), then we need to be sure that our groups of participants are very similar. Otherwise, it may be that any differences we observe between two conditions are due to differences in participant characteristics, rather than our independent variable. If we use a repeated measures design, we need to ensure that participants do not score higher in the second condition because of practice or lower because of boredom.

Ecological validity

Figure 11.2 Is a laboratory experiment likely to have lower ecological validity than a field experiment?

Ecological validity is part of external validity, the extent to which findings from a study can be generalised to other people and other situations. Ecological validity is the extent to which we can be confident that results can be generalised from the experimental situation to real-life situations.

There are two major factors affecting an experiment's ecological validity. One of these is its setting. A field experiment, which is carried out in a real-life setting, is *likely* to have better ecological validity than a laboratory experiment, which is by definition an artificial set-up. However, we also have to take into account how realistic the tasks are that participants carry out during a study. The technical term for this is the *realism* or *mundane realism* of the study. A laboratory experiment can still have reasonable ecological validity if the participants carry out realistic tasks, whereas a field experiment with poor realism can still be criticised for its ecological validity.

Threats to validity

The validity of research is threatened by two major factors:

- **Reliability and validity of measures**: in any type of psychological study, we use some way to measure our results. This might be a standard interview or questionnaire, an observed behaviour or a score on a task, such as a memory test. However results are measured, the method needs to be a valid measure of the dependent variable you are studying. An unreliable measure is by definition not valid as it will not consistently measure the variable you are interested in.
- **Extraneous variables**: in experimental studies, we also need to consider extraneous variables. An extraneous variable is anything that can impact on the results other than the independent variable you are investigating. Extraneous variables include situational variables, participant variables and experimenter effects (see Box 11.2).

Box 11.2

Types of extraneous variables

A **situational variable** is any aspect of the environment in which the experiment is conducted that might vary and affect results. Room temperature, lighting and noise are simple situational variables. Presence of observers, experimenters and fellow participants can also be situational variables.

A **participant variable** is any aspect of a participant that might impact on results. Participant variables include sex, age, culture, socio-economic status, intelligence and personality. Some participant variables are particularly important in certain types of study. If we are interested in opinions, then culture and socio-economic group become important. In a memory experiment, the memory ability of individual participants becomes an important participant variable.

Experimenter effects occur when the person running an experiment has an expectation about what the results will show, and subtly communicates this to participants.

Ensuring measures are valid

There are various approaches to ensuring that our measures are as valid as they can be:

- **Content validity**: this is the extent to which we can be sure that our test or procedure measures the right things. This becomes important when we are using a psychological test to measure a dependent variable such as IQ, personality or anxiety. For example, what cognitive abilities make up IQ? If an IQ test is to have good content validity, it should measure all the components of IQ but nothing else. A panel of experts can be used to assess content validity.
- **Concurrent validity**: this is the extent to which our test or procedure agrees with other measures of whatever variable we are assessing. For example, we can validate a new IQ test by giving people the new test along with existing IQ tests. If our test has good concurrent validity, then people will score very close to the same IQ as they do on other IQ tests.
- **Construct validity**: this is the extent to which we are actually measuring the variable we are interested in and not something else. We can demonstrate that our measure has good construct validity by identifying similar variables and making sure our measure does not measure those things. Sometimes

this is a matter of logic; we might want to measure attitudes to aggression and worry that a related variable is aggression. As long as we stick to asking about what people think of aggression and do not ask them about their own behaviour, we can ensure we are measuring the right thing. When common sense is not enough, we can ensure construct validity by measuring other related variables and see that they do not correlate strongly with the thing we are measuring. So to go back to our aggression example, if we find that our measure of attitudes to aggression *does not* correlate strongly with measures of aggression, we have helped ensure its construct validity. Of course we have not guaranteed good construct validity because we may be measuring other variables we have not thought of.

Eliminating extraneous variables

- To eliminate situational variables, each participant must take part in the experiment under identical conditions. This is much easier to achieve in a lab experiment than it is in the field. Participants will receive standard instructions in a standard environment and have a fixed amount of time to complete the experiment.
- Participant variables are only a problem if the design is independent measures (i.e. different people take part in each condition). Where this is the case, researchers need to identify the important participant variables and make sure each group is roughly matched on these. In a matched pairs design, this idea is taken further and, for every participant in one condition with certain key characteristics (which depend on the study), there is a closely matched participant in all the other conditions.
- Experimenter effects can be controlled by the use of a double-blind procedure. This means that the experiment is not conducted by anyone who knows the aim of the experiment, but by hired help who are not told what the study is about until afterwards. If those who come into contact with participants do not know the aim of the study, they cannot give it away!

Box 11.3

An example of ensuring validity in action

A psychologist is conducting a laboratory experiment into the process of making judgements alone and as part of a panel. In one condition, participants on their own rated singers for the quality of their voice by strongly agreeing, agreeing, disagreeing or strongly disagreeing with the statement 'This person has a really good voice'. In another condition, a different group of participants rated the same singers in the same way after having heard three other judges rate them highly. The aim was to see if the participants in the panel of judges rated the singers' voices more highly; this would indicate that they were influenced by the other judges.

- One issue of validity in this study is the measure used to assess quality of voice. One way to ensure validity of the measure would be to assess its **concurrent validity**. This would involve rating the singers using a standard scale (such as the 0–10 scale, as used on Strictly Come Dancing) and seeing whether the same singers came out well. If they do, then the measure has good concurrent validity.
- We might also be concerned about the **construct validity** of the measure of vocal quality because there are closely related variables, such as quality of performance. We can look at the wording of instructions to make sure they refer specifically to voice and not to performance. This will help ensure construct validity.

- **Situational variables** might be an issue in this study. To ensure they are not a problem, we would ensure that participants in both conditions received the same standard instructions and that both conditions were run in the same environment at the same time of day.
- **Participant variables** might be a particular

issue in this study because it uses an independent measures design. We could deal with this by changing the design to repeated measures or, better still, by having a matched pairs design with the pairs matched for hearing, musical taste, musical training, singing ability and generosity.

Ethical issues in research

We have seen that there are many practical issues to think about when carrying out psychological research. However, we also need to think about ethical issues. Ethics is defined by Wikipedia as follows: 'a major branch of philosophy … the study of value or quality. It covers the analysis and employment of concepts such as right, wrong, good, evil, and responsibility' (2010np). In other words, it is about understanding systems of morality. Morality is absolutely central to psychology. The ultimate aim of all psychology is to make life better for people. We are fighting a losing battle in trying to achieve this if we make life worse in any way for the people we work with! These include clients with whom professional psychologists work and those who take part in our studies. In this section, we are concerned with the latter.

The world's major professional psychological organisations publish extensive codes of ethical principles and guidelines. The following principles are based on the latest publication from the British Psychological Society (2009). Some principles are very general and others apply to particular sorts of research. The following are directly relevant to all research.

1. Consent

Researchers must take reasonable steps to obtain *real consent* from participants. Real consent is consent freely given by a participant that fully understands what they are agreeing to. Consent must therefore be:

- informed
- free from real or imagined pressure
- from participants able to understand what they are agreeing to.

Informed consent can be quite tricky to achieve because, if we give away the full aim of a study, it might affect participants' behaviour during the study. On the other hand, if we give too little away, participants might agree to take part when they would not have wished to had they known more.

Where children are being studied, a parent or adult in *loco parentis* (in place of the parent) is required to give consent. Where adults with impairments are being studied and they may find it hard to understand what is going to happen in the study, consent should be obtained from another person who would reasonably be expected to know whether the participant would wish to take

Figure 11.3 Payment should not be used by researchers in order to persuade participants to consent

part. Researchers should not use payment or their position of power over participants to persuade them to consent to activities they would not agree to anyway.

2. Deception

Deceiving participants should be avoided whenever possible. Participants should be informed of the purpose of the investigation at the earliest opportunity, which may be before or after the procedure. It is not acceptable to deceive participants when it is likely that they will object or become distressed when debriefed. Where deception is an essential part of the design of a study, the researcher has three obligations:

1   Ensure that there is no viable alternative procedure available that does not involve deception.

2   Ensure participants are properly debriefed at the earliest opportunity.

3   Consult with colleagues about participants' likely responses when they discover the deception.

3. Withdrawal

Participants should be made aware of their right to withdraw from a study at any point. Payment does not alter a participant's right to withdraw, and participants should be completely clear about this. Where children are concerned, avoidance of the procedure should be taken as withdrawal and the procedure should be ended once avoidance is observed. When debriefed, participants have the right to withdraw their data.

4. Confidentiality

Unless agreed with participants in advance, their individual results and any personal information obtained in a study should be completely confidential. Where it is likely that a participant would be identifiable following publication of results, they must agree to this at the start of the study.

5. Protection from physical and psychological harm

Participants should be protected from harm, including stress. This means that they should be exposed to no more risk than they would normally encounter in their usual lifestyle. Participants should be confident of confidentiality to prevent worry. Where the procedure does cause unexpected harm in spite of taking due care, the researcher is responsible for taking steps to rectify this – for example, offering referral to another professional. Discussion of children's results with parents, teachers, etc. should be done with caution as there is a risk of influencing their view of the child.

You can view several sets of ethical principles and guidelines online. Try reading the following. What similarities and differences can you see?

SOCIETY	WEB ADDRESS
British Psychological Society (BPS)	www.bps.org.uk/the-society/code-of-conduct/code-of-conduct_home.cfm
American Psychological Association (APA)	www.apa.org/ethics/
Australian Psychological Association (APS)	www.psychology.org.au/about/ethics/

Applying ethical principles to real research

You might think these principles are extremely reasonable. Indeed, in principle, they are. No psychologist would wish to harm or distress their participants, or to deceive them unnecessarily. However, in reality, there are many occasions when it is quite tricky to balance strict ethics against the importance of researching what you want. Let us consider one of the studies we have already looked at in detail. Had Milgram not stretched the boundaries of what is ethically acceptable, his study would have suffered from poor internal validity. Note that the sort of ethical guidelines and principles we rely on today had not been developed when most of the core studies you have looked at were carried out.

The ethics of the Milgram study

You can read a full account of Milgram's study on page 87. Looking at the ethical principles outlined on page 203, some issues leap out from his procedure. Firstly, his work is sufficiently controversial to risk altering public perceptions of psychologists. Participants did not give real consent because they believed they were taking part in a memory experiment rather than a study of obedience. They were deceived on several counts, including the purpose of the study, the status of the learner as a fellow participant, the fake shocks and, most importantly, that they might have injured or killed the learner. They suffered significant stress and, critically, they were denied their right to withdraw from the study.

This all seems pretty damning. However, the procedure could not have been carried out without these features. In some ways, Milgram paid close attention to ethics. For example, he informed participants of the purpose of the procedure at the earliest opportunity and went to considerable lengths to make sure they left the experiment in a positive frame of mind. When surveyed later, the vast majority of participants said they were glad to have taken part. We also need to consider the purpose of the study. It was, and still is, very important to understand better the participation of ordinary people in atrocities. The study was thus not performed casually, and the short-term stress suffered by participants must be balanced against the good that can come

out of such a study. Banyard and Flanagan conclude that 'Milgram was a good guy' (2005: p57).

Box 11.4

Strategies for dealing with ethical issues

We have seen that ethical issues in psychological research are quite complex. Psychological researchers care deeply about ethics. However, they also have a job to do, and there is a risk that if psychologists are too cautious about ethical issues they end up not tackling the most important issues. Unfortunately, it often seems that the more important a piece of research, the more ethical issues it can raise. Haslam and Reicher (2003) have used the term 'impeccable trivia' to describe the findings of studies where researchers have played too safe ethically and so not found really interesting, important results.

So how do psychologists steer the course between important findings with dodgy ethics, and ethical cleanliness with pointless findings? One strategy is to define ethical principles. All major psychological associations have such ethical principles and periodically review and update them. Guidelines are also periodically published to cover particular areas of research that raise ethical issues above and beyond the general ethical principles.

Consent

Consent is a particularly difficult issue for psychological research. We do not want to do things to people that they would not wish us to. On the other hand, if they knew exactly what we were going to do and why, they probably would not act naturally and there would be no point in studying them. In some kinds of observational research, we really need participants not to know they are being watched at all. Two kinds of consent thus become particularly important:

- **Presumptive consent**: in some situations, psychologists may judge that they can presume that someone would consent to being observed simply because they are in a situation where they are observed anyway.
- **Prior general consent**: another approach to gaining consent without giving too much away is to ask participants for consent to take part in several types of research. Participants need not know in which area they are participating.

Ethics committees

A researcher operating on their own will find it hard to make the complex and subtle judgements required to judge the ethics of their own research. For this reason, it is standard practice to run details of studies past an ethics committee before proceeding. Ethics committees consider the possible risks to participants' welfare and dignity. The British Psychological Society (2004) published guidelines for how to conduct the process of gaining ethical approval. These require that, wherever possible, all research should be looked at closely by a committee before it is carried out.

Sampling

Glossary

population – the group from which the sample is drawn.

For a study to have good population validity, we must have a representative group of participants. The procedure by which we select our participants is called sampling. The aim of sampling is to obtain a group of participants that are representative of our target population. The target population is the group you want to represent in the sample. There are two commonly used sampling methods that are unlikely to produce a representative sample.

Opportunity sampling

This involves asking whoever is most easily available to take part. Participants might thus be classmates, friends, family members or whoever happens to be available in the college refectory or library. This is the most common method in

student practicals. It is also used in professional research in studies where results are unlikely to be affected by age, education or socio-economic status. Thus many researchers rely on university students.

The major advantage of opportunity sampling is that it is quick and easy to carry out. This might mean we have a larger sample size than we would have if we had spent more time on obtaining a representative sample. Some types of study do not particularly require a representative sample because they focus on cognitive or physiological variables that do not tend to vary between people of different ages, sexes, social classes, etc. In these cases, it is probably acceptable to sample by opportunity.

The major disadvantage of opportunity sampling is that the sample is probably not going to be representative of the target population. This is a particular problem when we are dealing with variables that are affected by age, sex, culture and class. Typically, social-psychological variables are affected by these demographic factors, so having an unrepresentative sample can be a particular problem here.

Self-selecting (volunteer) sampling

This involves advertising for volunteers. People who respond to adverts and who meet the basic entry criteria (e.g. the right age and sex) get to take part in the study.

This approach to obtaining a sample is particularly useful when we are looking for highly unusual people. For example, in parapsychology research, we might particularly want to test the abilities of people who claim to be able to communicate by telepathy. We probably will not find many people who make such claims amongst our immediate circle, so advertising for volunteers is the best approach.

However, most people do not volunteer to take part in studies. This is therefore guaranteed to obtain an unrepresentative sample! Of all the sampling methods, this is likely to produce the most unrepresentative sample. That is a particular problem when we are studying social-psychological variables.

Figure 11.4 The volunteer sampling method is guaranteed to produce an unrepresentative sample

There are a range of ways we can obtain participants that are more representative of the target population.

Systematic sampling

This involves selecting every *n*th person on a list. We can choose *n* by dividing the population size by the sample size. So if we have a school population of 1,000 and we want a sample of 50, 1,000/50 = 20, so we could simply go down the list of pupils and select every twentieth person.

Systematic sampling represents a good trade-off between time and effort and a reasonable likelihood of obtaining a representative sample. It is pretty quick and easy to pick every *n*th person off a list and this is much more likely than opportunity or volunteer sampling to obtain a representative sample.

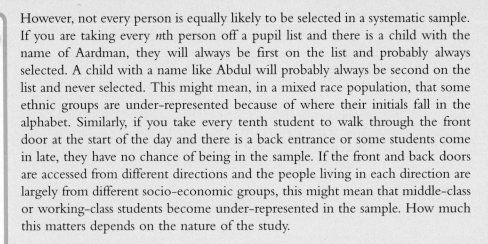

Traditionally, random samples have been obtained by putting names in a hat or by giving every member of the target population a number and taking numbers from a random number table. However, this can all be done more quickly and efficiently online now. Have a look at www.mathsyear2000. co.uk/explorer/ randomiser/. There are several ways of randomising here. The *random integers* and *random items* functions are particularly useful for sampling.

However, not every person is equally likely to be selected in a systematic sample. If you are taking every *n*th person off a pupil list and there is a child with the name of Aardman, they will always be first on the list and probably always selected. A child with a name like Abdul will probably always be second on the list and never selected. This might mean, in a mixed race population, that some ethnic groups are under-represented because of where their initials fall in the alphabet. Similarly, if you take every tenth student to walk through the front door at the start of the day and there is a back entrance or some students come in late, they have no chance of being in the sample. If the front and back doors are accessed from different directions and the people living in each direction are largely from different socio-economic groups, this might mean that middle-class or working-class students become under-represented in the sample. How much this matters depends on the nature of the study.

Random sampling

The technical definition of a random sample is one in which every member of the target population has an equal chance of being selected. You might think this is true in an opportunity sample. However, if you ask your friends or classmates, then certain types of people will be over-represented. A true random sample can be obtained by putting all the names from the population in a hat and drawing out the number you want in the sample. We can also give each member of the population a number and generate random numbers. There is even software that allows us to input names and randomly choose a sample from these.

The major advantage of random sampling is that, as everyone has an equal chance of selection, there is a very good chance that the sample will be representative of the population. It is therefore considered more representative than opportunity, self-selecting or systematic methods.

Random sampling is more time-consuming than many sampling methods. Another disadvantage is that it only 'works' in the sense of producing a representative group in fairly large samples. Randomly selecting a sample of ten people typically produces a biased sample. It takes about 200 people to be randomly selected to be reasonably sure of representativeness.

Quota and stratified samples

These are samples in which we try to be sure that as many variables in the population as possible are represented by the proportions in the sample. Thus if our target population is 55 per cent female, 45 per cent male, our sample will represent these same proportions. If 20 per cent of our population is under 21, 20 per cent of our sample will also be under 21.

In a quota sample, provided the proportions are right, any members of the target population are acceptable. There is thus an element of opportunity sampling here. If you are stopped in the street to be interviewed, the chances are that you are part of a quota. If the interviewers ignore you, it means that either you are not in their target population or they have enough participants of your age and sex.

Figure 11.5 With random sampling, there is a good chance that the sample will be representative of the population

In a stratified sample, there is a random element as well as a quota. The idea is that every member of the target population within the bounds of the quota has an equal chance of selection. To do this by hand is very complex and time-consuming, and it is normally achieved using a computer.

The advantage of quota and particularly stratified sampling methods is the strong probability of obtaining a representative sample. Stratified sampling produces the most representative samples of all. However, the disadvantage is that these are also the most complex and time-consuming sampling methods.

Summing it up

- We can estimate the accuracy of our procedures and measures by two means: reliability and validity.

- Psychological tests and procedures should be reliable (i.e. consistently measure the same thing).

- Reliability can be assessed by test-retest, split-half and inter-rater methods.

- They must also be valid (i.e. measure what they set out to measure).

- We need to be aware of both the internal and the external validity of a study.

- We also need to consider the validity of measures. This can be assessed by content validity, concurrent validity and predictive validity.

- In order to have good external validity, we must carry out research on a representative sample of participants.

- Psychological research often raises ethical issues. There are now a number of sets of ethical principles and guidelines which researchers are expected to follow.

- Some of the classic studies in psychology would not have conformed to these guidelines had they existed when the studies were carried out.

- There is sometimes a trade-off between what is ethically acceptable and what would be the most valid procedures to conduct a study.

- There are various strategies used to manage ethical issues in research. Presumptive consent and prior general consent can be employed.

- Ethics committees are intended to vet all research before it is carried out.

- Unrepresentative sampling methods include opportunity and self-selecting methods.

- Representative sampling methods include systematic, random and quota methods. Generally, the more representative methods are more time-consuming.

Consolidate your understanding

Practical and ethical issues in research

Use the following activities to run the information in this chapter through your mind. Each activity is designed to help you process the information in a different way, which should help you ensure you understand it and make it easier to remember.

Wordsearch

R	B	D	R	E	L	I	A	B	I	L	I	T	Y
U	R	S	L	A	N	R	E	T	N	I	Q	T	R
R	L	A	W	A	R	D	H	T	I	W	I	T	E
L	I	M	L	F	T	A	T	S	O	N	V	A	A
N	Y	P	A	S	A	A	I	E	U	Y	A	F	L
O	L	L	C	I	T	C	C	T	T	C	L	N	I
O	T	I	I	I	Q	R	R	E	T	A	I	O	S
A	D	N	G	U	I	O	A	R	H	M	D	I	M
T	L	G	O	P	P	O	R	T	U	N	I	T	Y
A	O	T	L	P	I	D	I	S	I	F	T	P	I
S	A	A	O	O	E	L	S	E	A	F	Y	E	D
E	E	R	C	E	P	C	A	T	C	I	I	C	I
G	T	N	E	S	N	O	C	A	E	L	B	E	P
C	O	N	T	E	N	T	P	I	T	D	O	D	D

reliability
test retest
consent
bias
opportunity
validity
ecological
deception

sampling
internal
realism
withdrawal
quota
split half
content
stratified

Crossword

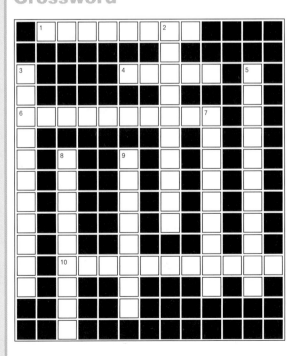

Across
1. Consent in which the participant knows what they are getting into
4. Like stratified but with an opportunity element
6. An unwanted variable that affects the dependent variable
10. Consistency of measurement

Down
2. Validity in the sense of generalising to real life
3. Believed consent
5. Unrepresentative sampling method
7. A way to ensure reliability
8. Procedure to ensure validity in which we make sure we are measuring the right variable
9. Measuring what we set out to measure

Wordsearch and crossword solutions begin on page 231.

Consolidate your understanding

Cloze

We can estimate the accuracy of our procedures and measures by two means: reliability and validity. Psychological tests and procedures should be reliable (i.e. consistently measure the same thing). Reliability can be assessed by test-_____, split-_____ and inter-_____ methods. They must also be valid (i.e. measure what they set out to measure). We need to be aware of both the internal and the _____ validity of a study. We also need to consider the validity of measures. This can be assessed by content validity, concurrent validity and _____ validity. Psychological research often raises ethical issues. There are now a number of sets of ethical principles and guidelines which researchers are expected to follow. There is sometimes a trade-off between what is ethically acceptable and what would be the most _____ procedures to conduct a study. There are various strategies used to manage ethical issues in research. Presumptive consent and prior general consent can be employed. Ethics _____ are intended to vet all research before it is carried out. In order to have good external validity, we must carry out research on a _____ sample of participants. Unrepresentative sampling methods include opportunity and self-_____ methods. Representative sampling methods include stratified, systematic, _____ and quota methods. Generally, the more representative methods are more _____-consuming.

For help completing the cloze activity, see the 'Summing it up' section for this chapter.

12 Describing data

I should be able to:

Define, outline the advantages and disadvantages of and draw conclusions from different ways of describing data, including:

- coding systems
- categorisation
- content analysis
- mean, median, mode
- range
- scattergraphs
- bar charts
- histograms.

What could I be asked?

There is no guarantee that future exams will keep precisely to this wording or mark allocation. However, it is likely that any questions you are asked about describing data will be much like the following:

1. State **one conclusion** that can be drawn from the modal scores in this research [3]

2. State **one conclusion** that can be drawn from the scattergraph in this research [3]

As we discovered in Chapter 10, quantitative data are readily derived from studies that produce numerical results, such as experiments. It is important to be aware that structured interviews or questionnaires using closed questions also produce quantitative data. Because such data are already categorised by the process of data collection, it is necessarily quantitative. However, unstructured interviews or questionnaires with open questions produce rich, detailed data. This raises a key question in how to deal with the information – whether to preserve depth of meaning or to represent the broader picture. Qualitative methods of describing the data aim to achieve the former. Alternatively, an indication of the general patterns, themes or issues raised by qualitative findings can be summarised by condensing the data using quantitative analysis. In the section that follows, we look at both ways of representing the findings of qualitative research in quantitative ways.

Coding systems

In many research situations, it is necessary to develop systematic strategies for collecting data. In an experiment, decisions must be made about how to measure the dependent variable. In methods such as observations, descriptions of the behaviours to be recorded must be developed and agreed between observers when there is more than one. This process of developing a coding system provides an outline of the variables or themes to be used. It serves a similar function to the defining variables in an experimental study. It aims to structure the data and ensure that researchers are consistent in their approach.

A coding system is a way of identifying or labelling qualitative data items. Each code is intended to represent a small, meaningful unit, which is allocated a unique symbol (e.g. a letter or a number). The way a coding system is developed depends largely on the research method being employed, although in every case the aim is for a representative and reliable measure. The system must be sufficiently flexible to allow the researcher to include all examples of the variable being measured but specific enough to ensure that the definition is valid. In essence, a coding system is a way of separating out different elements of the variable(s) being measured.

Coding in observations

One of the key issues in coding behaviours in observations is to break the stream of behaviour down into individual actions. The coding system used must be based on differences that can be seen, rather than assumed. For example, in recording indicators of stress in examination candidates, a coding system could use 'biting finger nails' or 'frowning', but not 'feels tense' or 'is guessing' because these two attributes cannot actually be observed. Items may also be coded as facial expressions, gestures, postures and speech. A good example is seen in Gardner and Gardner's coding of Washoe's use of signs (see Table 7.4 on page 134).

Coding in questionnaires and interviews

When closed questions have been used, coding in self-report measures is relatively easy; the coding system derives directly from the questions themselves. For example, look at Box 12.1; a questionnaire in which a respondent indicates 'yes' to any of the items on the left or 'no' to any on the right could be coded as 'high stress'.

Glossary

coding system – a way to organise data by representing each small, meaningful type of information (e.g. a behaviour being observed) with a different code so that they can be identified and separated.

Box 12.1

Coding in questionnaires

Do you work more than 60 hours a week?	Do you have lots of friends to whom you could turn if you were in need?
Do you have to look after an ill relative?	If things go wrong, do you tend to just shrug them off, knowing there will be something better around the corner?
When you wake up in the morning, do you dread the day?	Do you indulge in happy daydreams just for the fun of it?

This illustrates that the way questionnaire items are written dictates how they are scored. It is important to note that, when designing a questionnaire using Likert scales or semantic differentials, some items indicating each extreme should produce a 'no' answer, others a 'yes' answer.

When open questions are used, a coding system must be developed for classifying the responses so that they can be more easily interpreted and analysed. The way in which this is done will depend in part on the theoretical approach of the researcher. For example, in interpreting a response about a phobia, a researcher with a behaviourist perspective is likely to use a different coding system from one taking a psychodynamic perspective. In any situation, possible responses can be divided into different themes. For example, a behaviourist coding an interview about a phobia might look for examples of responses that indicated:

1 a possible source of reinforcement for phobic behaviour

2 indications that the phobic response has been associated with any other genuinely dangerous or unpleasant situation

3 evidence of a stimulus which could trigger the appearance of phobic behaviours.

These themes could be identified as reinforcers (1), unconditioned stimuli (2) and conditioned stimuli (3). Interview responses could then be coded using this system.

In contrast, a researcher approaching the same interview from a psychodynamic perspective might look for indications of the following:

1 reluctance to speak about a topic

2 the disguised appearance of a feared situation in the manifest content of a dream

3 descriptions of fears that could have appeared during childhood.

These themes could be identified as: unconscious repression or denial (1), a latent fear being represented in the dream (2) or key experiences from the individual's early childhood (3).

In both cases, the information derived from the interview can be coded using a system that allows the researcher to interpret their findings within a framework. This is useful as it allows situations or individuals to be compared.

Box 12.2

Should theory dictate the coding system or should the coding system evolve from the data?

In one approach to research, *grounded theory*, the explanations arise during the course of the study. This differs from the typical scientific approach in which a theoretical approach determines hypotheses and, in consequence, the nature of the coding system. In grounded theory, by contrast, hypotheses can emerge during the investigation and the coding system is flexible, with new codes and categories being added (or amalgamated or removed) as the research progresses. This inductive process, in which the theory is led by the researchers' observations, has high validity in the sense that it is driven by 'real-world' findings.

Glossary

categorisation – a way to combine codes to organise data by structuring them into related groups. This can help to identify patterns or possible relationships in the data.

Categorisation

A coding system provides the initial step in organising data. The next step is to combine these elements into categories. Let us return to the example of phobias. In the first instance, 'reinforcers' could be categorised into positive, negative and vicarious, and in the second, indicators of 'reluctance to speak about a topic' could be categorised into strategies such as silence or evasion which might also include failing to turn up to therapy sessions. In Gardner and Gardner's description of Washoe's use of language (see page 133), the signs she generated could be categorised into nouns (e.g. flower), verbs (e.g. open) and emphasisers (e.g. more). This enables the researchers to see patterns in the data more readily – for example, whether Washoe learned different aspects of language more quickly.

It is generally assumed that it is better to begin with many codes that might turn out to be measuring the same phenomenon and eventually combine them than to start with too few. The latter approach risks losing detail and making the analysis less meaningful.

Strengths of coding and categorisation

Coding and categorisation allow researchers to structure complex data so it is possible to collect meaningful results and produce an overall description of the findings. Where more than one researcher is recording data, precisely defined codes help to improve inter-rater reliability as each code can be clearly described, so when using the same coding system, raters should record the same codes from the same source (e.g. from a person being interviewed or observed). If raters do not have high reliability, the definitions of the codes can be refined or the raters can discuss the differences in order to overcome them.

When qualitative data have been collected, such as from open questions in questionnaires, coding systems provide a way to convert this into quantitative data so that a simple summary can be produced to describe the overall patterns present in the results.

Weaknesses of coding and categorisation

Defining codes and categories is difficult. For example, in an observation, the behavioural stream is continuous – it is not necessarily obvious where one behaviour ends and the next starts. The validity of the findings depends on whether the codes and categories reflect real-world differences in meanings.

One aspect that is particularly difficult to code in observations is feelings, as they can only be inferred (e.g. from facial expression) not observed directly. For example, in Langer and Rodin's study, the nurses observed residents and recorded their alertness and the time they spent with other residents. Their feelings of happiness, however, could only be measured through a questionnaire. However, some studies need to code for emotions, such as Gibson and Walk's assessment of fear in the animals on the visual cliff (see page 154). The code used was 'freezing' as this is an observable response.

When codes and categories are used to extract quantitative measures from qualitative data, there is a loss of information. In this respect, coding systems reduce the validity of the data as there is less chance that the description will reflect the depth and variety of the original findings.

Content analysis

Both coding systems and categorisation are essential to the process of content analysis. This method is an indirect method of investigation using sources from the media, such as children's books or television programmes. The technique can be used to study real-life issues, such as stereotyping in media models. For example, gender-specific behaviours, excessive dieting or violence could be investigated using content analysis.

In conducting a content analysis, the first step is for the researcher to decide which material is to be sampled (e.g. the number of TV programmes to be analysed and the channels to be watched). The next decision is about the coding units. For example, in an investigation of gender-role stereotypes in children's TV programmes, coding units could include the gender-role stereotype of each character, activity or scene. In an analysis of a book, the coding units could be words or the themes in each paragraph. Categories can then be constructed – for example, 'female in stereotyped female role', 'male in stereotyped female role', 'female in neutral role', etc. Categories could also include whether the portrayal is a positive or a negative one. Examples of actual text with its coding can provide qualitative data. The numerical totals of items in each code or category can provide quantitative data.

Strengths of content analysis

Content analyses are based on real-life sources of information (e.g. current TV programmes or newspapers) rather than the artificial situations that typify experimentation. This offers high ecological validity as it indicates the influences present in media to which we are genuinely exposed. Another advantage of content analyses over other methods is that they can be replicated easily. This is possible because TV programmes, printed material, etc. are permanent. This means that exactly the same sources can be accessed and used by another researcher for comparison and to replicate the study. Furthermore, comparisons can be made over time, such as the aggression level in current children's comics compared to ones from 20 years ago. This is possible as archived material can be used.

Glossary

content analysis – a technique for describing information from transcripts of interviews and from media, such as TV, newspapers and songs. Specific words, emotions or ideas are allocated coding units, which can be used to extract qualitative examples or count quantitative totals.

Figure 12.1 As content analyses can be conducted on archived material, comparisons can be made over time

Weaknesses of content analysis

Unlike the conclusions that can be drawn from experiments, causal judgements cannot be made on the basis of a content analysis. Although evidence from sources of media can illustrate patterns, these could be either reflecting or causing differences in the social world. When a researcher selects coding units and categories, their decisions may be biased, which potentially lowers the objectivity of the method and threatens validity. In addition, the way that they implement the coding units can reduce the validity of the findings. One major issue here is the influence of expectations – researchers are likely to find what they expect to simply because they are more likely to identify examples that confirm their ideas than those that contradict them.

Box 12.3

Collecting numerical data

In general, numerical data are relatively easy to organise. Results from tests or measures used in experiments and other methods designed to generate quantitative data fall into different *levels of measurement*. This refers to the nature of the numerical data and there are four different levels:

* *Nominal data* – results in named categories. The items do not lie on a linear scale but fall into discrete categories (e.g. total number of different types of aggressive acts: bite, kick or pinch).
  * The answer to Loftus and Palmer's question 'Did you see any broken glass?' is an example of nominal data.
* *Ordinal data* – points that lie in order on a scale. The points themselves may be numbers or words, but in either case the

'distances' between the values are only representative; the scale does not necessarily have equal divisions. Examples include a stress scale in which 0 = not stressed and 10 = unbearably stressed; an indicator of the importance of attractiveness in a partner on a rating scale reading very/fairly/somewhat/not at all; or how certain an eyewitness feels about their accuracy, estimated as a percentage. It is more informative than nominal data as scores have a value (i.e. they are relatively 'bigger' or 'smaller').

* The scales used to rate the animal species in Bennett-Levy and Marteau's study produced ordinal data.
* *Interval data* – points on a linear scale with equal divisions. The scale has no real zero – for example, scores on a simple maths test (in which all the sums are equally difficult). Interval

data are useful as the equal value between each point on the scale means they can be used in more effective mathematical procedures than ordinal data.
- Milgram's voltage scale is an interval scale as each division is equal but they relate only indirectly to the measured variable of obedience.

- *Ratio data* – points on a linear scale which has equal divisions between the points and a zero baseline.
- Rosenhan's measure of the time spent by pseudopatients in conversation with staff produced ratio data.

The mean, median and mode: measures of central tendency

A measure of central tendency indicates the 'middle' or typical point of a data set. There are three different measures, used with data with different levels of measurement.

The mode

The mode is the most frequent score in the data set. If two (or more) items are equally common, there will be two (or more) modes. For example, if two categories of data are most frequent, the data set is described as 'bi-modal'.

For example, in Table 12.1, the most frequent first language at Ysgol y Blaenau had a total of 58, so the mode is Welsh.

Table 12.1 First language of children in two schools

	WELSH	ENGLISH	BENGALI	POLISH	OTHER
Number of participants in Ysgol y Blaenau	58	25	8	4	5
Number of participants in Hilltop School	38	38	11	2	4

The median

The median is the score in the middle when the items in a data set are put in order from smallest to largest (i.e. when they are ranked). If there are two numbers in the middle, these should be added together and divided by two.

Table 12.2 Rating 1–5 of aggressiveness of children's play

BOYS	2	3	2	2	1	4	5	2	5	5	4	4
GIRLS	1	2	3	2	2	4	1	1	2	5	2	3

For example, in Table 12.2, the median for boys can be calculated as follows:

- Arrange the scores in rank order: 1, 2, 2, 2, 2, 3, 4, 4, 4, 5, 5, 5.
- Identify the middle score: 1, 2, 2, 2, 2, 3, 4, 4, 4, 5, 5, 5.
- Where there are two in the middle, add them together and divide by two: 3 + 4 = 7, 7/2 = 3.5.
- The median aggressiveness score for boys is 3.5.

The mean

The mean is the arithmetic average. It is worked out by adding up all the scores in the data set and dividing the total by the number of scores. Zero scores should be included in the number of items.

Table 12.3 Galvanic skin response (GSR) of phobics in response to feared objects before and after therapy (the GSR is a measure of conductance that rises in response to arousal, such as fear)

BEFORE THERAPY	98	76	83	91	88	84	97	95	89	102
AFTER THERAPY	65	76	58	49	55	76	48	51	53	49

For example, in Table 12.3, the mean for 'after therapy' can be calculated as follows:

- Add up all the scores: 65 + 76 + 58 + 49 + 55 + 76 + 48 + 51 + 53 + 49 = 580.
- Number of scores = 10.
- Divide the total by the number of scores: 580/10 = 58.
- The mean GSR for 'after therapy' is 58.

Advantages and disadvantages of different measures of central tendency

The mode is easy to calculate and can be used on any level of measurement. It is also useful as it is not affected by extreme scores. However, the mode is not very informative as it does not take every score into account (unlike the mean). Nor is the mode useful for small data sets as it is unlikely to be representative. Because it is not very informative, it tends to be used only with nominal data as other kinds of data can employ other measures of central tendency.

The median, unlike the mode, can be used with ordinal, interval or ratio data. It is more representative than the mode and is not affected by very large or small scores. However, the median, unlike the mean, does not represent all of the data because it ignores very large and very small 'outliers'.

The mean is the most representative measure of central tendency as it takes all of the scores into account. However, precisely because of this, the mean may also be distorted by very large or small 'outlying' scores. Even though it is the most useful measure of central tendency, it can only be used with interval or ratio data.

The range: a measure of dispersion

The scores within a data set vary. Measures of spread help us to describe the extent of this spread – that is, to provide a simple summary of the variation within the set. The range is the difference between the largest and smallest scores. This can be represented either by quoting both the biggest and smallest scores or by taking the smallest from the largest to express the range as a single number.

Glossary

mean – a measure of central tendency used with interval or ratio data which takes every score into account.
median – a measure of central tendency used with ordinal data which finds the midpoint in a set of scores.
mode – a measure of central tendency used with nominal data which finds the most common score.
range – a measure of dispersion which describes the extent of variation within a set of scores.

Advantages and disadvantages of the range

The range is easy to work out and can be used with ordinal, interval or ratio data. However, the range does not indicate how tightly or widely spread the data points are within the extremes.

Scattergraphs, bar charts and histograms

Graphs are used to illustrate aspects of a data set; this may include the central tendency of the data or the spread of a data set. In general, graphs are used to represent the general characteristics of the data, although in some every single data point is plotted.

Glossary

bar chart – a graph used to illustrate discontinuous data (e.g. nominal data or measures of central tendency).

Bar charts

The bar chart is used only when the data is in discrete categories. This includes illustrating measures of central tendency (modes, medians or means) and for totals of nominal data. When drawing a bar chart, the bars should be separate. This is because the scale along the x axis is not a continuous scale but represents distinct categories. If plotting the IV and DV, the IV goes on the x axis, the DV on the y axis. Figure 12.2 illustrates this use of the bar chart.

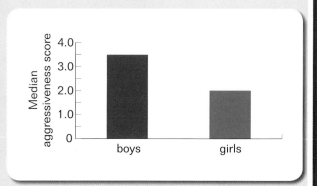

Figure 12.2 A bar chart has a gap between the bars as the data are in discrete categories

Histograms

The histogram is used when you are representing continuous data. The most common use is to illustrate the frequency of different scores when a measure of the DV is on an ordinal, interval or ratio scale. This is called a frequency histogram. The possible scores on the DV may be grouped into categories (e.g. 0–5, 6–10, 11–20, 21–30, etc.) and are plotted along the x axis. The frequency of each score or category is represented on the y axis. Unlike the bars on a bar chart, the bars on a histogram are adjacent because the scale is a continuous measure. This is illustrated in Figure 12.3.

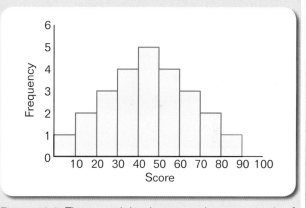

Figure 12.3 This normal distribution graph is an example of a histogram. On a histogram, the bars are adjacent along the x axis and frequency is plotted on the y axis

Histograms are used to represent the way that the scores are distributed across the range, so they are also called frequency distributions. A line joining the tops of all the bars would be a frequency distribution curve. When a set of scores is evenly distributed around the mean, the frequency distribution curve makes a symmetrical bell-shape. This is called the normal distribution (Figure 12.3).

Scattergraphs

A scattergraph plots pairs of scores collected in a correlational design. In a correlation, each participant has a score on two variables, one variable would be plotted on the x axis, the other on the y axis. There is no fixed rule for which

Glossary

histogram – a graph used to illustrate continuous data (e.g. to show the distribution of scores within a set).

scattergraph – a graph used to illustrate the results of a correlational study, which plots each person's scores as a single point.

variable is plotted on which axis as both variables are measured. In a comparison of the scores of pairs of observers, one observer's record would be plotted on one axis, the second observer's records on the other. This is a useful way to compare inter-observer reliability. The shape of the scattergraph in this case should be a diagonal line out from the origin (see Figure 12.4a) – this is a positive correlation (e.g. $r = 0.9$). In a negative correlation (e.g. $r = -0.8$), the line slopes the other way (see Figure 12.4b). When there is no correlation ($r = 0$), the points are randomly scattered (see Figure 12.4c).

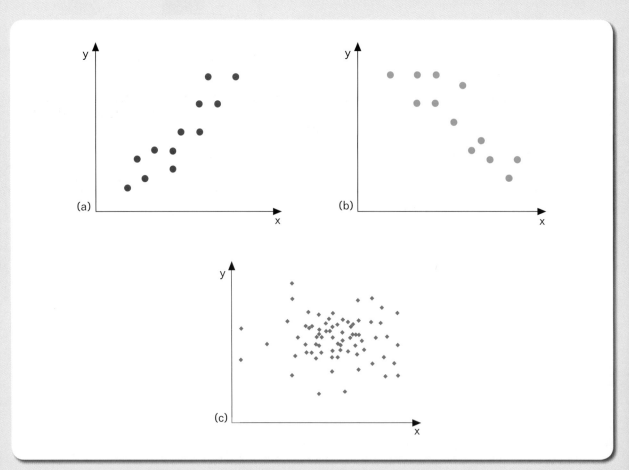

Figure 12.4 Scattergraphs (a) a positive correlation, (b) a negative correlation, and (c) no correlation

Summing it up

➡ Coding systems and categorisation can be used to describe data from interviews, questionnaires and observations.

➡ Coding systems represent meaningful types of information with different codes to identify and separate them. Categories are combinations of codes used to organise data by structuring them into related groups.

➡ Coding and categorisation is useful for structuring complex data and helps to improve inter-rater reliability, but when used to convert qualitative data to quantitative data, this may reduce its validity.

➡ Content analyses describe information from interview transcripts and media. Coding units include words and emotions.

➡ Quantitative data are measured on numerical scales. There are four levels of measurement: nominal, ordinal, interval and ratio.

➡ Measures of central tendency indicate the middle or average score in a data set. They include the mode, median and mean.

➡ The mode is easy to calculate and can be used with any data but is not very informative. The median requires data on a scale and is more representative than the mode but it does not represent all of the data. The mean is the most representative but can be distorted by outlying scores.

➡ The range is a measure of dispersion that indicates how spread out the points in a data set are.

➡ Graphs are used to represent data visually. Bar charts are used with discontinuous data. Histograms are used to illustrate variation within a set of continuous data. A scattergraph is used to plot the results of a correlational analysis.

Consolidate your understanding

Describing data

Use the following activities to run the information in this chapter through your mind. Each activity is designed to help you process the information in a different way, which should help you ensure you understand it and make it easier to remember.

Crossword

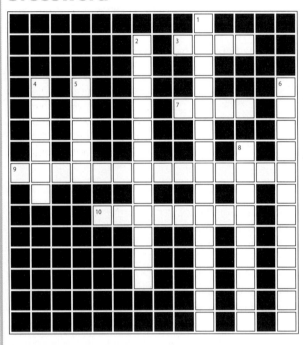

Across
3. The most frequent score in a data set
7. Average calculated by adding up the scores and dividing by the number of scores
9. A way to combine codes by organising them into related groups
10. An illustration of discontinuous data on a graph

Down
1. Extracting specific coding units from information such as media sources
2. An illustration of correlational data
4. The score in the middle of a ranked data set
5. The difference between the largest and smallest scores, which indicates dispersion
6. A way to organise data by identifying and separating each small, meaningful type of event
8. An illustration of continuous data on a chart with adjoining bars

Crossword solutions begin on page 231.

Consolidate your understanding

Cloze

Coding systems and _____ can be used to describe data from interviews, questionnaires and observations. Codes represent and separate different meaningful units. These can be combined into related _____ to organise the data. Coding systems and categorisation help by _____ complex data and can improve inter-rater _____, but if used to convert qualitative data to a numerical form, some detail is lost, which may lower _____. A _____ _____ describes information from _____ transcripts and media by using coding units such as words or emotions.

_____ data are measured on numerical scales. The mean, median and mode indicate the average score in a data set. The _____ is easy to calculate and can be used with any data but is least informative. The median needs data on a scale and is _____ representative than the mode but it does not take all the data into account. The mean is the _____ representative but can be distorted by outlying scores. The _____ indicates how spread out the points in a data set are. Graphs represent data visually. _____ _____ are used with discontinuous data and _____ with continuous data. A _____ plots the results of a correlational analysis.

Exam focus

Research methods

The methods questions are **always** Question 7 and Question 8.

Remember to **do only one of them** – some people panic and do two!

You only have 3 minutes to answer every question – **do not write the question out!** Don't be afraid of using a **heading** rather than writing out the question: '**Advantage**' is much quicker than 'One advantage of using a lab experiment in this research is . . .'.

Also remember that you must include some **reference to the actual study** in each answer to get the full marks – if not you only get 1 out of 3 maximum.

The questions

The questions are always the same type and in the same positions:
a) Method
b) Reliability
c) Validity
d) Sampling
e) Ethics
f) Results

Method

This will normally be **one advantage** and **one disadvantage** of a particular method.

Firstly, do **not** give two advantages and one disadvantage (or the opposite) because only one of each will be scored!

Secondly, you have about 3 minutes to do this, and you need to get some reference to the study in there.

One tip relates to experimental design – there are **mirrored** differences:

Reliability

The sort of answer you might give would be:

> 'You could repeat the study with the same participants with all details identical and see if you obtained the same results, i.e ... (and here you could give details of the original study).'

But remember you must focus your answer clearly on the study to get high marks.

Validity

There are different types of validity. The main questions you will be asked relate either to some form of **measurement** carried out during the study (is it measuring what it says it is measuring?) and possible **confounding variables** (where something hasn't been properly controlled).

An example of the **first type** is a happiness score (PY 2 June 2010) used in a correlation. How do you know the score obtained is a measure of happiness?

The best multi-purpose answer is this is a **concurrent validity** issue, and that it is dealt with by **checking it against another measure** that is well established as a happiness measure.

An example of the **second type** is testing whether a vitamin supplement makes a difference in performance in educational attainment tests. Validity is an issue if nutritional intake is not strictly controlled for a long period up to and including the study, to make sure the levels of vitamins are the same for all participants. Dealing with this issue of course means **controlling** this variable.

You have to identify which type of validity it is, and then give your generic answer plus a reference/ example from the study given.

MEASURES	ADVANTAGE	DISADVANTAGE
Independent	No **order effects** since participants only take one condition	**Individual differences** between participant groups may affect results
Repeated	**Individual differences** have no effect as the same individuals take all conditions	**Order effects** may occur, such as fatigue or practice effects

Exam focus

Sampling

This is another **advantage/disadvantage** question. Alas there is no alternative but to learn the main ones (opportunity, self-selecting, random and systematic). Be very careful to link to the study, best done by mentioning the target population (usually a college student group or the 'population at large') e.g:

Advantage
Easy to select your sample from the chosen target population (i.e. the Post -16 students at the college).

Disadvantage
The sample may be biased in some way (e.g. only friends chosen from the student group).

Results

You are normally asked to state **one** conclusion from the results table, graph or scattergram given.

Firstly – **don't** give two conclusions! You only get marks for one.

Secondly – **do** remember to get the reference to the study in:

'The modal mark for the students who ate breakfast was a grade higher than the modal mark for those who didn't.'

Lastly – **do** state the obvious. It's not a trick question.

Epilogue: Thinking about taking psychology further?

I should be able to:

- understand what is involved in studying A2 and undergraduate psychology
- know where to find information about possible careers in psychology
- find degree courses accredited by the British Psychological Society
- check out the entry requirements for a range of psychology degrees
- research the quality of a range of psychology degrees.

If you are coming to the end of your AS-level year, it is time to start thinking seriously about your career options. If you are applying to university, the autumn will soon be upon you and there are a number of advantages to submitting an early application. This requires that you do some of the background research now. Obviously we cannot help with all your possible career plans, but we can help to point you in the direction of the sort of information you will need if you are thinking about going into psychology.

Doing well at A2

Psychology is one of the most popular subjects at undergraduate level, and gaining a place to study for a psychology degree is now pretty much on a par with getting to study medicine or law. Any offer you receive will be conditional on your A2 grades, so you have to do well at A2. This sounds obvious but there is one important and immediate practical application; if you are taking January modules, the last thing you want is to be preparing for these at the same time as completing your UCAS application. Get your research done now and get your application in as early as possible in the autumn.

A2-level is meant to be a step-up from AS-level, but in reality what does that mean you should expect? It does *not* mean that all the psychology you will study will be harder to understand than what you have already come across at AS-level. You may notice a slight increase in pace and perhaps a little more to learn for exams. Actually the main thing that marks A2 out as harder than AS is the exam questions. These differ in two ways. Firstly, they will require longer answers. Secondly, more marks will be allocated for analysis and evaluation and fewer for straight description.

Understanding how A2 will be different from AS should have a couple of practical applications for you. Firstly, if you have coped with AS-level, there is no reason why you should not continue to do so at A2. Do not be put off by the level. Similarly, if after AS-level you decide that psychology is 'your thing', do feel able to apply for it at university. Your teacher or teachers will have made a decision about how much detail they give you and how much independent reading they expect you to do. Make sure you are clear about this, and that you stick to whatever level of reading they advise. The other major tip we can give you is to work on your question technique. Specifically, work on giving longer answers and developing your A2 skills.

Differences between A-level and undergraduate psychology

We both thoroughly recommend going on to study psychology at degree level, but as far as possible you should do so in the full knowledge of what you are in for. Research has shown that many psychology undergraduates are surprised by how scientific university psychology is. You will spend a lot of time carrying out experiments and other studies, and a lot of time learning about research methodology and statistics. There is also less opportunity at degree level to choose exciting options, and you may find that your A-level teachers have chosen options that protect you from some of the more dry and technical aspects of psychology.

The other key difference between any study at A-level and undergraduate level is the requirement for independent study. There are good reasons for this, and you will have to adapt to a very different system. The emphasis at A-level is on knowing well a particular body of information and being able to demonstrate that you can think analytically about this material. This necessarily means that your teacher will give you everything you need to know or at least prescribe reading that will give you all the answers. At undergraduate level, there is more emphasis on you finding information and developing skills on your own. The more skills you can develop now in independent study, the easier this will be.

Careers in psychology

It is never too early to start thinking about your career, and now with student debt what it is, it is crucial to make the right sort of choices. First question: do you want to be a psychologist? If so, then you really have to start with a psychology degree (although you can do a postgraduate conversion course if you decide psychology is for you later). If you do not have a fixed career plan but want an interesting degree well regarded by employers, then you would also do well to consider a degree in psychology. Most people with psychology degrees do not ever become psychologists; you should not worry that you are limiting yourself to a career as a psychologist by undertaking a psychology degree.

Information on psychology careers

The stereotypical 'psychologist' is usually a clinical psychologist, who applies psychology to helping people with mental health problems or other psychological distress. In fact, applied psychology is very broad, and psychologists may work in a huge variety of fields, including health, sport, education, criminal justice and work. Detailed information about different psychology careers can be found here: www.bps.org.uk/careers/careers_home.cfm.

If you have no idea what you want to do for a living but psychology is your favourite subject, our advice is to go for it!

Accredited psychology degrees

There are currently 388 degrees in the United Kingdom accredited by the British Psychological Society. Some of these are pure psychology but there is also a range of joint and combined honours courses. If you are likely to want a career as a psychologist, it is important to choose a British Psychological Society-accredited degree. You can see the list here: www.bps.org.uk/careers/accredited-courses/.

Entry requirements

Psychology is now extremely popular and entry grades are correspondingly high. For the most sought-after courses, this can mean up to three A grades at A-level. You can see an up-to-date list of entry requirements here: www.ucas.ac.uk/students/coursesearch/.

You will see from this list that there is some variation in entry grades. Before getting downhearted about your chances of getting into the 'best' courses, think about what that actually means. The most sought-after courses are *not* necessarily those that will suit you best as an individual student. Think about whether you care about prestige – which has little to do with teaching quality! Go to open days, meet some real psychology lecturers and reflect on where you feel most comfortable.

It is also well worth remembering that location has as much to do with the popularity of a course as any measure of quality. Pretty campus universities in the Home Counties are most popular. If you are not bothered about landscaped grounds, you can sometimes gain a place at an equally prestigious university in London, Northern Ireland, Scotland or North Wales with lower grades.

Measures of course quality

There are two major published figures that are used to define the quality of a university department:

1. The Research Assessment Exercise (RAE) grade. This is a measure of how successful the department is in publishing influential research. The RAE scale goes from 1 to 5★, 5★ being the highest. In 2014, RAE is due to be replaced by the Research Excellence Framework (REF), so from then on you will need a different source for department ratings. For now, RAEs are available here: www.rae.ac.uk/results/.

2. The National Student Surveys. Statistics are recorded of how highly psychology undergraduates rated their courses. Scores are out of five for several criteria, including quality of teaching and feedback. There are several sites where you can access this information, including here: http://education.guardian.co.uk/students/tables/0,,1574395,00.html.

It just remains to say good luck. We hope that you have enjoyed AS psychology and that you will decide to take it further.

Julia and Matt

Answers

Chapter 1

Wordsearch

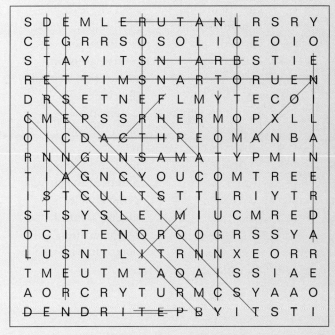

```
S D E M L E R U T A N L R S R Y
C E G R R S O S O L I O E O I O
S T A Y I T S N I A R B S T I E
R E T T I M S N A R T O R U E N
D R S E T N E F L M Y T E C O I
C M E R S S R H E R M O P X L L
O I C D A C T H R E O M A N B A
R N N G U N S A M A T Y P M I N
T I A G N C Y O U C O M T R E E
I S T C U L T S T T L R I Y T R
S T S Y S L E I M I U C M R E D
O C I T E N O R O O G R S S Y A
L U S N T L Y T R N N X E O R R
T M E U T M T A Q A S S I A E
A O R C R Y T U R M C S Y A A O
D E N D R I T E P B Y I T S T I
```

Crossword

Across

1. Chemotherapy
4. Localisation
5. Psychosurgery
9. Stress
10. Lab Experiment

Down

2. Exhaustion Stage
3. Neuron
6. CNS
7. Receptor
8. Hormone

Cloze

electrical, neurotransmitters, receptor, brain, localisation, endocrine, hormones, stress, unable, general adaptation syndrome, alarm, autonomic, adrenalin, resistance, exhaustion, illness, psychosurgery, lobotomies, poor/low, fewer, unimpaired, reductionist, (childhood) experiences, chemotherapy, neurotransmitter, cause, animals, controlled, generalise, MRI, PET, reliable, validity, determinist, symptoms

Chapter 2

Wordsearch

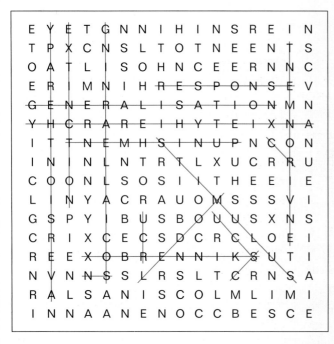

Crossword

Across
3. Ecological
5. Operant
7. Discrimination
8. Reinforcement
9. Classical
10. Natural

Down
1. Social desirability
2. Learning
4. Observer bias
6. Vicarious

Cloze

observable, stimuli, generalisation, extinction, classical, operant, learning, punishment, social reinforcement, model, aversion, unpleasant, alcoholic, discrimination, systematic desensitisation, relaxation, extinction, testable, Skinner, objective, generalisable, independent, demand characteristics, deterministic, reliable

Chapter 3

Wordsearch

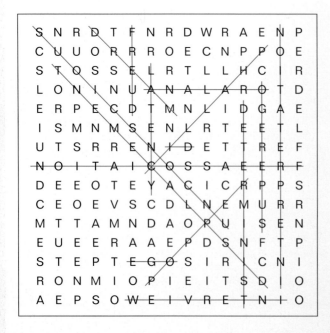

Crossword

Across
4. Bias
5. Dream
6. Wolfman
9. Anna O
10. Superego

Down
1. Determinism
2. Displacement
3. Unconscious
7. Stages
8. Popper

Cloze

unconscious, relationships, id, ego, superego, personality, Hans, association, Anna O, analysis, Wolf, clinical, study, unrepresentative, interview, bias, explanatory, scientific, evidence

Chapter 4

Wordsearch

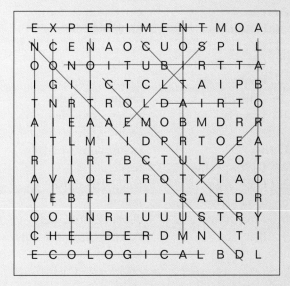

Crossword

Across
1. Heider
6. Musturbation
7. Reductionism
9. Beck
11. Computer
12. Obesity
13. Utopian

Down
2. Ellis
3. HM
4. Laboratory
5. Consensus
8. Internal
10. Consent

Cloze

mental, computer, pure, character, undesirable, covariation, REBT, ecological, participants, scientific

Chapter 5

Wordsearch

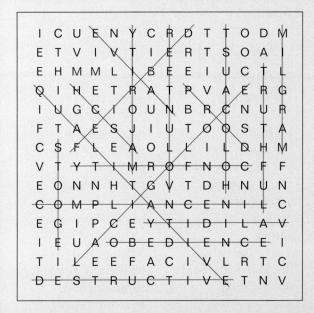

Crossword

Across
2. Conformity
7. Nuremberg
8. Yale
9. Stooge
10. Concurrent

Down
1. Volunteer
3. Informed
4. Milgram
5. Internal
6. Truthful
7. Naive

Cloze

opinions, laboratory, stooges, 98%, two-thirds, reduced, sample, unrepresentative, cultural
Holocaust, obedience, true, electric, memory, stress, prods, qualitative, ethical, cultural

Chapter 6

Wordsearch

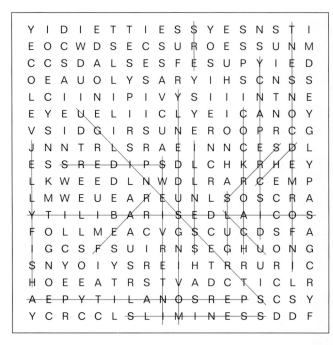

Crossword

Across
1. Hardiness
4. Quantitative
5. Questionnaire
7. Preparedness
8. Rabbit
10. Correlation

Down
2. Retrospective
3. Daily hassles
5. Qualitative
6. Prospective
9. Rat

Cloze

correlational, future, SRE/Schedule of Recent Events, health, positive, stressful, validity, controls, sample, reliability, causes, informed consent, clinicians, exam, negative, daily hassles, readily, discrepancy, number, characteristics, ugly, slimy, speedy, suddenly, fear, avoidance, cockroaches, jellyfish, spiders, women, men, less, more, approached, feared, species, demand characteristics, qualitative, quantitative, validity, generalisibility, opportunity, disease

Chapter 7

Wordsearch

Crossword

Across
2. Leading
5. Operant
6. ASL
7. Emotions
8. Nim chimpsky
9. Post-event
10. Transfer

Down
1. Lexigram
3. Differentiation
4. Eatlisten

Cloze

leading, laboratory, speed, accident, five, control, broken glass, more, post-event, validity, real, emotional, ecological validity, reduce, less verbal, sign, human, case study, observation, vocabulary, differentiated, transferred, combined, arbitrary, blind, structure-dependence, ethical, lexigram, produce

Chapter 8

Wordsearch

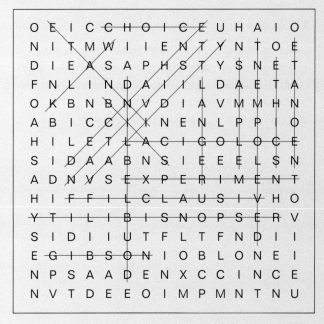

Crossword

Across
7. Neonate
9. Internal
10. Plant
13. Activity
15. Sociability
16. Nativist

Down
1. Innate
2. Ecological
3. Control
4. Turtle
5. Visual cliff
6. Development
8. Langer
11. Quasi
12. Kids
14. Bias

Cloze

choice, experiment, two, choice, responsibility, staff, observations, beneficial, ecological, blind, determination nurture, cliff, babies, preference, ethical, innate

Chapter 9

Wordsearch

Crossword

Across
4. Thud
6. Sane
7. Realism
8. Schmitt
10. Bias
11. Iran
12. Self-selecting
13. Diagnosis

Down
1. Andrews
2. Feminists
3. Chastity
5. Fertility
6. Sample size
9. Ambition

Cloze

cultural, evolutionary, survey, ambition, younger, sampling, questionnaire diagnosis, patient, remission, follow, pseudopatients, realism, ethical

Chapter 10

Crossword

Across

2. Correlation
3. Quantitative
6. Lab
8. Questionnaire
9. Qualitative
10. Interview
11. Field

Down

1. Interobserver
4. Observation
5. Case study
7. Nature

Cloze

questionnaires, detailed, numerical, experiments, independent variable, dependent variable, controlled, field, causal, natural, positively, negatively, not, participant, overt, validity, interviews, open, unstructured, less, case study, single, generalise

Chapter 11

Wordsearch

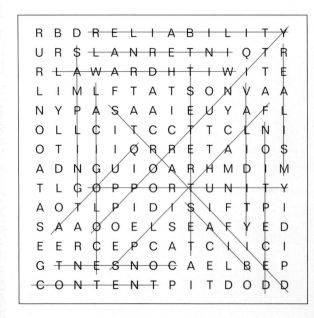

Crossword

Across

1. Informed
4. Quota
6. Extraneous
10. Reliability

Down

2. Ecological
3. Presumptive
5. Opportunity
7. Split half
8. Construct
9. Validity

Cloze

retest, half, rater, external, predictive, valid, committees, representative, selecting, random, time

Chapter 12

Crossword

Across
3. Mode
7. Mean
9. Categorisation
10. Barchart

Down
1. Content analysis
2. Scattergraph
4. Median
5. Range
6. Coding system
8. Histogram

Cloze

categorisation, codes, organising, reliability, validity, content analysis, interview, quantitative, mode, more, most, range, bar charts, histograms, scattergraph

Bibliography

Adams, C.E., Rathbone, J., Thornley, B., Clarke, M., Borrill, J., Wahlbeck, K. and Awad, A.G. (2005) 'Chlorpromazine for schizophrenia: a Cochrane systematic review of 50 years of randomised controlled trials.' *BMC Medicine*, 3: 15.

Adelman, R., McGhee, P., Power, R. and Hanson, C. (2005) 'Reducing adolescent clients' anger in a residential substance abuse treatment facility.' *Joint Commission Journal of Quality and Patient Safety*, 31: 325–326.

Ahn, W.K. and Bailenson, J. (1996) 'Mechanism-based explanations of causal attribution: An explanation of conjunction and discounting effect.' *Cognitive Psychology, 31*, 82–123.

Ahn, W.K., Kalish, C.W., Medin, D.L. and Gelman, S.A. (1995) 'The role of covariation versus mechanism information in causal attribution.' *Cognition*, 54: 299–352.

Andrews, G., Slade, T. and Peters, L. (1999) 'Classification in psychiatry: ICD-10 versus DSM-IV.' *British Journal of Psychiatry, 174*: 3–5.

Asch, S.E. (1955) 'Opinions and social pressure.' *Scientific American, 193*: 31–35.

Backus, T.B., Fleet, D.J., Parker, A.J. and Heeger, D.J. (2001) 'Human cortical activity correlates with stereoscopic depth perception.' *Journal of Neurophysiology*, 86: 2054–2068.

Bandura, A. (1977) *Social learning theory*. Englewood Cliffs, New Jersey: Prentice-Hall.

Bandura, A., Ross, D. and Ross, S.A. (1961) 'Transmission of aggression through imitation of aggressive models.' *Journal of Abnormal and Social Psychology*, 63(3), 575–582.

Bandura, A., Ross, D. and Ross, S.A. (1963) 'Imitation of film-mediated aggressive models.' *Journal of Abnormal and Social Psychology*, 66: 3–11.

Banyard, P. and Flanagan, C. (2005) *Ethical issues and guidelines in psychology*. London: Routledge.

Bartone, P.T. (2000) 'Hardiness as a resiliency factor for United States forces in the Gulf War.' In J.M. Violanti, D. Paton and C. Dunning, *Posttraumatic stress intervention: challenges, issues, and perspectives*. Springfield, Il.: Charles C. Thomas.

Bateson, P. (1986) 'When to experiment on animals.' *New Scientist*, 1496: 30–32.

Beck, A. (1976) *Cognitive therapy and the emotional disorders*. New York: International Universities Press.

Bennett-Levy, J. and Marteau, T. (1984) 'Fear of animals: What is prepared?' *British Journal of Psychology*, 75: 37–42.

Bergstrom, C.T. and Leslie, A.R. (2000) 'Towards a theory of mutual mate choice: lessons from two-sided matching.' *Evolutionary Ecology Research*, 2: 493–508.

Blass, T. (1996) 'Attribution of responsibility and trust in the Milgram obedience experiment.' *Journal of Applied Social Psychology*, 26: 1529–1535.

Blass, T. and Schmitt, C. (2001) 'The nature of perceived authority in the Milgram paradigm: two replications.' *Current Psychology: Developmental, Learning, Personality, Social*, 20: 115–121.

Boen, F., Auweele Y.V., Claes, E., Feys. J. and Cuyper, B.D. (2006)

'The impact of open feedback on conformity among judges in rope skipping.' *Psychology of Sport and Exercise*, 7: 577–590.

Bonanno, G.A., Galea, S., Bucciarelli, A. and Vlahov, D. (2007) 'What predicts psychological resilience after disaster? The role of demographics, resources, and life stress.' *Journal of Consulting and Clinical Psychology*, 75(5): 671–682.

Bond, R. and Smith, P.B. (1996) 'Culture and conformity: a meta-analysis of studies using Asch's 1952/1966 line-judging task.' *Psychological Bulletin*, 119: 111–137.

Bowlby, J. (1944) '44 juvenile thieves.' *International Journal of Psychoanalysis*, 25: 19–52.

Breuer, J. and Freud, S. (1896) *Studies on hysteria. The complete works of Sigmund Freud, volume II*. London: Hogarth.

British Psychological Society (2004) *Guidelines for minimum standards for ethical approval*. Leicester: British Psychological Society.

British Psychological Society (2009) *Code of ethics and conduct*. Leicester: British Psychological Society.

Burger, J.M. (2009) 'Replicating Milgram: would people still obey today?' *American Psychologist,* 64: 1–11.

Buss, D. (1989) 'Sex differences in human mate preferences.' *Behavioural and Brain Sciences,* 12: 1–49.

Cahill, J., Barkham, M., Hardy, G., Rees, A., Shapiro, D.A., Dtiles, W.B. and Macaskill, N. (2003) 'Outcomes of patients completing and not completing cognitive therapy for depression.' *British Journal of Clinical Psychology*, 42: 133–143.

Carmichael, L.C., Hogan, H.P. and Walter, A.A. (1932) 'An experimental study of the effect of language on the reproduction of visually perceived forms.' *Journal of Experimental Psychology,* 15: 73–86.

Charlton, T., Gunter, B. and Hannan, A. (eds) (2000) *Broadcast television effects in a remote community*. Mahway, NJ: Lawrence Erlbaum Associates.

Cohen, R.A., Kaplan, R.F., Zuffante, P., Moser, D.J., Jenkins, M.A., Salloway, S. and Wilkinson, H. (1999) 'Alteration of intention and self-initiated action associated with bilateral anterior cingulotomy.' *Journal of Neuropsychiatry and Clinical Neuroscience*, 11: 444–453.

Conway, L.G. and Schaller, M. (2005) 'When authorities' commands backfire: attributions about consensus and effects on deviant decision making.' *Journal of Personality and Social Psychology*, 89: 311–326.

Cook, M. and Mineka, S. (1989) 'Observational conditioning of fear to fear-relevant versus fear-irrelevant stimuli in rhesus monkeys.' *Journal of Abnormal Psychology*, 98(4): 448–459.

Cook, M. and Mineka, S. (1990) 'Selective associations in the observational conditioning of fear in rhesus monkeys.' *Journal of Experimental Psychology and Animal Behavior Processes*, 16(4): 372–389.

Davey, G.C.L., Cavanagh, K. and Lamb, A. (2003) 'Differential aversive outcome expectancies for high- and low-predation fear-relevant animals.' *Journal of Behavior Therapy and Experimental Psychiatry*, 34(2): 117–128.

Davey, G.C., McDonald, A.S., Hirisave, U., Prabhu, C.G.,

Iwawaki, S., Jim, C.L., Merckelbach, H., de Jong, P.J., Leung, P.W. and Reimann, B.C. (1998) 'A cross-cultural study of animal fears.' *Behavioural Research and Therapy*, 36(7–8): 735–750.

DeLongis, A., Folkman, S. and Lazarus, R.S. (1988) 'The impact of daily stresses on health and mood: psychological and social resources as mediators.' *Journal of Personality and Social Psychology*, 54: 486–495.

De Meuse, K.P. (1985) 'The relationship between life events and indices of classroom preference.' *Teaching of Psychology*, 12(3): 146–149.

Dickemann, M. (1981) 'Paternal confidence and dowry competition.' In R.D. Alexander and D.W. Tinkle (eds), *Natural selection and social behaviour.* Chiron Press.

Eley, T.C. and Stevenson, J. (2000) 'Specific life-events and chronic experiences differentially associated with depression and anxiety in young twins.' *Journal of Abnormal Child Psychology*, 28: 383–394.

Ellis, A. (1977) 'The basic clinical theory of rational emotive therapy.' In A. Ellis and R. Grieger (eds) *Handbook of rational emotive therapy.* Monterey: Brooks/Cole.

Engels, G.I., Garnekski, N. and Diekstra, R.R.W. (1993) 'Efficacy of rational-emotive therapy: a quantitative analysis.' *Journal of Consulting and Clinical Psychology*, 61: 1083–1090.

Eron, L.D. and Huesmann, L.R. (1986) 'The role of television in the development of antisocial and prosocial behaviour.' In D. Olweus, J. Block, and M. Radke-Yarrow (eds), *Development of antisocial and prosocial behaviour, theories and issues.* New York: Academic Press.

Eron, L.D., Huesmann, L.R., Leftowitz, M.M. and Walder, L.O. (1972) 'Does television violence cause aggression?' *American Psychologist*, 27, 253–263.

Fava, G.A., Rafanelli, C., Grandi, S., Conti, S. and Belluardo, P. (1998) 'Prevention of recurrent depression with cognitive behavioural therapy: preliminary findings.' *Archives of General Psychiatry*, 55: 816–820.

Freud, S. (1900) *The interpretation of dreams.* London: Hogarth.

Freud, S. (1905) *Three essays on sexuality.* London: Hogarth.

Freud, S. (1909) 'Analysis of a phobia in a five-year-old boy.' *Collected Papers*, vol. 3: 149–295.

Freud, S. (1915) *Introductory lectures on psychoanalysis.* London: Hogarth.

Freud, S. (1917) 'Mourning and melancholia.' *Collected works volume 14.* London, Hogarth.

Freud, S. (1918) 'From the history of an infantile neurosis.' *Collected Papers*, vol. 3: 473–605.

Freud, S. (1923) *The ego and the id.* London: Hogarth.

Freud, S. (1933) *New introductory lectures on psychoanalysis.* London: Hogarth.

Frydenberg, E., Lewis, R., Kennedy, G., Ardila, R., Fridte, W. and Hannoun, R. (2003) 'Coping with concerns: and exploratory comparison of Australian, Columbian, German and Palestinian adolescents.' *Journal of Youth and Adolescence*, 32: 59–66.

Gardner, B.T. and Gardner, R.A. (1969) 'Teaching sign language to a chimpanzee.' *Science*, 165: 664–672.

Gibson, E.J. and Walk, R. (1960) 'The visual cliff.' *Scientific American*, 202: 67–71.

Golombok, S. (2000) *Parenting: what really counts?* London: Routledge.

Grazioli. R, and Terry, D.J. (2000) 'The role of cognitive vulnerability and stress in the prediction of postpartum depressive symptomatology.' *British Journal of Clinical Psychology,* 39: 329–347.

Greene, W.A. (1954) 'Psychological factors and reticuloendothelial disease – I. Preliminary observations on a group of males with lymphomas and leukemias.' *Psychosomatic Medicine,* 16: 3.

Greene, W.A., Young, L.E. and Swisher, S.N. (1956) 'Psychological factors and reticuloendothelial disease – II. Observations on a group of women with lymphomas and leukemias.' *Psychosomatic Medicine,* 18: 4.

Gupta, M.A. and Gupta, A.K. (2004) 'Stressful major life events are associated with a higher frequency of cutaneous sensory symptoms: an empirical study of non-clinical subjects.' *Journal of European Academy Dermatology and Venereology,* 8(5): 560–565.

Harrington. R., Campbell, F., Shoebridge, P. and Whittaker, J. (1998) 'Meta-analysis of CBT for depression in adolescents.' *Journal of the Academy of Child and Adolescent Psychiatry,* 37: 1005–1006.

Harris, K. and Campbell, E.A. (1999) 'The plans in unplanned pregnancy: secondary gain and the partnership.' *British Journal of Medical Psychology,* 72(1): 105–120.

Haslam, A. and Reicher, S. (2003) 'A tale of two prison experiments: beyond a role-based explanation of tyranny.' *Psychology Review,* 9: 2–6.

Hauff, E., Varvin, S., Laake, P., Melle, I., Vagium, P. and Friis, S. (2002) 'Inpatient psychotherapy compared to usual care for patients who have schizophrenic psychoses.' *Psychiatric Services,* 53: 471–473.

Hawkins, N.G., Davies, R. and Holmes, T.H. (1957) 'Evidence of psychological factors in the development of pulmonary tuberculosis.' *American Review of Tuberculosis,* 75(5): 768–780.

Hayes, K.H. and Hayes, C. (1951) 'Imitation in a home-raised chimpanzee.' *Journal of Comparative Physiology and Psychology,* 45: 450–459.

Hebb, D.P. (1946) 'On the nature of fear.' *Psychological Review,* 53: 259–276.

Heider, F. (1958) *The psychology of personal interpersonal relationships.* New York: Wiley.

Herman, L.M., Richards, D.G. and Wolf, J.P. (1984) 'Comprehension of sentences by bottle-nosed dolphins.' *Cognition,* 16: 129–219.

Hinde, R.A. (1974) *Biological bases of human behavior.* New York: McGraw-Hill.

Hobson, J.A. and McCarley, R.W. (1977) 'The brain as a dream state generator: an activation-synthesis hypothesis of the dream process.' *American Journal of Psychiatry,* 134: 1335–1348.

Hofling, K.C., Brotzman, E., Dalrymple, S., Graves, N. and Pierce, C.M. (1966) 'An experimental study in the nurse–physician relationship.' *Journal of Nervous and Mental Disorders,* 143: 171–180.

Holmes, T.H. and Rahe, R.H. (1967) 'The social readjustment rating scale.' *Journal of Psychosomatic Research,* 11: 213–218.

Holzhausen, K.G. and Glyn, R.P. (2001) 'Beyond compliance and acceptance: influence outcomes as a function of norm plausibility and processing mode.' *Group Dynamics*, 5: 136–149.

Ito, M. (1998) 'Consciousness from the viewpoint of the structural-functional relationships of the brain.' *International Journal of Psychology*, 33: 191–197.

Jacobs, M.A., Anderson, L.S., Champagne, E., Karush, N., Richman, S.J. and Knapp, P.H. (1966) 'Orality, impulsivity and cigarette smoking in men: further findings in support of a theory.' *Journal of Nervous and Mental Disease,* 143: 207–219.

Jarvis, M. (2004) *Psychodynamic psychology: classical theory and contemporary research*. London, Thomson.

Jones, E.E. and Davis, K.E. (1965) 'From acts to dispositions: the attribution process in person perception.' In L. Berkowitz (ed.), *Advances in experimental social psychology*, vol. 2. New York: Academic Press.

Jones, M.C. (1924) 'A laboratory study of fear: the case of Peter.' *Pedagogical Seminary,* 31: 308–315.

Joy, L.A., Kimball, M.M. and Zabrack, M.L. (1986) 'Television and children's aggressive behavior.' In T.M. Williams (ed.), *The impact of television: a natural experiment in three communities*. Orlando, Fl.: Academic Press.

Kanner, A.D., Coyne, J.C., Schaefer, C, and Lazarus, R.S. (1981) 'Comparison of two modes of stress measurement: daily hassles and uplifts versus major life events.' *Journal of Behavioral Medicine*, 4(1): 1–39.

Kelley, H.H. (1967) 'Attribution theory in social psychology.' In D. Levine (ed.), *Nebraska symposium on motivation*, vol. 15. Lincoln: Nebraska University Press.

Kellogg, W.N. and Kellogg, L.A. (1933) *The ape and the child*. New York: McGraw Hill.

Kobasa, S.C. (1979) 'Stressful life events and health: an enquiry into hardiness.' *Journal of Personality and Social Psychology*, 37: 1–11.

Lang, P.J. and Lazovik, A.D. (1963) 'Experimental desensitization of a phobia.' *Journal of Abnormal and Social Psychology*, 66: 519–525.

Langer, E.J. and Rodin, J. (1976) 'The effects of choice and enhanced personal responsibility for the aged: a field experiment in an institutional setting.' *Journal of Personality and Social Psychology*, 34, 191–198.

Lashley, K.S. and Russell, J.T. (1934) 'The mechanism of vision: a preliminary test of innate organisation.' *Journal of Genetic Psychology*, 45: 136–144.

Le Doux, J.E., Wilson, D.H. and Gazzaniga, M.S. (1977) 'A divided mind: observations on the conscious properties of the separated hemispheres.' *Annals of Neurology*, 2: 417–421.

Leichsenring, F. (2001) 'Comparative effects of short-term psychodynamic psychotherapy and cognitive-behavioural therapy in depression: a meta-analytic approach.' *Clinical Psychology Review,* 21: 401–419.

Liberzon, I., Abelson, J.L., Flagel, S.B., Raz, J. and Young, E.A. (1999) 'Neuroendocrine and psycho-physiologic responses in PTSD: symptom provocation studies.' *Neuropsychopharmacology*, 21: 40–50.

Lindgren, A., Werbart, A. and Philips, B. (2010) 'Long-term outcome and post-treatment effects of psychoanalytic psychotherapy with young adults.' *Psychology & Psychotherapy*, 83: 27–43.

Little, A.C., Cohen, D., Jones, B.C. and Belsky, J. (2007) 'Variable preferences for facial sexual dimorphism according to temporal context and environmental risk in humans.' *Behavioural Ecology and Sociobiology*, 61: 967–973.

Loftus, E.F. (1975) 'Leading questions and the eyewitness report.' *Cognitive Psychology*, 1: 560–572.

Loftus, E.F. (1979) 'Reactions to blatantly contradictory information.' *Memory & Cognition*, 7: 368–374.

Loftus, E.F. and Palmer, J.C. (1974) 'Reconstruction of automobile destruction: an example of the interaction between learning and memory.' *Journal of Verbal Learning and Behavior*, 13: 585–589.

Loftus, E.F. and Zanni, G. (1975) 'Eyewitness testimony: the influence of wording of a question.' *Bulletin of the Psychonomic Society*, 5: 86–88.

Luttke, H.B. (2004) 'Experiments within the Milgram paradigm.' *Gruppendynamik und Organisationsberatung*, 35: 431–464.

Maki, P., Hakko, H., Joukamaa, M., Laara, E., Isohanni, M. and Veijola, J. (2004) 'Parental separation at birth and criminal behaviour in adulthood: a long-term follow-up of the Finnish Christmas Seal Home Children.' *Journal of Social Psychiatry and Psychiatric Epidemiology*, 38: 354–359.

Malan, D. (1995) *Individual psychotherapy and the science of psychodynamics*. London: Butterworth-Heinemann.

Massie, H. and Szeinberg, N. (2002) 'The relationship between mothering in infancy, childhood experience and adult mental health.' *International Journal of Psychoanalysis*, 83: 35–55.

Matchett, G. and Davey, G.C. (1991) 'A test of a disease-avoidance model of animal phobias.' *Behavioural Research & Therapy*, 29(1): 91–94.

McKnight, J. and Sutton, N. (1994) *Social psychology*. Sydney: Prentice Hall.

McVey, C., McKechnie, K., Thomson, K. and Watt, S. (2003) 'Group dynamics: the effects of a bipartite selection on social interaction of castaways on a Scottish island.' *Proceedings of the British Psychological Society*, 11: 4.

Mendels, J. and Weinstein, N. (1972) 'The schedule of recent experiences: a reliability study.' *Psychosomatic Medicine*. 34(6): 527–532.

Menéndez Villalva, C., Montes Martínez, A., Núñez Losada, C., Fernández Domínguez, M.J., Gamarra Mondelo, T. and Buján Garmendia, S. (2002) 'Environmental stress and cardiovascular reactivity: the effect of stressful life events on hypertense patients.' *Atencion Primaria*, 30(10): 631–637.

Merckelbach, H., van den Hout, M.A., Jansen, A. and van den Molen, G.M. (2005) 'Many stimuli are frightening, but some are more frightening than others: the contributions of preparedness, dangerousness, and unpredictability to making a stimulus fearful.' *Journal of Psychopathology & Behavioral Assessment*, 10(4): 355–366.

Milgram, S. (1963) 'Behavioural study of obedience.' *Journal of Abnormal and Social Psychology*, 67: 371–378.

Mineka, S., Keir, R. and Price, V. (1980) 'Fear of snakes in wild- and laboratory-reared rhesus monkeys.'

Animal Learning and Behaviour, 8: 653–663.

Moran, M. (2006) 'Writer ignites firestorm with misdiagnosis claims.' *Psychiatric News*, 41: 10–12.

Musher-Eizenman, D.R., Holub, S.C., Miller, A.B., Goldstein, S.E. and Edwards-Leeper, L. (2004) 'Body size stigmatisation in preschool children: the role of control attributions.' *Journal of Paediatric Psychology*, 29: 613–620.

National Institute for Clinical Excellence (2004) *Depression: management of depression in primary and secondary care. Clinical Guidelines 23*. London: NICE.

Neenan, M. (2004) 'REBT 45 years on: still on the sidelines.' *Journal of Rational Emotive and Cognitive Therapy*, 19: 31–41.

Õhman, A. and Soares, J.J.F. (1998) 'Emotional conditioning to masked stimuli: Expectancies for aversive outcomes following nonrecognized fear-irrelevant stimuli.' *Journal of Experimental Psychology: General*, 127: 69–82.

O'Neill, R.M., Greenberg, R.P. and Fisher, S. (1992) 'Humour and anality.' *Humour: International Journal of Humour Research*, 5: 283–291.

Palesh, O., Butler, L.D., Koopman, C., Giese-Davis, J., Carlson, R. and Spiegel, D. (2007) 'Stress history and breast cancer recurrence.' *Journal of Psychosomatic Research*, 63(3): 233–239.

Palmer, S. and Dryden, W. (1995) *Counselling for stress problems*. London: Sage.

Parker, G., Mitchell, P. and Wilhelm, K. (2000) 'Twelve month episodes of non-melancholic depressive subjects: refinements of subgroups by examination of trajectories.'

Annals of Clinical Psychiatry, 12, 219–225.

Patall, E.A., Cooper, H. and Robinson, J.C. (2008) 'The effects of choice on intrinsic motivation and related outcomes: a meta-analysis of research findings.' *Psychological Bulletin*, 134(2), 270–300.

Pate, J.E. and Gabbard, G.O. (2003) 'Adult baby syndrome.' *American Journal of Psychiatry*, 160: 1932–1936.

Pavlov, I.P (1927) *Conditioned reflexes*. Oxford: Oxford University Press.

Pei, F., Pettet, M.W. and Norcia, A.M (2007) 'Sensitivity and configuration-specificity of orientation-defined texture processing in infants and adults.' *Vision Research*, 47: 338–348.

Perez, M.G., Rivera, R.M., Banos, F. and Amparo, B. (1999) 'Attentional bias and vulnerability to depression.' *Spanish Journal of Psychology*, 2: 11–19.

Perrin, S. and Spencer, C.P. (1980) 'The Asch effect – a child of its time.' *Bulletin of the BPS*, 33: 405–406.

Perrin, S. and Spencer, C.P. (1981) 'Independence or conformity in the Asch experiment as a reflection of cultural and situational factors.' *British Journal of Social Psychology*, 20: 205–209.

Pert, C.B. and Snyder, S.H. (1973) 'The opiate receptor: demonstration in nervous tissue.' *Science*, 179: 1011–1014.

Pillsworth, E.G., Hasleton, M.G. and Buss, D.M. (2004) 'Ovulatory shifts in female sexual desire.' *Journal of Sex Research*, 41: 55–65.

Pines, A.M. (2002) 'Teacher burnout: a psychodynamic perspective.' *Teachers and Teaching: Theory and Practice*, 8: 121–140.

Pole, N. and Jones, E.E. (1998) 'The talking cure revisited: content analysis of a two year psychodynamic therapy.' *Psychotherapy Research,* 8: 171–189.

Rahe, R.H., Mahan, J.L. and Arthur, R. (1970) 'Prediction of near-future health change from subjects' preceding life changes.' *Journal of Psychosomatic Research,* 14: 401–406.

Rahe, R.H., Meyer, M., Smith, M., Kjaer, G. and Holmes, T.H. (1964) 'Social stress and illness onset.' *Journal of Psychosomatic Research,* 8: 35–44.

Raphael, K.G., Cloitre, M. and Dohrenwend, B.P. (1991) 'Problems of recall and misclassifications with checklist methods of measuring stressful life events.' *Health Psychology,* 10: 62–74.

R*egan,* M. and *Howard,* R. (*1995*) 'Fear conditioning, preparedness, and the contingent negative variation.' *Psychophysiology,* 32: 208–214.

Rhodewalt, F. and Zone, J.B. (1989) 'Appraisal of life change, depression and illness in hardy and non-hardy women.' *Journal of Personality and Social Psychology,* 56: 81–88.

Roberts, S.C., Havlicek, J., Flegr, J., Hruskova, M., Little, C., Jones, B.C., Perrett, D.I. and Petrie, M. (2004) 'Female facial attractiveness increases during the fertile phase of the menstrual cycle.' *Proceedings of the Royal Society,* 10.1098np.

Rose, H. and Rose, S. (2000) *Alas poor Darwin*. London: Vintage

Rosenhan, D.L. (1973) 'On being sane in insane places.' *Science,* 179: 250–258.

Rosenman, R.H. and Friedman, M. (1958) 'The possible relationship of occupational stress to clinical coronary heart disease.' *California Medicine,* 89(3): 169–174.

Rothbaum, B.O., Hodges, L., Smith, S., Lee, J.H. and Price, L. (2000) 'A controlled study of virtual reality exposure therapy for the fear of flying.' *Journal of Consulting and Clinical Psychology,* 68: 1020–1026.

Roussy, F., Camirand, C., Foulkes, D., Dekoninck, J., Loftis, M. and Kerr, N. (1996) 'Does early night REM dream content reflect presleep state of mind?' *Dreaming,* 6: 121–130.

Ruscio, J. (2004) 'Diagnoses and the behaviors they denote: a critical evaluation of the labeling theory of mental illness.' *Scientific Review of Mental Health Practice, 3:* 5-22.

Rutter, M. (1981) *Maternal deprivation reassessed*. Harmondsworth: Penguin.

Ryan, R.M. and Deci, E.L. (2000) 'Self-determination theory and the facilitation of intrinsic motivation, social development, and well-being.' *American Psychologist,* 55(1), 68–78.

Saliba, D. and Schnelle, J.E. (2002) 'Indicators of the quality of nursing home residential care.' *Journal of the American Geriatrics Society,* 50(8), 1421–1430.

Sandahl, C., Herlitz, K. and Ahlin, G. (1998) 'Time-limited group psychotherapy for moderately alcohol dependent patients: a randomised controlled clinical trial.' *Psychotherapy Research,* 8: 361–378.

Sandell, R. (1999) 'Long-term findings of the Stockholm Outcome of Psychotherapy and Psychoanalysis Project (STOPP).' Paper presented at the 'Psychoanalytic long-term treatment: a challenge for clinical and empirical research in psychoanalysis' meeting, Hamburg.

Sautter, F.J., Bissette, G., Wiley, J., Manguno-Mire G., Schoenbachler, B., Myers, L., Johnson, J.E., Cerbone, A. and Malaspina, D. (2003) 'Corticotropin-releasing factor in posttraumatic stress disorder (PTSD) with secondary psychotic symptoms, nonpsychotic PTSD, and healthy control subjects.' *Biological Psychiatry*, 54: 1382–1388.

Schmitt, D.P. (2003) 'Universal sex differences in the desire for sexual variety: tests from 52 nations, 6 continents and 13 islands.' *Journal of Personality and Social Psychology,* 85: 85–104.

Schneirla, T.C. (1965) 'Aspects of stimulation and organisation in approach/withdrawal processes underlying vertebrate behavioural development.' In D.S. Lehrman, R.A. Hinde and E. Shaw (eds), *Advances in the study of behavior,* vol. 1. New York: Academic Press.

Seifert, K. (2003) 'Attachment, family violence and disorders of childhood and adolescence.' *Paradigm*, Summer: 14–18.

Seligman, M. (1971) 'Phobias and preparedness.' *Behavior Therapy*, 2: 307–320.

Selye, H. (1947) *Textbook of endocrinology*. Montréal: University of Montréal.

Simantov, E., Schoen, C. and Klein, J.D. (2000) 'Health-compromising behaviors: why do adolescents smoke or drink?: identifying underlying risk and protective factors.' *Archives of Pediatrics and Adolescent Medicine*, 154: 1025–1033.

Sinai, M.J., Ooi, T.L. and He, Z.H. (1998) 'Terrain influences the accurate judgement of distance.' *Nature*, 395: 497–500.

Slater, L. (2004) *Opening Skinner's Box: great psychological experiments of the twentieth century*. New York: W.W. Norton.

Slater, M., Antley, A., Davison, A., Swapp, D., Guger, C., Barker, C., Pistrang, N. and Sanchez-Vives, M. (2006) 'A virtual reprise of the Stanley Milgram obedience experiments.' *PLOS One*, December: np.

Smallbone, S.W. and Dadds, M.R. (2004) 'Attachment and coercive sexual behaviour.' *Sexual Abuse: A Journal of Research Treatment,* 12: 3–15.

Solms, M. (2000) 'Freudian dream theory today.' *The Psychologist*, 13: 618–619.

Stander, V.A., Hsiung, P. and MacDermid, S. (2001) 'The relationship of attributions to marital distress: a comparison of mainland Chinese and US couples.' *Journal of Family Psychology,* 15: 124–134.

Stefanou, D.R., Perencevich, K.C., DiCintio, M. and Turner, J.C. (2004) 'Supporting autonomy in the classroom: ways teachers encourage student decision making and ownership.' *Educational Psychologist*, 39(2), 97–110.

Stewart, A.E. (2005) 'Attributions of responsibility for motor vehicle crashes.' *Accident Analysis and Prevention,* 37: 681–688.

Suzuki, H. and Lucas, L.R. (2010) 'Chronic passive exposure to aggression escalates aggressiveness of rat observers.' *Aggressive Behavior,* 36: 54–66.

Tarnow, E. (2000) 'Self-destructive obedience in the airplane cockpit and the concept of obedience optimisation.' In T. Blass (ed.), *Obedience to authority*. Mahwah: Lawrence Erlbaum.

Terrace, H.S. (1979) *Nim*. New York: Knopf.

Theorell, T., Lind, E. and Floderus, B. (1975) 'The relationship of disturbing life changes and emotion to the early development of myocardial infarction and other serious illnesses.' *International Journal of Epidemiology*, 4: 281–293.

Thornhill, R. and Palmer, C. (2000) *A natural history of rape*. Cambridge: MIT Press.

Tinbergen, N. (1951) *The study of instinct*. Oxford: Clarendon Press.

Tondel, G.M. and Candy, T.R. (2007) 'Infants' accommodative and vergence responses to ramp stimuli under binocular and monocular viewing conditions.' *Investigative Ophthalmology and Visual Science*, 46, np.

Tooth, J.C. and Newton, M.P. (1961) 'Leucotomy in England and Wales 1942–1954. Reports on public health and medical subjects No. 104.' London: Her Majesty's Stationery Office.

Trivedi, M.H., Rush, A.J., Wisniewski, S.R., Nierenberg, A.A., Warden, D., Ritz, L., Norquist, G., Howland, R.H., Lebowitz, B., McGrath, P.J., Shores-Wilson, K., Biggs, M.M., Balasubramani, G.K. and Fava, M. (2006) 'Evaluation of outcomes with citalopram for depression using measurement-based care in STAR★D: implications for clinical practice.' *American Journal of Psychiatry*, 163: 28–40.

Trivers, R.L. (1972) 'Parental investment and sexual selection.' In B. Campbell (ed.), *Sexual selection and the descent of man*. Chicago: Aldine Publishing.

Trower, P. and Jones, J. (2001) 'How REBT can be less disturbing and remarkably more influential in Britain: a review of views of practitioners and researchers.' *Journal of Rational Emotive and Cognitive Therapy*, 19: 21–30.

Vidal, A., Gomez-Gil, E., Sans, M., Portella, M.J., Salamero, M., Pique, J.M. and Panes, J. (2006) 'Life events and inflammatory bowel disease relapse: a prospective study of patients enrolled in remission.' *American Journal of Gastroenterology*, 101(4): 775–781.

Vonk, R. and Konst, D. (1998) 'Intergroup bias and correspondent inference bias: people engage in situational correction when it suits them.' *British Journal of Social Psychology*, 37: 379–385.

Wall, T.N. and Hayes, J.A. (2000) 'Depressed patients' attributions of responsibility for the causes of and solutions to their problems.' *Journal of Counselling and Development*, 78: 81–86.

Ware, J., Jain, K., Burgess, I. and Davey, G.C. (1994) 'Disease-avoidance model: factor analysis of common animal fears.' *Behavioural Research & Therapy*, 32(1): 57–63.

Watson, J.B. and Rayner, R. (1920) 'Conditioned emotional responses.' *Journal of Experimental Psychology*, 3(1): 1–14.

Weinrott, M.R., Riggan, M. and Frothingham, S. (1997) 'Reducing deviant arousal in juvenile sex offenders using vicarious sensitisation.' *Journal of Interpersonal Violence*, 12b: 704–728.

Wolpe, J. (1958) *Psychotherapy by reciprocal inhibition*. Stanford University Press: Stanford.

Wolpe, J. (1969) 'Basic principles and practices of behavior therapy of neuroses.' *American Journal of Psychiatry,* 125: 1242–1247.

Workman, J.E. and Freeburg, E.W. (1999) 'An examination of date rape, victim distress and perceiver variables within the context of attribution theory.' *Sex Roles*, 41: 261–277.

Wright, D.B., Loftus, E.F. and Hall, M. (2001) 'Now you see it, now you don't: inhibiting recall and recognition of scenes.' *Applied Cognitive Psychology,* 15: 471–482.

Yamada, Y., Tatsumi, K., Yamaguchi, T., Tanabe, N., Takiguchi, Y., Kuriyama, T. and Mikami, R. (2003) 'Influence of stressful life events on the onset of sarcoidosis.' *Respirology*, 8(2): 186–191.

Yost, J.H. and Weary, G. (1996) 'Depression and correspondent inference bias: evidence for more effortful processing.' *Personality and Social Psychology*, 22: 192–200.

Yuille, J.C. and Cutshall, J.L. (1986) 'A case study of eyewitness memory of a crime.' *Journal of Applied Psychology*, 71: 291–301.

Zorrilla, E.P. and Koob, G.F. (2004) 'The therapeutic potential of CRF1 antagonists for anxiety.' *Expert Opinion on Investigational Drugs*, 13: 799–828.

Index

RECEIVED
03 NOV 2011